During the first part of April, seed formation is in full swing for the early bloomers like the hybrids of the Lenten rose, Helleborus orientalis, and winter aconite, Eranthis hyemalis, on the left, and snowdrop, Galanthus nivalis, in the center. The yellowing aconite and snowdrop foliage will quickly be hidden by the rapid growth of the Lenten roses, which will tower over it with leaves as large as or larger than the bronzed fading ones here indicated among the aconite. Hiding the dying early snowdrop foliage will be the wide glaucous blades of the autumn lycoris, L. squamigera, shown emerging center rear; the unfurling parasols of May apples, Podophyllum peltatum; and a tall, greenish-yellow fritillary from Japan, Fritillaria verticillata, at the right rear, with its distinctive curled tendrils topping the bud.

Under this expanding canopy the spring ephemerals are making their way to bloom. Massed around the snowdrops, left to right, are the cluster-budded, thick-stemmed Delphinium tricorne and Dutchman's breeches, Dicentra cucullaria, among the fiddleheads of the fragile fern, Cystopteris fragilis var. protusa. Above the netted iris, I. reticulata, with its reedy leaves, in the right foreground are the delicate rue anemone, Anemonella thalictroides; the emerging large-flowered trillium, T. grandiflorum; the twinleaf, Jeffersonia diphylla; the budded Greek anemone, A. blanda; and the leaflets of the Jacob's-ladder, Polemonium reptans, just showing beneath the dark green swirls of the Allegheny pachysandra, P. procumbens. The pinkish-brown, very fragrant spires of bloom on the Allegheny spurge contrast with the bold whites of the bloodroot, Sanguinaria canadensis, lower right.

WILD WEALTH

Paul Bigelow Sears
Ecologist

Marion Rombauer Becker
Gardener

Frances Jones Poetker
Arranger

Janice Rebert Forberg
Illustrator

The Bobbs-Merrill Company, Inc.
Indianapolis · New York

The Bobbs-Merrill Company, Inc.
A Subsidiary of Howard W. Sams & Co., Inc.
Publishers/Indianapolis • Kansas City • New York

1243

Acknowledgments

The authors acknowledge the privilege we have enjoyed of harmonizing our keenest mutual interests. Although we were separated at the outset by both background and distance, our attitudes toward the living world have drawn us together into a singularly happy collaboration—made more fruitful by the sympathy and editorial comment of our life-partners, to whom we lovingly dedicate this joint venture: Marjorie L. Sears, John W. Becker and Joseph G. Poetker.

Nothing has ever made us more intensely aware of the prolific, magnificent and fleeting quality of nature than being obliged to select, arrange and coordinate the material for illustrating our text. What you see is a distillation from the interlocking richness of bud, bloom and seed-cluster, of pervasive spring growth overshadowed and enveloped in a rush of summer profusion, of the seed stems and still verdant tips that make up the dichotomy of fall.

We trust you enjoy these drawings, which with few exceptions depict plants and flowers growing or grown at Cockaigne, as recorded by Janice Forberg. The authors are indebted to this artist for the spirited way in which she has reinforced our efforts to evoke ever changing seasonal relationships. We also heartily thank Elizabeth Dalvé for her supplementary charts and botanical drawings which in all instances bear her initials, with the exception of bird feeders, maps, pollens, a three-tiered container, the white oak and the flower holders.

We are also grateful to skilled and helpful friends such as Charles Harper, who assisted with book layout and color flow, and to many authors, only a few of whom we specifically identify in the text.

As to taxonomy, we have relied for our first choice for most native plants, when they are there listed, on *Gray's Manual of Botany*, 8th Edition (Fernald), 1950. For lack of a similar current authoritative volume for non-natives, we have consulted Dr. Peter Hyypio, extension botanist of the Bailey Hortorium, whose expertise in the ramifications of recent developments in nomenclature we consider outstanding and to whom we are most grateful for assuming this responsibility.

Thanks are also due to James A. Maxwell for his objective and constructive criticism of Frances Jones Poetker's section of the book. For coordinating our efforts through many versions our thanks to Jane Brueggeman, who also made the index. Use it. You will be surprised how much it will open up to you.

To our publishers—salvos for allowing us the freedom to pursue our visions of text, layout and presentation untrammeled.

M.R.B., F.J.P. and P.B.S.

Paul
Bigelow
Sears,
Ecologist

Seeing, we are often reminded, is believing. It is also one of those five remarkable keys to appreciation and enjoyment—the five senses—with which the normal human animal is blessed. Now that we have the trick of mass-producing knowledge as well as consumer goods, ordinary language is too flexible and elusive to convey much of that knowledge with precision. The language of everyday use often carries emotional overtones—"radical," for example—or has more than one meaning—"pen," for pigs or writing—and does not convey knowledge precisely enough. Consequently, a great deal of this bewildering and growing store of accurate information about ourselves and the world in which we live is recorded by mathematical formulae, like $E = MC^2$, or unfamiliar and uninviting technical terms. Yet we must never forget that whatever certainties science affords depend in the last analysis on what trained minds can see, hear, taste, touch and smell.

These pathways to experience have, it is true, been powerfully expanded by ingenious and intricate mechanisms as mysterious to the layman as the charms and incantations of the medicine man were to his clientele. Human curiosity, so often stifled in the young, has only too frequently been channeled into a bizarre mixture of the professional drives of the technical scientist, fear and international rivalry, and a lusty desire for profits in what seems to be an endlessly expanding economy. As in music the cult of the virtuoso tends to discourage a striving toward excellence in the amateur, so there is a growing tendency to regard the observation and even the enjoyment of nature as business to be handled by the specialist.

There is even a sneering and pungent vocabulary to discredit those who protest against the obvious violence to the environment that results from the insensate growth of human numbers and the reckless technology that accompanies it. Thanks to what may fairly be called the unscientific applications of science, we are not only compromising the future but penalizing ourselves in terms of understanding, enjoyment, and plain good citizenship.

Values that have long been accepted are not easily changed, but they *can* be. Public revolt against ugliness and discomfort is gradually reinforcing the valiant efforts of dedicated individuals and organizations. Elementary and secondary schools, despite overcrowding and other handicaps, are doing much to open the eyes of youngsters to their surroundings. A wise friend recently remarked that the best training in the nation is being done in the first three grades, the next best in high schools, and the worst in colleges. To quote Mark Antony, "If 't were so 't were a grievous fault," since what we call higher education trains teachers and puts the finishing touches on future citizens. It is a jest, cruel and dangerous, to certify anyone as educated if he emerges unable to see what is all around him, near at hand.

Yet I doubt if the need is for new machinery so much as for better use of the machinery we have. I could fill pages with accounts of what has been accomplished quietly by people whose energy has been given to using the tools

Man And Nature

at hand instead of clamoring for better ones. Take, for example, a small town in Indiana whose banker was a naturalist, subsequently known for his scholarly monographs on insects and plants. With his friend the energetic and interested village druggist, he roamed the countryside—the result was an education for the latter much like that which gave Darwin his real start at Cambridge. Thus equipped, the druggist became a pioneer state forester. In this capacity he recruited able professional assistants and forged a sound forest and park policy for his state. In his late years, at an age when most men are slacking off, this remarkable amateur scholar, Charles Deam, produced a book—*Flora of Indiana*—which Professor Fernald of Harvard, never known for soft-hearted judgments, called the best study of state flora in the nation.

Now professional research and its application—research and development, "R&D"—are perfectly legitimate concerns, essential to human welfare. But the need for these activities, dinned into the ears of the public and the government, could come dangerously close to obscuring an even more vital need. *Much of the world's most serious trouble is due not to the lack of new knowledge, but to failure to apply what is already known.*

What, we may ask, does this have to do with our book? Simply this: only where people have learned to appreciate and cherish the landscape and its living cover will they treat it with the care and respect it should have. Certainly the first step toward this end is to see not only what is around us, but what is happening in nature and in what direction life is moving. This means looking both backward and forward in time, and, with great concern, at the present.

I have known scorn to be poured on advocates of a return to the simpler ways of life, although as Harrison Brown points out in *The Next Hundred Years*, we may all be forced to return to it in a most disagreeable fashion if our wasteful civilization continues on its present course. This is not to say that we should return to the crudities and hardships of earlier times or forego all the benefits we enjoy today. But in fairness to ourselves and those who come after us, we should keep in mind those various periods of history when the world was less crowded, when individual survival was a great challenge, and when pressures on the individual were less intense than they are now.

To you the April blooming of the golden chartreuse bangles of the red oak, Quercus rubra, *may have only aesthetic significance. To pioneers they spelled good fortune, for pigs were fed on acorn mast before being shipped downriver, when prime, to New Orleans. To foresters today an abundance of these 6-inch blooms promises a bumper crop of seed that can be planted with less likelihood of squirrel plundering, since the red oak acorns are more bitter than those of other kinds of oak.*

The past offers us models as well as warnings. We are reminded that those who ignore history are condemned to relive it; to which we may add they are equally in danger of losing its benefits. We need not relive the past, even if we could. But we can be guided by some of its indubitable virtues, just as we have striven to overcome its evils of disease and hardship.

There was a time, brief as history goes, when streams were clear and free from the wastes of sewage, industry and excessive erosion from mismanaged land; when humanity was more evenly distributed instead of being crowded into rebellious masses dependent upon an intricate and vulnerable economy; when there were materials at hand to serve the craftsman, clean air to breathe, and work

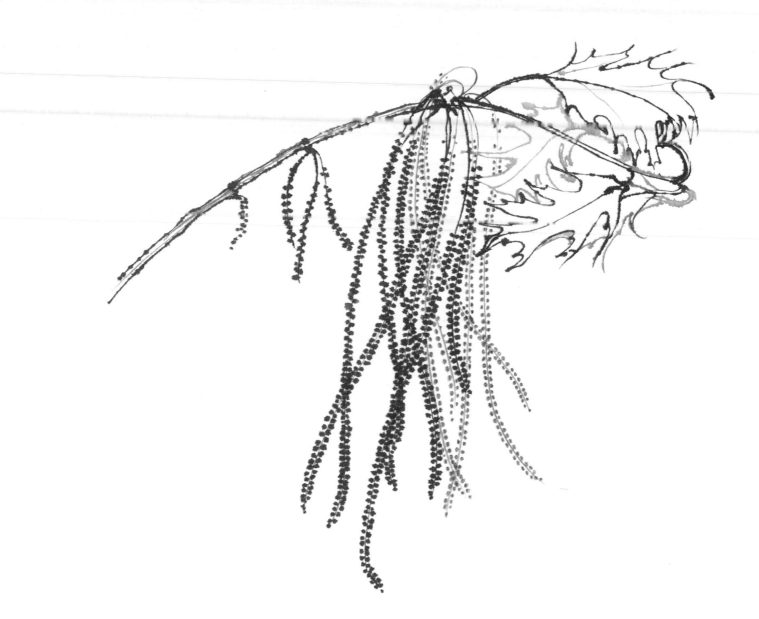

enough for all, including chores to occupy and train the young for their future responsibilities.

In those earlier days—and here we return to our present concern—our people entered a land that was clothed in green, a land teeming with plant and animal life and free from naked, unsightly scars. Unaware, as even the wisest of men have been until recently, of the vast antiquity of earth and the life in it, they did not realize that behind the generous abundance of the New World lay an order and a balance that had developed through hundreds of millions of years, perpetuating itself in excellent working condition despite the vicissitudes and even the violence of nature. Instead, these pioneers saw in the life of forest and steppe their rivals for space that could be used for food, clothing and shelter. Their wits as well as their physical energy were challenged, and so we became an inventive people, little thinking that in time we might be the slaves instead of the masters of our own machines.

Men and women came to America to improve their lot. What they hoped to find depended on what they were trying to escape from. Some sought freedom—political, religious, social. Many sought wealth, an objective toward which European religion had relaxed its attitude during the Middle Ages, when usury ceased to be regarded as sinful. (It is interesting that the biblical injunction against "usury" applied to any charge whatever for money-lending, and that it took several centuries of rising mercantilism to prevail against Scripture.)

Where the search for wealth was conducted in alliance with political, economic and at times, I regret to say, religious power, the welfare of the individual in terms of education and economic opportunity reached its lowest level. Illiteracy and exploited labor are still widespread. The common man is still fair game for usurers and extortionists. The land and its resources—the commonwealth—have suffered as well. They too have been exploited and abused. And the United States has no reason to believe that it constitutes a shining exception.

However the worship of wealth may have been blunted by other considerations, the weaker these restraints, the greater the mischief. I am familiar with a tract of land from which a peaceful tribe of civilized Indians was callously deported in 1842 to make room for white settlement. During the next twenty years, the record shows this parcel to have changed hands no fewer than twelve times—hoofprints of the speculator, not wheel tracks of the homeseeker.

On a far vaster scale the exploitation of nature and of man has been and still is being sanctioned by a naive belief in the necessity of unlimited economic expansion and "growth." All that is necessary, we are solemnly told, is more applied science and more legislation. Yet all biological experience tells us that individuals, populations, and living communities of all kinds can survive only by coming into some kind of working balance within and without themselves.

Fundamentally, this is an expression of physical principles, yet so long has the burden of proof fallen on the biologist that it is a timely reinforcement to read the editorial in *Science*, October 11, 1968, by the physicist Philip Abelson, entitled "The Inexorable Exponential." "Many people," he writes, "view growth as akin to progress, achievement, and the good things of life." But, he goes on to remind us, even so modest a growth rate as three percent a year leads to a doubling —whether it be in the production of human beings or material goods—in twenty-three years. Obviously such a process cannot continue indefinitely without disaster. ". . . Continuous growth often leads to great problems for society. . . . The toughest enemy is the inexorable exponent."

To me, at least, one conclusion seems inevitable. If we care about those who will follow us, we must bend every effort toward achieving an ultimate harmony between man and nature. Here, as in any other great undertaking, we must have some kind of model in mind. For the prospective buyer it must be a sample or at least a picture of the goods; for the scientist, a classic experiment; for the writer, great literature; for the artist, a thing of beauty; and for the physician, the normal healthy human body.

Mistletoe, both the Viscum album *of the Druids and the* Phoradendron serotinum *of America, with pearl-white berries on 1- to 3-foot brittle greenish-yellow clusters, is part and parcel of Christmas festivities. The Greek word "phoradendron" reveals another side of its character: it translates as "tree thief." Mistletoe is parasitic to a variety of deciduous trees, but is partial to oak and black gum as far north as Zone VI. Because it prefers to grow in the upper branches it is collected locally with a gun, much as David Douglas, the famous English plant hunter, shot down seed cones of the 200-foot Northwest fir that bears his name.*

Particularly apposite are the needs of artist and physician, even though we often see the artist impelled to depict disorder and frustration and the physician continually involved with the treatment of disease. Like them, we must see clearly the ills we wish to correct, but we must all have the concept of what can and should be. For the landscape, as for the body, harmony and beauty are inseparable from health.

Our political system is, as Lincoln reminded us more than a century ago, still being tested. Under it each one of us is assumed to have a voice in determining and a share of responsibility for what happens to all of us and to the environment from which our lives and destinies are inseparable. It is easy to forget, in the blare and spectacle of national politics, that duty, like charity, should begin at home. Whatever the weaknesses of the democratic idea, it deserves a fair trial by a citizenry whose individual voices are not smothered in the size, complexity and power of central government.

Often problems of greatest concern to us are most manifest in our own immediate sphere, if we can be trained to see them. It is here that the individual's voice can be most effective if he will use it; and use it he should to preserve his political health. Life can yield its greatest satisfaction in the local community—in a fit and beautiful environment. Where beauty is present it should be cherished. Where it is lacking the good citizen should strive to create it.

What I have seen from the air and on the ground in fifty states and a number

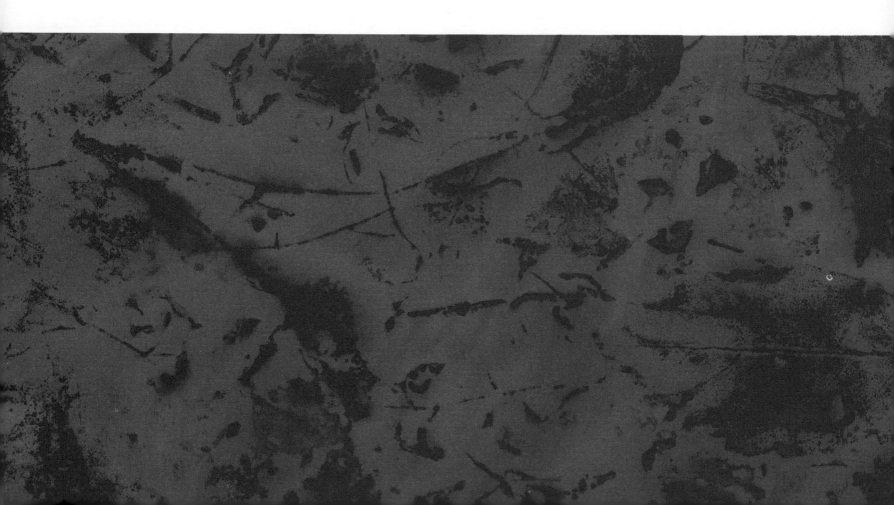

of foreign countries has long since convinced me that from twenty to twenty-five percent of a healthy landscape should be a kind of living cover that is so far as possible like its original, indigenous vegetation. This would be, in my judgment, the minimum required to ensure the purity of air, regulate the flow and storage of water, maintain the structure and quality of the soil, and in general stabilize the land surface. These are the benefits that derive normally from the presence of living communities in nature undisturbed by man—communities that made the earth habitable for him in the first place.

It has been heartening to learn, belatedly, that my estimate of what would be required to ensure a stable and productive landscape was first put forth in 1863 by that shrewd and observant world traveler, the learned Vermont Yankee George Perkins Marsh, in his great but long-neglected classic, *Man and Nature*. Even then, a decade before we had "won the West" from bison and Indian and four decades before we had stripped the forest lands of the lake states to the bare ground, Marsh saw that we were not so much blazing new trails as following an ancient and dangerous path. For he had seen the remains of once splendid empires in the Old World. With clearer vision than most travelers, he saw that around the ruins of stone and mortar lay ruins of once fertile land that had nourished great civilizations. Pointing out that man had become a major geological and biological force, he showed that this power had been and still was being used to make a lonely planet unfit for decent living, if not for very survival.

Forget the compulsion to rake leaves if you are a woods gardener. Rimed with frost or nestled in the woods' hollows safe from wind, leaves form one of the most useful of groundcover contrasts. But never plant where leaf-fall remains abnormally heavy, for growing shoots that have the power to split stone show a curious inability to penetrate packed leafage. This impervious forest litter, which roofs over countless microbial and insect activities, turns in time into the greatest of all treasures—rich soil. To achieve its closest counterpart, see pages 94 to 101.

If you look at the leaf scars on this walnut twig, it is not hard to imagine oldtime herbalists seeing portents and human forms in roots, stems, leaves and stalks. To observe how tremendously natural phenomena affected artists through the ages, glance at D'Arcy Thompson's Growth and Form, *or Blossfeldt's* Urformen der Kunst, *where the unfamiliar language is no barrier to appreciation. Be sure, if you are planting bare-root, to move beech in spring before it loses its coppery bud scale; dogwood in early March; tulip, magnolia and other fleshy-rooted trees just before they leaf out; willow oak at the same time, for if it is transplanted in the fall the roots do not establish well enough to keep its thin bark and many twiglets moist enough to survive. Move buckeye and walnut while still quite dormant.*

The face of earth is a graveyard, and so it has always been. To earth each living thing restores when it dies that which has been borrowed to give form and substance to its brief day in the sun. From earth, in due course, each new living being receives back again a loan of that which sustains life. What is lent by earth has been used by countless generations of plants and animals now dead and will be required by countless others in the future. The supply of an element such as phosphorus is so limited that if it were not constantly being returned to the soil, a single century would be sufficient to produce a disastrous reduction in the amount of plant life. No plant or animal . . . can establish permanent right of possession to the materials which compose its physical body.

Left to herself, nature manages these loans and redemptions in not unkindly fashion. She maintains a balance which will permit the briefest time to elapse between burial and renewal. The turnover of material for new generations to use is steady and regular. Wind and water, those twin sextons, do their work gently. Each type of plant and animal, so far as it is fit, . . . can bring forth its own kind to the limits of subsistence. . . . There is a balance in undisturbed nature between food and feeder, hunter and prey, so that the resources of the earth are never idle. Some plants or animals may seem to dominate the rest, but they do so only so long as the general balance is maintained. The whole world of living things exists as a series of communities whose order and permanence shame all but the most successful of human enterprises.*

There is thus an intensely practical as well as aesthetic reason for insisting that we learn to see, understand and cherish—and where we can, to restore—the natural communities or their remnants that have readied the earth for us. First of all, in keeping with the purpose of this book, I want to see us learn to enjoy the spectacle of living outdoor nature. I would hope to have this whirling ball of rock and water looked upon, as it was in legend, as a garden not to be violated and trampled into deadness. Whatever may be expected in some future existence, this is what we have, here and now. It will be what we make it.

Man's struggle through the ages has been against nature. Now, to preserve himself, he must change sides and work with her, for assuredly she will have the last word. It is the simple truth that appreciation is the first step in the care and keeping of the great works of hand and mind. It is no less so with the works of nature, so essential not only to the good life but to life itself.

Now that we in this country are predominantly an urban folk, more dependent on engine-driven wheels than on our own muscles for movement, on electricity for our daily tasks, and on mass production for the things (even the growing of food and fiber) we use, it may seem hopeless to talk of an interest in the land and its cover. Waste, littering and vandalism, this latter to the extent of

* From Chapter 1, "Man, Maker of Wilderness," in *Deserts on the March* by Paul B. Sears (University of Oklahoma Press).

millions of dollars' worth of damage in our beautiful metropolitan park systems, have become commonplace. I doubt if those who oppose the defenders of natural beauty realize the sinister mischief they are compounding. For in my experience beauty is a symptom of harmony and order, and ugliness of landscape is a sure index of disease.

But these difficulties need not be taken with the bowed shoulders of fatalism. In England, for example, while American critics of the late Rachel Carson's *Silent Spring* were still trying to discredit her as a scientist, there was prompt action to control the abuse of pesticides. And in Kew Gardens nearly half a century ago I was impressed by the number of plain working folk who not only came with their families to see the showy tulip, rhododendron and horse chestnut displays but who could be overheard discussing with knowing appreciation the tiny alpines and succulents. We can do with less talk about the perversity of human nature and with more scrutiny of the climate of values in which that nature develops.

In our own country, vast, complicated, and troubled though it be, there are hopeful signs. Green belts and open spaces are being featured in the better planned housing developments, and the shift toward suburbia is more than a negative act of escape. In many of these new communities one finds a creative spirit of political and community responsibility. Substantial leadership in the preservation of natural beauty and protection of resources is coming from urban dwellers, without whose support the admirable voluntary organizations with which the United States is blessed would languish. Again, only a generation ago a small shelf would hold the notable American books defending the cause of nature against ruthless abuse; today such books make up a library respectable in both quality and size.

As the tutor told his princely pupil, there is no royal road to learning. But when it comes to enjoyment and understanding of a living landscape, there are many intriguing pathways whose charm softens the labor involved in the journey. To temper the disastrous effects of our assault on greenery with concrete and asphalt (a cool million acres a year), we have national and state parks, forests, wilderness areas and an increasing number of natural preserves. Even vacant lots and roadsides have a story for those who care to watch them through the seasons and the years.

The unmanicured New England yard I left only a short time ago is beautiful in its own way; despite rock outcrops and thin soil it is host to more than a hundred species of uninvited plants, while its roster of animals includes birds, moles, squirrels, shrews and an occasional fox and raccoon from the neighboring woods.

From the hills of New England south along the Appalachians and westward into the oak-clad cross timbers of Texas and Oklahoma there is forest. True, much of it is second growth, having long since been robbed of its monarchs. Yet it displays a carpet of delicate spring flowers early in the year before the leaves emerge, masses of rich green foliage during the summer months, and a panorama of glorious tapestry during the waning year.

Even in winter the woodland retains its charm. There is rare beauty in the curious combination of order and irregularity as bare twigs and branches reveal the geometry of growth against the porcelain background of an early morning sky, while the persistent brown dry leaves of an occasional oak furnish a rustling obbligato and the decaying leaves a soft carpet.

It is on the fertile, level or gently rolling lands of the Midwest that agriculture has most completely replaced the original cover. Even in Ohio, where the occupants of 1750, some fifteen thousand Indians, have been supplanted by today's population of ten million or more whites, the air traveler is impressed by the area remaining in farm woodlots. These tend to survive along watercourses and in the centers of square-mile sections, where they are farthest from roads. To date their struggle to exist has been a rear-guard action. For thousands of generations man has conceived of himself as pitted against the forces of nature. He still, perhaps more than ever, talks of conquering them. Yet his problem is to protect nature against his own kind and his way of life, unless he wishes to join the long parade of vanished species.

His success in this task of self-preservation will lie, I am convinced, not in any new battery of technical tricks, but in cultivating an understanding and love for the wondrous world in which he is a fortunate guest. Whatever may happen must be with nature's consent. As Darwin long ago reminded us, we need not marvel at extinction.

The chaste white 3- to 5-inch chalices of the fragrant water-lily, Nymphaea odorata, *of our muck-bottomed ponds and slow-moving waters bloom as regularly as a clock. The blossom stays open from six in the morning until noon for a period of three days. If you'd like to float it open on your dinner table, foil it with a few drops of wax plopped into its center. Other flowers like crocus, tulip or hemerocallis, not so acceptive of restraints, close with the fading light. Plant water-lilies where they can get at least one-half day of sun.*

While our attention will focus upon the Ohio-Indiana-Kentucky area, this is the center rather than the limit of our concern. When one deals with living things in a knowledgeable way, the benefits are almost certain to reach beyond his parish; such at least is our hope. Thoreau's readers are not confined to New England, nor those of Gilbert White to his native Selbourne.

Take, for example, Edgar Anderson's account, in his book *Plants, Man and Life,* of typical native gardens in Mexico. These seemingly confused, irrational and certainly unsystematic mixtures of vegetables and flowers are actually far more efficient than they might seem. Less vulnerable to epidemics of pests and diseases than pure stands of a single crop, their stability comes from a close-knit and interdependent variety and furnishes a substantial basis of foods, drugs, fiber, color and form for their human sponsors. Surely such models have much to teach those who live far north of the Rio Grande.

We know, of course, that the native forests, intervales and swamps of our region could not furnish the subsistence needed by our present population. Before the coming of the white man the fifteen thousand Indians in Ohio needed all the space they had for hunting and fishing and for their gardens of corn, beans, and squash. Instead of the three or four square miles per capita which they required, we now get along with about as many acres, thanks to the many ways in which we apply science to the production, transportation and exchange of food and other necessities.

Yet this progress, combined with the growth of urban life and the expansion of industry, makes it imperative to recognize the value of conserving space for the existence of natural vegetation in the broad pattern of land use. As we have noted earlier, just to regulate the water cycle, protect the land surface, promote soil development and ensure an adequate supply of breathable air would require that a minimum of twenty to twenty-five percent of the land surface be clothed in permanent plant cover. Preferably this cover should approximate the natural character of the living communities before man's encroachment.

An equally good case can be made for preserving and restoring these conditions because of their priceless values to mankind. There is already under way a revolt against the extreme analytical and reductionist use of science in the interpretation of the human adventure. One of the symbols of this meager view is the word "mere"—man is a mere animal, the brain a mere mechanism, life a mere biochemical phenomenon, values a mere psychological matter.

While the reaction is largely intuitive and emotional, there are signs that it may develop into something like a disciplined demand that science be applied scientifically, in the light of historical experience and human values that are not merely expedient but truly paramount. By this I mean that we have freely applied physical and chemical discoveries to the elaboration of consumer goods without regard for ecological effects. A good example is the costly destruction, in the 1955 New England floods, of a factory manufacturing precision instruments, built in a location no naturalist would have recommended as safe.

*Of
Place
And
Time*

On this basis there would be no question of the importance of preserving and restoring open areas for recreation and refreshment of the human spirit. Nor would there any longer be indifference to the models that natural communities afford with respect to the organized use of energy and materials, models now in such tragic contrast to wasteful human enterprise.

The times seem to require us to be tough; thus apologists for the astronomically expensive outer space program feel called upon to explain that spin-offs or by-products of space research may someday begin to pay economic dividends. The ploy is familiar in academia as well, where seekers for funds who may not give a damn about the crass world of business are overjoyed when they can say that, given time, "this thing we are playing with may turn out to be useful."

We need not be so coy. In 1880 there were over two thousand industrial plants in Ohio utilizing the magnificent native hardwoods—walnut, white oak, hickory and cherry, as well as ash and yellow poplar or tulip wood. Banks at that time, and for a long time afterward, classed wooded land as "unimproved." Indubitably the need for food and forage crops was great, although the records of wheat shipment abroad via the Erie Canal show that far more was being produced than was required to sustain the local population.

Conrad Richter, in *The Trees*, describes logrollings in which great trees of now precious woods were felled and put to the torch just to clear the ground. By 1880 the woodworking mills had begun to feel the pinch of raw materials and petitioned the legislature for help, as ailing industries to this very day often do. The lawmakers responded by requesting Congress to lower the tariff on lumber, and in an additional burst of enlightened generosity voted one thousand dollars a year for the hire of a young forester from Cornell! I knew this individual thirty years later, when he had become a venerable figure who went about his business in a black frock coat and white linen. He certainly knew trees and appreciated their importance, as did a minority of his fellow citizens. Had Ohio in 1880 inaugurated a forestry policy similar to those already under way in Europe, many farms now languishing and mills now gone would still be productive. With management and selective cutting, the saplings thriving then would be the choice saw logs of today. But nothing less than the power of a dictator would have sufficed to bring this about at a time when not only trees but buffalo and even the Indians were still fair game.

One might say with truth of capitalism, as is often said of Christianity, that it might be an excellent thing if practiced seriously and consistently. (For capital wealth, essential to any viable economy, accumulates through budgetary controls for the sake of future benefit.) Where processing or marketing is concerned, those who manage our economy do look ahead. But when it comes to such basic resources as space, soil, minerals, and timber the pattern has been almost purely one of exploitation rather than perceptive and controlled management with an eye on the long future.

The big blue stem, Andropogon gerardi *(preceding pages), tall enough in moist years to conceal a man on horseback, waves its tiny flowers, along with a multitude of other grasses, in webby, plumed or downy tassels, rippling and soughing under the drive of winds that are seldom still. Beneath a bowl of azure, they have the endlessness and sweep of the sea. And their colors are just as varied—greens, greys and blues that take on rich beaten-copper tones throughout the sunny winter, against drifts of snow.*

Hidden in the earth, grass roots go down 3 to 5 feet or more, and this accounts for their capacity to store sufficient moisture to resist daytime heat and evaporation. The buried buds on these grasses allow them also to survive the spring and fall burning-over introduced by the early settlers, and the inadvertent lightning-set blazes.

Whenever we render life impossible for a species of plant or animal, or survival out of the question for a system of species, i.e., a living community, we are loading the future against ourselves. To put it in other words, by harvesting all seed trees or draining a pond we shrink the range of options and limit our freedom of choice. However rosy a completely mechanized future may look through the spectacles of the technologist, the naturalist cannot forget the incredibly long past and the interactions of life and environment that have made the earth habitable for man.

It is nearly five centuries since the landing of Columbus, and not quite two since the opening of the land west of the Alleghenies to settlers from Europe and American pioneers. Surveyors and travelers who crossed this ancient mountain chain found its diminishing foothills stretching southwestward into Kentucky. Rich in coal, their sandstones and shales were poor in lime and other plant nutrients. Except for the valleys and coves, they were covered with oak and chestnut.

These foothill forests, in no sense a worthless cover, were used for charcoal and mine timbers. Eventually the use of coke for steelmaking reduced the demand for charcoal, while the end of railroad expansion cut the market for ties. Mine timbers are no longer needed where powerful machinery strips away the

Down among the highly nutritious prairie grasses, as the season advances, the prairie forbs, net-veined and broad-leaved, range from the delicate white and blue windflowers to the mauve and blue vetches and lupines. The latter and many other legumes furnish the nitrogen necessary for fertilizing the prairie's stupendous grass growth. The coarsest forb is Silphium terebinthinaceum, *the prairie dock, which shoots its 2-foot pebbled silica-filled arrowy leaves straight up into the air. In August the comparatively small clustered blooms rise to 10 feet, to sway above the other yellow composites—coneflowers, goldenrods, sunflowers—and the purplish asters and blazing stars.*

soil and rock above seams of coal, exposing it for easy removal. Unhappily, this respite for the timbered hills was offset by the coming of the chestnut blight, to all intents and purposes exterminating that valuable tree.

Suitable only for marginal agriculture, and more favorable to the distillation of illicit spirits than to normal enterprise, this outpost of distressed Appalachia is a region of actual and potential beauty, thanks to its topography and its ability to sustain a growth of woodland. It is already becoming a place of aesthetic and recreational value for those who live in more fertile and heavily urbanized regions far to the north and west of it.

Beneath the sandstones and shales lie much more ancient beds of limestone that come to the surface as the former thin out and disappear. Their contact stretches diagonally across the state of Ohio from northeast to southwest like the ribbon across the shirt front of a European diplomat. Although this limestone region west of the foothills was at one time cut deep with valleys of rivers long since gone, it has been smoothed into a gently rolling topography and covered by the rich debris of the great glaciers that, during the past million years, scraped their way southwest from eastern Canada before their final retreat about 8000 B.C.

It was the surveyance of this relatively level surface that revolutionized the system of mapping land. Instead of metes and bounds marked by rocks, streams and trees, the land was marked off into mile-square sections separated by roads. At first these sections were grouped into townships of twenty-five sections each, later into thirty-six sections each, six miles square. This system, vastly simplifying land records, has been followed ever since, with mixed results.

In the semi-arid far West, the uncompromising squareness of official land units has no relation whatever to the all-important pattern of available water. In Ohio, Indiana and westward through the fairly level Mississippi basin, such a geometrical pattern has been favorable to farm-market relations and more recently to mechanized farming. But since every road is a drainage way, and straight ditches speed the movement of water, this "reform" in land surveys has been one of the reasons why springs have dried up, stream flows have become more irregular, and water tables have lowered.

To the north this fertile and neatly packaged land drained by way of the Great Lakes and the St. Lawrence River into the Atlantic; to the south by way of the Ohio and other tributaries of the Mississippi into the Gulf of Mexico and thence also into the great Atlantic Ocean. Its landscape was one of splendid hardwood forests, varied by swamps and enclaves of prairie—these latter relics of a climate drier than today's, a climate that reached its greatest spread about 2500 B.C. and gave way later to a moister one more congenial to the trees that came to surround the remnants of grassland. Thus the pioneers in Ohio encountered these islands of natural prairie in seas of forests.

But as settlers moved farther west the grasslands grew larger, finally opening up into the great interior prairie province. Here grass and its companion herbs became the running sea, the groves of oak and hickory, and where there were any, the islands. Other woodlands formed narrow ribbons along the floodplains of rivers, ending in the Father of Waters.

So far as the native plant materials to be discussed are concerned, they reflect this mixture of forest and grassland, but chiefly the more eastern landscape, where forests predominate. Because of its present moisture supply, long growing season, generally fertile soils and long history of climatic changes, most of this region is impressively rich. Plant species from all quarters of the compass mingle here, some of them at the borders of their home ranges. One is reminded of the mixtures of nationalities pocketed in a cosmopolitan seaport, although the native vegetation has long since shaken down into stable and integrated communities.

Likewise we find an imposing list of introduced plants that flourish here, thanks to the temperate, humid and subhumid conditions reflected in the area labeled as Zone VI on the map on page 20. These immigrants, as will be shown, include not only valuable crop plants such as the cereals, but many highly prized ornamental and useful herbs and shrubs.

Not to be overlooked are the often maligned weeds or ruderals that have tagged the steps of man in his wanderings over the earth. Whatever unpleasant qualities they have are balanced by their virtues, for they are nature's scar tissue, the first steps in healing broken and idle land. They seldom invade flourishing natural communities.

First, however, a closer look at the environment of the upper Ohio Valley. Moving northward on reasonably level ground, spring comes about a day later for every fifteen or twenty miles. The growing season in the bluegrass region of Kentucky averages around two hundred days. In northern Ohio, save where it is lengthened in a narrow fringe about Lake Erie, the average is some one hundred forty days. While the extremes of heat, cold, moisture and aridity are important, often decisive, the averages are no less so and are given in a table from the valuable U. S. Yearbook of Agriculture, *Climate and Man*, 1941.

The following averages indicate the range of climates in this region:

State	Days of Growing Season	Temperatures F* Winter	Summer	Inches Rainfall
Pennsylvania	100-200	22-32	66-76	34-50
Ohio	140-200	24-34	72-76	32-44
Indiana	150-190	26-34	74-78	34-46
Illinois	150-210	18-36	72-78	32-46
Iowa	140-170	14-24	72-76	26-36
Michigan	80-180	10-26	60-72	26-36
Kentucky	180-210	32-38	76-78	40-50

* Sunshine throughout this region approximates fifty percent on the average.

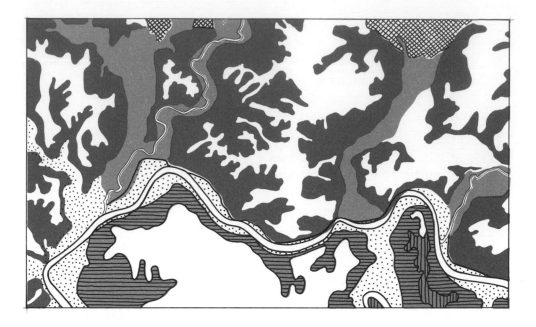

Along with climate and soil, one must take drainage into consideration. Note its effect on the dominant vegetation patterns in two townships, six by six miles each, in northern Ohio. Roads now superimposed on original section lines alter, as they always do, and become part of the present drainage system. But in 1819 when this area was first mapped, prairie, with oak-hickory on the knolls, dominated the poorly drained western section, indicated by dotted lines. Intermediate elm-oak-hickory prevailed in the central section where drainage was still juvenile, and the eastern portions of the townships where drainage was mature showed beech-maple supremacy. (Adapted from Sears's "Natural Vegetation of Ohio," Ohio Journal of Science, vol. 36, 1926. See also Gordon, loc. cit.)

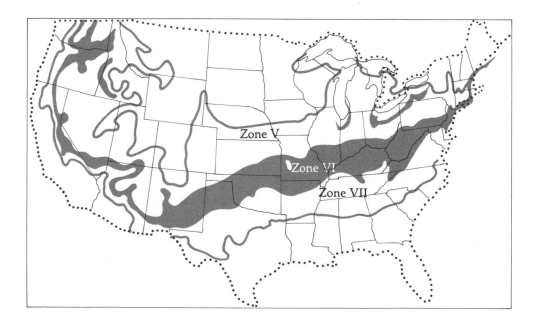

The final character of the soil depends on the long interaction of living plant and animal communities on the mineral substrates. But it does not take a budding ecologist long to learn where huckleberry, hemlock and rhododendron, all at home on acid soil ▨ with a pH of 4.5 to 6.5 (101), give way to the plants shown in this book which, with few exceptions, flourish on a near-neutral calcareous base. Shown here between the Great and the Little Miami Rivers, and north and south of the Ohio, are a variety of soils ▬ with a pH range of 6.6 to 7.3; ▢ with small pockets as low as 4.5, largely comparable to ▬ ; ▨ testing from 5.6 to 7.8; and in Kentucky ▤ and ▥ ranging from 5.8 to 8.4. ▦ indicates alluvial soils.

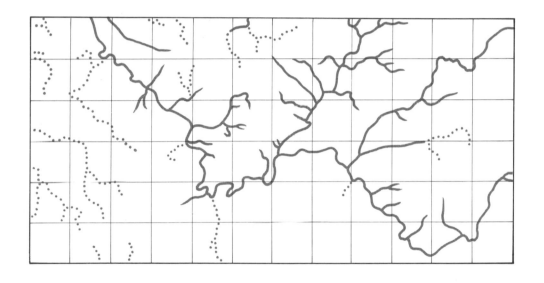

If you are trying to introduce hardy exotics, choose plants that come from areas of similar temperature and rainfall as well as from regions where soils are compatible. The conditions that lead to such a commonsense approach are summed up by scientists in the term bioclimatic analogues. This map, based on the hardiness zones of the USDA, gives the broad ranges. The gardener always hopes he can produce the microclimate (58) that will extend his own particular range. The plants described in this book are all hardy in Zone VI, shown here in red. Many of them flourish as well in Zones V and VII, contiguous north and south respectively.

Useful as they are, figures such as these must be read with judgment; climates differ on the opposite sides of a house or hill and change rapidly with elevation; there are fewer sunny days in the cloud belt around the Great Lakes than there are a short distance away; and extremes of temperature and moisture between day and night, winter and summer increase as one leaves the oceanic climates for the continental interior.

Actually the influence of the several factors that make up what we call climate is subtle and complex. Climate varies infinitely with location, exposure, and altitude. There are hundreds of thousands of plant species, each with its special requirements of moisture, temperature, and light. Only the needs of a relative few such as the cereals and other major crop plants have been studied thoroughly in field and laboratory. To them must be added some kinds which, like white mice and guinea pigs, lend themselves conveniently to experiment.

Thus the relative lengths of day and night, which vary with season and latitude, affect the periods of vegetative growth and flowering in many plants. Those of late spring and early summer tend to flower with the advent of longer days and shorter nights. The autumn bloomers, such as many composites, come into flower as the days shorten. Species of grass are known whose northern varieties require longer days for flowering than do their southern counterparts.

Again, for some plants—the tomato, for instance—fruit production is affected by the range between day and night temperatures. And in introducing plants to a new environment, the length of the growing season has to be reckoned with, as well as other conditions. For crop plants, selection has sometimes modified these requirements; varieties of maize, of central American origin, were grown by the Indians far north of the original range.

Studies have been made of what are called agroclimatic analogues. These are regions of essentially similar climates on the various continents. Primarily a guide to the introduction of crops, such studies are a useful supplement to the trial and error experience of those who garden for aesthetic satisfaction.

No less important than climates are the soils, themselves an expression of climate as well as of parent mineral material and the resultant living cover. For soil, be it remembered, differs from raw earth stuff as a home differs from the frame that is to contain it. Weathered rock only becomes soil by being lived in.

We have noted the sharp diagonal transition from the sandstones and shales to the older lime rocks that come to the surface as one moves west. West of the Alleghenies fertile land occurs, as in the bluegrass region of Kentucky, where bedrock rich in nutrients has weathered into soil; or as in the lake states of Ohio, Indiana and Illinois, where glaciers brought down nutrient minerals from the north more than ten thousand years ago. Unfortunately for New England, the rocks and rock material left by its glaciers was much poorer stuff.

Even the stiff, heavy clays, properly handled, are hearty and yield good

From the roots of chicory, Cichorium intybus, *comes that taste New Orleans prides itself on in its coffee; and from the pods of the common milkweed,* Asclepias syriaca, *comes a waterproof down to stuff life vests with. But of what earthly use are foxtails, especially the tall bristly types like* Setaria glauca, *the yellow foxtail grass shown on the right? Roadside managers try to suppress such berm weeds with preemergent chemical killers. Don't imitate them in your garden, for tests published by the Arnold Arboretum already prove that viburnum and other horticulturally valuable families are killed if they are growing in proximity to areas so treated.*

crops. In fact, a group of English settlers who had been potters chose to farm in the stubborn clays of northern Ohio in preference to lighter and more easily worked soils elsewhere. As one of their descendants explained, "My people knew how to handle clay to get the most out of it." He did not elaborate, but it is a reasonable guess that time of plowing, choice of crops and above all the working in of abundant organic matter were the secrets. With enough organic stuff in and on the soil as mulch one invites the services of earthworms and microorganisms to convert stiff paste to mellow, crumbly loam. Especially important is the role of clay and organic growth, both colloidal, as "middlemen" between plant roots and soil nutrients.

Soil on any farm, or even in a single field, is seldom uniform in fertility, texture or drainage. Like all moving water, outwash from melting glaciers dropped the heaviest material first, the finest last. Gravels, sands, silts and clays are zoned in that order, as they are farther west in the sediments brought down from the Rockies. But in many places in our region these materials, plus boulders from Canada, are scattered at random, having been lowered in place by fast-melting ice.

All of these variations in climate and soil found expression in the living cover of plant and animal life. The persimmon tree is barred by temperature from flourishing north of central Ohio; Canadian conifers persist in the cool, moist protection of canyonlike valleys tributary to Lake Erie. Chestnut stopped short where the acid sandstone soils reached their western limit, while the juniper or red cedar serves the geologist as an indicator of limestone soils. The cactus known as prickly pear was, until destroyed by "progress," at home on low dunes and in the thin layer of soil over scarcely buried limestone far from the desert.

What has been true of such individual species has been even more strikingly true of their associations or communities. Because of its general climate and typical forest cover, our region is labeled as part of the Eastern Deciduous Formation. But while it was mostly forested it was never completely so, nor was the forest cover by any means the same everywhere. An excellent map of the original vegetation of Ohio, showing its great variety, has been prepared by Dr. Robert Gordon and can be obtained from the Institute of Natural Resources of the State University at Columbus.

Among the forest types, in addition to the oak-chestnut that intruded on the eastern foothills, were the beech-maple, the oak-hickory, the swamp forest of ash, elm and soft maple, and a mixed mesophytic forest enriched by the presence of species that flourish in the humid headwater region of the Tennessee River. For a classic study of the deciduous forests of eastern North America one should consult the work of that title by the late Dr. E. Lucy Braun of Cincinnati.

So far as Ohio is concerned, less than twenty percent remains in forest as compared with an original eighty to ninety percent of that kind of cover. Much of what is left is in poor condition as a result of grazing, removal of the best

Aside from its primary function in plant reproduction, the usually yellow dust called pollen is an important source of protein in the diet of bees and other insects. Because the pollen of each kind of plant is distinctive in form and surface pattern, as well as resistant to decay when deposited in layers of sediment, we have an immensely useful key to vegetation changes in the past. These exquisitely formed vital grains, barely visible to the naked eye, are magnified (left to right) x 1,000, x 360 and x 3,200. They were residual on herbarium specimens at the Missouri Botanical Garden, where many facets of pollen research, including its relation to hay fever, are under way.

If you see trees fruiting only on the leeward side of the prevailing winds, it is likely that industrial pollutants have filmed over the narrow channels necessary for pollen entry. It is both alarming and ironic that such tiny entities, strong enough in structure to withstand fossilization and storage, should be thwarted in their function when still alive.

specimens and neglect. Recently there has been a revival of interest in both public and farm forests in this and neighboring states. One evidence of this concern is the return of deer, which had practically disappeared from the region before the beginning of the present century.

Of special interest have been the treeless areas—prairies, bogs and swamps —all of which, like the forest, have diminished with the growth of agriculture, highways and urban expansion. As is true of a community of human beings— San Francisco, New Orleans, St. Louis and Milwaukee, for example—these many kinds of vegetation express not only present conditions but the historical processes that have produced them.

To give at least a glimpse of these processes will be the task of the next chapter.

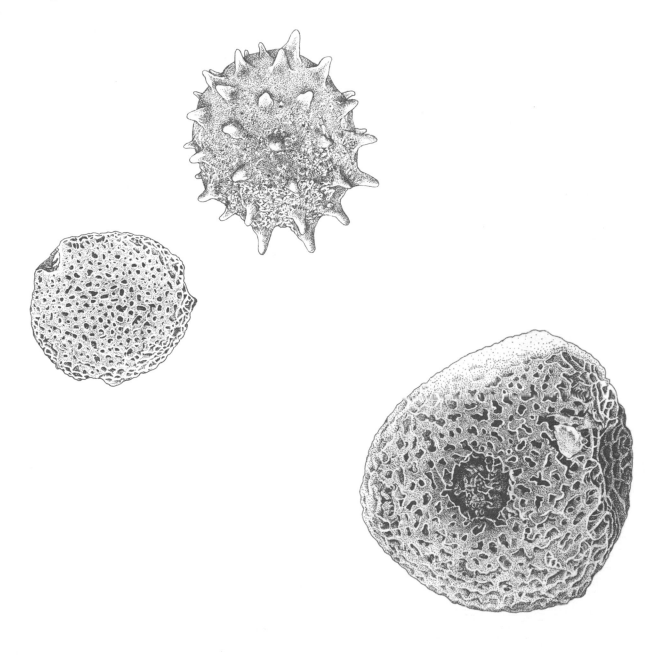

Whether they hail from the tropics or the arctic, the eighty-two species of Lycopodium, *the creeping club mosses, glacial remnants in our latitude, are distinguished in having only one type of sporangium among them—and that of a highly explosive nature. The quaint early photographer and balloonist, J. N. Niepce, used these spores for flash powder and even mixed them with air to fuel the first internal combustion engine. Today, the constancy of Lycopodium's ninety-four thousand spores per milligram is used in the analysis of dusts and powders. The several species found in Ohio form a beautiful evolutionary series when arranged in order of the increasing complexity of their fertile branches. Shown is Lycopodium complanatum, usually found in acid peaty soil, but recently noted to be changing its habits by invading quite limey areas. Why?*

To learn what I could about living plants has been my business and pleasure for many years. In the academic world I have seen the word "botany" give way to the more austere "plant science," and both gradually lose their identity under the term "biology." As a matter of logic and, often, administrative convenience, there is nothing wrong with this development, for biology, the science of organisms, has to do with the study of both plants and animals. Both share the unique quality of being alive. Indubitably the phenomenon of life is one of the great challenges to the human mind.

Powerfully aided by the physical sciences, this new approach has without question produced a rich harvest of knowledge as to what goes on within the living body. Yet it has deflected attention from the green mantle that clothes the earth and from whose welfare that of mankind is inseparable. As we have said before, vegetation is necessary to maintain the purity of the air we breathe, to regulate the flow of water, stabilize the land surface, develop soil, and ensure the continuing supply of nutrients, mineral and organic. In performing these functions it adds immeasurably to the beauty of the landscape as well as to its utility.

Psyche, it will be recalled, curious to see the face of her lover, dropped hot wax from her candle on his sleeping body and lost him. Icarus, aloft on wax wings devised by the patient work of his father Daedalus, rashly flew too near the sun and was destroyed. Shaping these ancient fables, poets long ago sensed that knowledge, unless tempered by understanding, can endanger those who use it.

We have used knowledge to devise means of mutual extermination. These, if brought into play, will end the need for discussion, so we pass them over. But geology, in its most significant lesson, teaches us that change can be effective, however slowly, even imperceptibly, it comes about. We must look, as honestly as we can, to see where the uses of science are leading us. These uses have, by controlling the rate of deaths, brought about an increase of human numbers that has no parallel in natural history. Along with it has come access to incalculable amounts of energy stored by plant activities in the remote past, supplanting and vastly multiplying the energy from food that for a million years fueled the muscles of man and the animals that helped with his work.

Kipling, using the phrase "drunk with power" in his Recessional, spoke plain truth, although I have heard that this hymn cost him the royal preferment he had earned. Numbers and power, in heedless combination, make modern man the dominant force of change today. Nowhere is this more evident to the discerning observer than in his disruption of the very processes which have made possible man's survival on the one planet in our solar system fitted for his existence. Nor is there any sounder *prima facie* evidence of the degree of disruption than that revealed by what has happened to the plant cover of the earth.

A physician who had studied with Dr. William Osler once described to me the remarkable skill of his mentor, entering a hospital ward for the first time and

The
Living
Landscape

calling off his diagnosis of each patient's illness as he viewed external appearances from where he stood. Rarely if ever was he wrong. This of course was no mystical insight, for Osler had spent years in detailed and disciplined analyses of symptoms and the diseases that caused them. Even to the routine, less scholarly practitioner, skin, features, and posture are invaluable clues.

As in the problem of human health the skill of the professional is essential, so it is when we consider the health of the living landscape. Yet experience has shown us that the enlightened layman can do much about both of these matters—indeed, he is essential to success in dealing with them. The best of doctors can do little against the stubborn inertia of ignorance and indifference; no amount of brilliant research on the dynamics of vegetation and its role in human affairs can be fruitful without public support. And such support can come only from genuine appreciation of the need for control.

Despite our preoccupation with bigness, mass production, and the ills of a predominantly urban society, despite exploitation, vandalism, and littering of the countryside, there are reasons for hope. A growing, often very well informed minority is beginning to understand the importance of living plants and to appreciate their beauty. As more of us learn to see and interpret land forms, the processes that shape them and the vegetation that clothes and expresses them, we have a source of continuing pleasure. With it comes a sense of concern that this privilege is not more widely shared. For apart from satisfactions missed, those who cannot read and enjoy their surroundings are blind to issues of growing importance in today's world of increasing waste and environmental contamination.

In a few square miles free from concrete and asphalt and not too diligently "improved" there are likely to be between one and two thousand kinds of green plants with roots, stems and leaves. While it takes time for even a professional to learn them all, there are enthusiastic amateurs who have done it. Fortunately the number of plant species that dominate the landscape (outside of the tropics) is not great. There are now excellent illustrated guides from which they can be identified in most parts of the country. Once one learns to know the plants that give character to his neighborhood, he begins to see that a woodland is more than a chance mixture and that prairie or roadside is not a monotonous wilderness of grasses and "weeds."

Instead of this he begins to sense order—not an order that is spick-and-span or mechanically calibrated, but order nevertheless. As he moves on to see that plants and animals, like people, exist in communities, he comes to realize that these communities have their own life histories, developing from simple beginnings into more or less stable systems that express the conditions under which they live.

As our observer learns the kinds of trees and other conspicuous plants, he will discover that they are not growing at random in his immediate locality. White

If you are picking the delicately structured blooms of Daucus carota, *often called Queen Anne's lace, be sure there are three stiff tripartite bracts under the bloom, and perhaps a single almost purple-black floret in the center of the umbel. The carrot family has very poisonous similar forms, especially the poison hemlock,* Conium maculatum, *and hemlock parsley,* Conioselinum chinense, *both with fuller and more intricately cut, fernier leaves than Queen Anne's lace. The* Conium *can be fatal: remember Socrates? Shown to the right, a young teasel,* Dipsacus sylvestris. *The teasel has another kind of defense. Its pods (297) are as "stickery" as those of its less persistent relative,* D. fullonum, *which is still used in the fulling of fine woolens.*

oaks, for example, thrive on ridges or southwestern slopes exposed to the warmth and drying power of the afternoon sun. Here they do not compete with beech and sugar maple, which require moist, cool ravines and northeastern hill slopes. For willows and sycamore he must look along the banks of streams.

Now that we are a nation on wheels, he may choose to travel from east to west on byroads with stops enough to view the countryside. In so doing he will bid adieu to the lovely beech with its smooth grey bark as he passes through Illinois, or farther south through Missouri and Arkansas. Somewhere in Iowa he will make his farewell to the sugar maple, or again farther south, if he is inquisitive enough, he may see its western outpost in a canyon west of Oklahoma City. In this same canyon, along with the sugar maple, he would find red oak, more tolerant of shade than its rugged relatives, the white and bur oaks.

Along with the linden, the red oak crosses the Missouri into eastern Nebraska, where these companions drop out as woodlands shrink to ribbons bordering the rivers. Cottonwood now replaces the sycamore with its green and white bark as a streamside tree; farther away from the water, bands of bur oak and hickory fringe the valley, whose edge may be marked by graceful thickets of such shrubs as sumac and plum. Before many miles have been passed, only the hardy bur oak will remain as a reminder of the great eastern forest complex.

So much for what can still be seen, despite the changes made by human enterprise. Had this journey been made on foot or by horseback two centuries ago a watchful traveler would have seen, as the kinds of trees became fewer, that the wooded areas were shrinking and giving way to grassland. Almost certainly he would have become aware of the increasing dryness of the air, more intense sunshine and greater contrasts in temperature between day and night as he moved into the prairie province.

With the establishment of military outposts in the nineteenth century, weather records began, confirming what had been impressions and registering as well a decrease in annual rainfall. Still later measurements have revealed that as rainfall diminishes toward the continental interior the evaporating power of the air increases, making moisture supply a limiting factor in the development of plant life. Correspondingly, tall grasses on the upland give way to those of medium height until, around the one hundredth meridian, west of McCook, Nebraska, the native growth consists of short grama and buffalo grass spread from north to south in a wide carpet along the massive Rocky Mountain front.

Here the symphony of vegetation breaks out into new and complex themes which can only be suggested. With rising altitude sagebrush or other grey-green scrub yields to belts of pine, and these in turn to fir and spruce; finally come the higher summits with heavy winter snowfall, but summer-clad in superbly colored alpine meadow. Descending at the west to lower altitudes and extreme aridity, one enters the stern beauty of the desert.

I cannot help feeling a sense of *lèse majesté* in touching so lightly upon this

Although Burbank managed to breed thornless cacti suitable for fodder, the many types hardy in the north are aggressively thorned. Some hardy ones may not bloom, however, because of the difference in periodicity between Zone VI and their native haunts. Once established in grass, the prickly pear or Indian fig, Opuntia compressa, is treacherous. Placed on roadside dry walls, it keeps out intruders and furnishes a ten-day period of 3-inch golden flowers useful in arrangements, and a harvest of red fruits which are edible if peeled. Always handle leaves and fruits with gloves or tongs.

rich and varied magnificence that lies beyond the eastern sunset. No one who has seen the autumn gold of the aspen groves that spring up around moist spots on the mountainside, or that clothe great stretches of burn to prepare the way for the evergreen forest that is sure to replace them, can be content to dismiss them with a word. This is equally true of the open elfin foothill forest of juniper and pinyon pine marching up the slope in skirmish formation, the pinyon growing larger until its advance is halted by the shadows of ponderosa pine. Remote in distance and different in character from the gentler climate and landscape of the Ohio Valley as this vast western area may be, it is not completely a thing apart. I do not refer to today's facilities for fast travel, but rather to such importations as the frequent specimens of Colorado blue spruce on our lawns and the carefully tended plantings of cacti, other desert succulents, and choice dwarfs from alpine meadows that brighten midwestern and eastern rock gardens. It is a human privilege to draw upon exotics to create islands of artificial beauty and harmony as well as an obligation to preserve these islands of beauty and harmony in nature.

We are curiously ambivalent in our attitude toward the forest and the trees that compose it. The forest itself is
at once a source of needed material and a rival for space. As we admire individual trees such as this century-old
white-oak, Quercus alba, for their beauty of form and color, their majestic size and promise of shelter, we tend
to forget their vital role, as the largest of plant forms, in maintaining, along with ocean plankton, the favorable
supply of the oxygen so essential to us.

Within the seemingly inert but self-renewing cork of trunk and branches there is an amazingly effective
system of conduction and mechanical support. By means of a pressurized hydraulic system water and dissolved
nutrients are moved upward through the younger wood cells, while older ones supply physical strength. Living
cells of the inner bark serve to distribute and store food made in the foliage. The leaves, in the course of their
work, after divesting water and carbon dioxide of their carbon and hydrogen needed for the manufacture of
sugar, evaporate immense quantities of moisture and release oxygen into the air.

So powerful has the cult of cactus fanciers become that one botanical garden in California no longer dares to include rare species and varieties, lest they be stolen soon after planting. The magnificent collection in Berlin which I saw between wars is now protected by a shield to prevent theft, a sad commentary on the change in a country whose traditions of respect for law had made it safe to line the roadside with fruit trees in an earlier and happier day.

Turning back to the eastern forest, the order in which its important trees drop out toward the west—beech, sugar maple, red oak-linden, hickory-white oak and finally bur oak—can be reversed. If this is done it gives us the sequence in which forests usually develop, with variations, of course, in the eastern deciduous forest region. Here we encounter a curious instance in which the race is not always to the swift, nor the victory to the strong. To use the words of the naturalist, the tough bur and white oaks that flourish without protection cannot maintain their dominance indefinitely. The generation gap is not confined to man. The young of these hardy pioneer trees cannot thrive, or even get a start, under the conditions of shade which their parents create.

When the forester speaks of tolerance he does not, as one might suppose, have in mind the ability of a species to tolerate the harsh conditions of a raw and exposed habitat, untempered from extremes of light, temperature, moisture and raw mineral soil. Instead he has developed a scale for measuring tolerance to shade or, roughly speaking, conditions that arise as plant life modifies raw physical factors and exerts increasing control. This tolerance scale quite closely corresponds to the reverse of our geographical sequence listed in the preceding paragraph, with beech as the most tolerant species. To it we might add the hemlock of the northeastern forest, where pines are normal pioneers.

This introduces us to the phenomenon of plant succession, which is most helpful in understanding and appreciating vegetation. Once an observer learns to see the process by which living communities develop into stable systems, he has a key for describing them in terms of the stages represented in various examples.

The fact of succession, like the falling of ripened fruit and the force of steam from kettles, was in plain sight long before these and other everyday experiences got the disciplined attention we call science. Those who practiced the ancient art of slash and burn farming certainly knew that the forest would return to replace the weeds and brush that took over their abandoned fields. A surveyor's notes made soon after the opening of the Northwest Territory in 1784 states that in one forest he saw "the kinds of trees to be changing here." What he saw were young shade-tolerant species coming in under pioneer types that created shade which their own seedlings could not endure. On another scale are changes due to shifts of climate, enabling plants to advance or obliging them to retreat from former limits. Examples of such plants may be reconstructed from organic remains embalmed in lake sediments and peat beds.

Tree Barks

The color and texture of trunk and branches are determined by the outer layer of bark. This consists of cork cells that form to cover inner bark and wood as diameter increases with growth. One can observe this process as wounds heal over, often slowly.

As new cork is formed, the older outer layers crack and split and are sometimes shed. In other cases they remain as a roughened surface of varying appearance. Thus the outer bark of birch shows as a papery white layer, that of ash as narrow ridges, while the shagbark hickory (opposite right) gets its common name from its covering of shinglelike vertical strips partially freed from the younger cork.

Notable for its beauty is the pattern of sycamore bark (opposite left), with its clinging plates of whitish older cork that reveal the fresh green of the younger bark replacing it.

The thin but impervious cork on young twigs shows markings called lenticels, which allow the exchange of gases between the atmosphere and the green food-making cells of the cortex just beneath. In some trees such as birch, cherry and beech (right) these lenticels persist as horizontal "pen-strokes" long after their role in photosynthesis is over.

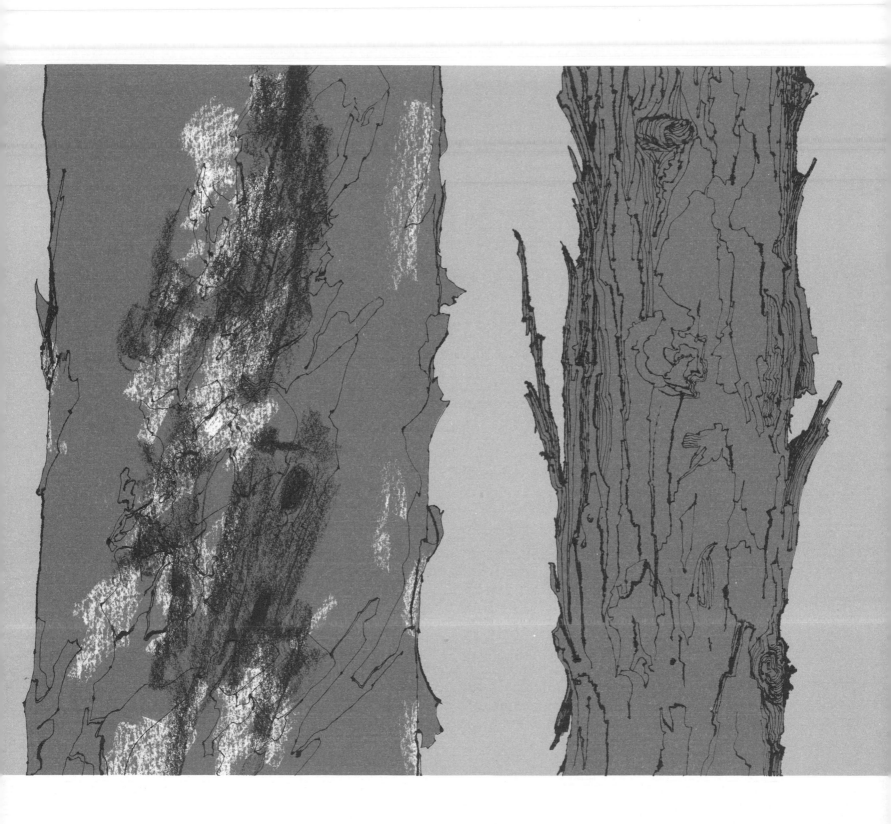

Succession

Pioneers—plant, animal, or human—must cope with exposure to hardship if they are to survive. Whether pioneer plants invade rock, sand, water, or an abandoned field, they encounter extremes of moisture, temperature and light. But once established, their presence creates new conditions favorable to more specialized types of life.

    The annual "weeds" in a neglected field in our area (below) are followed by perennials, woody shrubs and brambles that shelter seedling trees until, in the course of time, the way is opened for the return of a mature native forest or its equivalent. On the right, at the edge of such an established association, a few felled trees have made additional room for a second growth of forest, seen gradually increasing along the old field edges.

Thanks to the fact that each kind of plant has a distinctive form of pollen and that the windblown pollen of trees and other plants is beautifully preserved in lake and bog sediments, the history of climatic succession is recorded by these microscopic evidences of changing plant life. Along with geological information, their study shows us that the waning of the ice sheets was a matter of retreats and advances—not a steady but rather a pulsating process, marked by alternating changes in moisture, temperature and plant life. These successive episodes have left their signatures in the native vegetation of our region. Remnants of cooler times held on in the bog communities where sphagnum moss, sedges and members of the heath family flourish, although sad to say many of these interesting habitats have been drained or burned. A few, fortunately, have been set aside as nature preserves.

Other striking relics of postglacial conditions are the outliers or enclaves of western prairie communities that persisted until they were largely destroyed by modern enterprise. The warming that followed glacial retreat reached a climax some four thousand years ago, a time warmer and dryer than today. In consequence the vegetation of the prairie spread far to the northeast of its present province, along with its insects and other fauna. Presently thereafter the climate became cooler and more moist, definitely so around the beginning of the Christian era, bringing in the present type of forest. With this change the prairies shrank, retaining possession only where local conditions of soil and moisture fended off the invasion of trees.

The prairie, be it noted, has suffered more at our hands because of the deep rich soil it produces than the forest, which is saying much. Contrary to the popular impression that it is a monotonous expanse of grasses, the prairie is a living sea of changing color throughout the seasons. Interspersed with the grasses are many kinds of flowering herbs. These include, besides numerous legumes—clovers, vetches and lupines—that add nitrogen to the soil, beautiful pentstemons, lilies, vervains and composites.

Fortunately it has been possible not only to set aside some—although too few—prairie preserves, but to reconstruct this superb type of plant community, so deserving for what it has contributed to our economy and so valuable for its aesthetic worth. Two notable "made" prairies exist, one in Wisconsin and the other in Ohio, the former due to the enterprise of the late Professor John Curtis, the latter to the unselfish efforts of Mrs. Marie Aull at the Audubon Nature Center near Dayton.

Of the several cities in which I have lived, Lincoln, Nebraska, is in many respects the most beautiful. Its streets are wide and clean, lined with shade trees that have grown surprisingly in this prairie climate since I first saw them in 1913. Its skyline, uncluttered by a congestion of tall buildings, is dominated by the tower of a state capitol, masterpiece of the architect Bertram Goodhue. Below this tower spreads out a building like the terrace of some ancient sun temple, wonderfully symbolic of the broad and open expanse of the grassland. Here if anywhere

Bamboos are not only Oriental in provenance. Our native giant cane, Arundinaria gigantea, often over 10 feet high, stolons out to throw up almost impenetrable barriers in wet territory. Its thick canebrakes hid, as well as trapped, frontiersmen. The mania today for draining wetlands and for tidying up landscapes in general makes this handsome wildlife shelter something of a rarity. As with most bamboos, no one knows what sets off its random and infrequent flowering—an event which causes the plant's death, for it is monocarpic—that is, it bears seed as its climactic and final grand gesture.

is an edifice that should be surrounded and tied to the ground by a living texture that recreates the source of Nebraska's fertile soil. Yet so strong are the canons, or at least the practices, of landscape architecture that one only sees plantings of conventional stuff.

Though man was forest born, his race would be ungrateful not to acknowledge its profound debt to the open lands of grass and forb which on every continent have given him nourishment and enabled him to move about on foot until he covered the earth.

We have been speaking of the kind of succession due to changing climates. But within our present climates there is a more intimate kind of succession which begins as plant life moves in to occupy an empty surface. On such bare ground as sandbars, abandoned fields and broken roadsides—even on the fresh lava beds of our newest state—one can observe it. First there is an invasion of annual ruderals which we call weeds that can thrive on raw mineral soil, exposure to bright sunshine, and the drying power of wind and heat. Their very presence, like that of the human pioneer, brings change. The litter they produce and that of the animal life they foster add organic material to the soil, while their shade encourages the establishment of more tolerant, perennial plant life such as sunflowers, goldenrods and briers. A familiar sight in old fields that have been pastured, and a next step in succession, is the appearance of shrubs and tree seedlings such as juniper, elm, or perhaps old field birch within the protecting circles of uneaten brambles or thistles. This advance guard of the forest, like the annual weeds that began the process, is a hardy growth, prospering in open sunlight but sensitive to shading. So sensitive is the old field birch, for example, that its lower branches and inner twigs cannot survive in the shadows of its own upper and outer foliage.

The next step depends on what kinds of woody plants are available to seed the area and their means of invasion. Fruits of red maple or ash may be borne in by the wind, venturesome and thrifty squirrels may bury the seeds of oak and hickory for later retrieval and fail to use them, or birds may drop the seeds of fruits they have eaten. Moisture and texture of soil also play their part. In one place the developing "second growth" forest may be scattered, remaining open for a time. At another there may be a dense growth of pin oak, or a thicket, in swampy ground, of ash, elm and red maple. In any event, pioneer vegetation is seldom "permanent," although change may be retarded, as it is by fire in the pine forests of the southern states.

Eventually it is likely to be replaced by more and more tolerant species, often in the order we have suggested—red oak-linden, sugar maple, and finally beech. Under the shade of these last two and in the rich leaf mold they create, one finds their own seedlings waiting like crown princes for their parents to die and give them an opportunity. To share this diminutive woody groundcover of the mature forest there develops the exquisite spring flora that includes trilliums, Dutchman's breeches, and woodland phlox, in company with mosses, ferns, and bright-colored

Tree stumps symbolize the presence of man the toolmaker—the shaper of farms and cities, yet too often also the creator of desolation and erosion. While at times such stumps may remain naked and barren, as shown here, more often they serve to nurse an advance guard of plant and animal life that heralds the restoration of living cover. In this happy event they support simple communities that exemplify both the beauty of form and the power of recovery that pervade the world of nature.

fungi. Such, in too simple outline but in essential scheme, is the life history of what we call the native beech-maple forest, self-perpetuating and capable of holding its ground for long periods of time unless disrupted by calamities such as hurricane, fire and cutting, or by a climatic change.

Because moisture, soil and exposure differ so greatly even within a small area, the variations on this major theme are many. Often, due to local conditions, succession is halted in one of its earlier stages, like a still shot from a motion film. Again, the successions on bare rock, dunes, along river sides and around the margins of dying lakes (for lakes like men are born to die) have separate, distinctive patterns subject to the ground rules of the game we have sketched.

Armed with a knowledge of these rules, the observer has an endless source of interest and appreciation. Speaking for myself, I have never seen a dull landscape except where man has mucked it up or failed to achieve harmony in his use of it.

Happily, there are places where man has established a harmonious working relationship with his environment. Switzerland is a prime example, with parts of rural eastern Pennsylvania not far behind. Here the hilltops, in other places victims of nakedness and erosion, are clad in woodland. These, like the sloping hillside pastures or terraced fields, are well managed, leaving the level, fertile valley lands for tillage.

The Swiss, of course, have long since learned that they must make the best of their limited space. The ugliness so prevalent in much outdoor space is the result of waste and poor accounting among people who consider themselves fiscal experts. In their haste to convert natural wealth into currency, its mere symbol, they have confused true profit with depreciation and left the future poorer for it.

But there are signs of rising hope. Cultures, like natural communities, develop by succession. As a people, we are becoming steadily more aware of the importance of beauty in our surroundings. A growing revulsion against sheer ugliness is becoming powerfully reinforced by the physical discomforts and even dangers of our way of life. We are now blessed, as few countries are, with voluntary organizations and dedicated individuals who share what the Quakers call "concern," in this instance a concern to leave the world better than they have found it. No longer do men like William Cullen Bryant, Andrew Downing and John Muir have to battle, almost singlehanded, to establish city and national parks. In their wake are legions whose force is now respected by those eminently practical and indispensable gentlemen who preside over our political and economic destiny.

And even more hopeful than the growth of concerned organizations is the rising group of individuals who are impelled to become involved—to find some way to make their own feelings patent.

The young are seeing the land as the basic resource it has always been, even to the point of decrying the technologies of monocropping and mass production, techniques which have arisen to keep abreast of our expanding populations. An older group feels the need of land for outdoor recreation, but again, because of an excess of people, is fighting for protected areas where the wilderness must be rescued from overuse before we love it to death.

Never before have such masses craved direct land involvement through gardening and shaping the landscape, and it is to this group that the next section of our book addresses itself.

Let us now turn to a more detailed study of an eight-acre plot of neglected fields and pastured woods near Cincinnati purchased about thirty-five years ago. Existing natives have been encouraged and added to and sympathetic hardy exotics have been imported to create a disciplined sense of beauty.

Here at Cockaigne in a varied terrain of upland, ravine, and open space broken by stands of imposing oaks, sycamores and other survivors of the original forest is an example of controlled harmony between a naturalistic landscape and its occupants.

This decaying stump at the edge of a wood is obviously the promiscuous host to Trillium flexipes, *our local form of white or maroon-flowered trillium;* Dentaria laciniata, *the cutleaf toothwort;* Cystopteris fragilis, *the bladder fern;* Parthenocissus quinquefolia, *the Virginia creeper;* Phlox divaricata, *or blue phlox;* Claytonia virginica, *the spring beauty;* Botrychium multifidum, *the leathery grape fern;* Galium aparine, *a bedstraw; a shelf fungus decayed beyond recognition, and various mosses and lichens. How many insects and micro-organisms could we add? And who could ever be sure that we had listed them all?*

Marion Rombauer Becker, Gardener

...Paul Valéry once declared, "I write half the poem; my reader writes the other half." Valéry's is just another way of reminding us of what we all know: beauty lies so largely in the eye of the beholder. And for the gardener, as well as the reader of verse, this eye is more multifaceted than a dragonfly's. In the world of flowering plants it takes account not only of bloom, but of the impact of sympathetic grouping and dramatic contrasts, the subtle alterations brought about by seasonal change, the effects of specific soil makeup, orientation, air-flow and degree of moisture, the evidence of healthy and agreeable ecologic balance.

Sometimes the "other half" brings nothing to the poetry of plants. A telling example is that of an otherwise not wholly incompetent observer who once lived for some years in the very area where my own horticultural experience has proved so rewarding. I quote Mrs. Frances Trollope, mother of the noted nineteenth-century novelist, who in the forties wrote these disparaging lines:

> To the north, Cincinnati is bounded by a range of forest-covered hills, sufficiently steep and ragged to prevent their being built upon or cultivated. . . . Deep and narrow watercourses, dry in summer but bringing down many streams in winter, divide these hills into separate heights and this furnishes the only variety the landscape offers for many miles around the town. . . . I doubt if any inhabitant ever mounted these hills so often as myself and my children but it was rather in the enjoyment of a freer air than for any beauty of prospect that we took our daily climb. These hills afford neither shrubs nor flowers. . . .

It was this same Mrs. Trollope who, to while away her tedium, and to edify backwater and backwoods vulgarians, built in the middle of her adopted town something she called "The Oriental Bazaar"—an edifice in the "Moorish Gothic" style whose madly fanciful exterior was matched by the curious and esoteric "exhibits" within.

Yet all around Mrs. Trollope lay far more curious and far more authentic "exhibits"—wild wealth that had utterly escaped her notice. Fortunately, others who came after her, when they directed to those "barren" hills only a glance of the multifaceted eye, found in and among them a greater variety of native flowering species than anywhere else in the whole United States. For the Cincinnati region lies geographically in a part of Zone VI (20), where the growth tolerances of North and South merge and overlap.

To spark an awareness of these treasures; to put before you the trials and the triumphs of thirty years' enchanted effort; to show how the great panoply of natives and hardy exotics I have grown at Cockaigne on our eight woodland acres in southwestern Ohio may be grown with equal satisfaction in any number of similar locations throughout North Central and Midwest America—in short, to set off a certain bright blaze of creative participation in those who possess,

A Love Affair With Land

latently or actively, the gardener's multifaceted eye—this is why my section of this book has been written.

How and why did I begin this adventure, this love affair with an initially not very endearing tract, largely alkaline in composition, much of it despoiled by logging and pasturage? "Naturalizing," for anyone who owns such a site, has limited time to give to it, and cannot resist an obvious challenge, is the most practical response. There were other reasons to prefer this kind of wild-gardening too. We acquired our acreage several years before we built a house on it, and I realized that it would be foolhardy for us to start cultivating areas that might later be disturbed by excavation or terracing. This meant, by the process of elimination, the wooded glen north of the favored housesite. In addition, we had no water on the place—the water so essential in transplanting—except what we could scoop up from the small creek which, as it happened, flowed constantly, even in summertime, through the glen.

Then, and later also, I found that working with a woodland relieved me of many of the irksome problems of more formal gardening. It abolished time-consuming maintenance techniques, one of which was intensive weeding. To obviate it I simply installed near steps and paths clumps of desirable natives and sympathetic aliens, and let them colonize. These aliens included certain selected hardy exotics, some of which were "escapes," so-called: species which, first introduced under other circumstances, subsequently prove sturdy and congenial companions for strictly indigenous material.

In some of my woods area heavy leaf-fall automatically inhibits greenery, and these patches in themselves can form effective year-round contrast. In wild-gardening little time need be given to fertilizing and none to spraying. I found myself, too, the recipient of a fringe benefit. For if I paint or sew and am interrupted, my handiwork confronts me unchanged upon my return. But now and then when the demands of ordinary life separate me from my woods, I discover that during the interval they not only have largely taken care of themselves, but have been busy confecting wonderful surprises.

Another quite unanticipated thrill of developing my little woodland principality was, as the years went on, a microcosmic one. Here at work in miniature were all those forces and phenomena which Paul Sears has already described as typical of the landscape at large. Controlling the baleful ones, like erosion, while encouraging those which made for harmony and fruitfulness gave me a modest but very appreciable sense of mastery, as if I had played the director's dominant role in a long, happy drama of redemption.

The mainstays of my woods garden, I need hardly say, are the natives. Many of the pages that follow are given over to a description of these plants which, together and in succession, put a characteristic stamp and seal on the regional landscape. Yet the first native to bloom, *Erigenia bulbosa*, so rightly called harbinger-of-spring (66), does not normally appear until mid-March. Long before that date, however, the wild-gardener, if he naturalizes well-chosen exotics, can achieve not only bloom but spectacular drifts of bloom between onsets of severest weather.

Since the context of my section of this book is more or less chronological—flowers of winter, spring, summer and fall—it seems appropriate to treat at the beginning not the more reluctant natives, but these same hardy exotics which first announce the lengthening of days and the turn of the year. Extending the blooming season forward, so to speak, into the unlikely midwinter months is one powerful inducement to experiment with such exotics. Yet, as we have observed, the time-honored sensitive comradeships that have given the primordial landscape its distinctive loveliness must not be disrupted or disturbed by the intrusion of incongruous newcomers. It takes skill to place alien materials graciously. I am haunted by my recollection of several Northwest towns where the New Zealand monkey puzzle trees, fascinating as they are, gesticulate at the passerby from front yards like the simians they are supposed to perplex. Coloradans probably leave the Midwest wondering how on earth we can cage the Koster's blue spruce on tiny lawns away from their accustomed rock and mountain vastnesses. Pay a visit to almost any arboretum and you will despair as guides point to foreign specimens, glorious in themselves, but juxtaposed to others so different in shape and scale and foliage as to suggest a vegetative vendetta.

It so happened that when we first bought our property I found Lob's Wood, a two-hundred-acre forest tract developed by a generous amateur enthusiast, the late Carl Krippendorf, after he had read the works of Robinson, Jekyll, Farrer and Bowles. He never saw the gardens of these great exponents of naturalizing, but on the basis of his reading, this "sharing" gardener tried out hundreds of hardy exotics and built up seed exchanges and corresponded with Victoria Sackville-West and Clarence Elliott. In turn, these gifted Britons have become admired authorities of my own who continue to influence my gardening life.

The exotics I have added to my woods in greatest number are bulbous plants. If you are an old hand at bulbs, you know their imperative need to mature undisturbed. This is also from an aesthetic point of view their greatest disadvantage. It is essential to use them in combination with surface-rooting plants that cover their leaves as they die down, and there will be specific suggestions for such camouflage as we go along.

Within a wood, with its winding paths along hill and hollow, it is not difficult to establish flowing relationships. Certain similarities of structure—the bold verticals of tree trunks, the spreading high shade, clumps of understory—all create situations where one seldom wants for suitable backgrounds against which to plot accents of form and color. But realize that a woodland garden has, in addition to its own, a plant power structure imposed on it by varying climatic forces. The triggering of bloom is erratic from year to year. The strong color contrast provided by a generous grouping of deep purple *Delphinium tricorne*,

What is more enticing when crunching through the frosty autumn leaf-fall, with only the remotest expectations of bloom, than to come on the golden sparks of witch-hazel, Hamamelis virginiana, *blazing among the dark boles of the wintry woods, or to catch its pungency in the cold air?* H. vernalis, *from the Ozark country, has many reddish-orange forms, while* H. mollis *from China also heralds the spring with pale yellow, more twisted, straplike petals, showier than the ones depicted here. The seeds take two years to mature. They are best gathered in fall by picking a podded branch and covering it with a bag, for when the rocklike capsules finally split, the shiny black seeds are ejected with explosive force. A handy way to spread seed is to discard the branches pruned for arrangements in an area where you want witch-hazel to take hold.*

for example, against the milder tones of pink wild geranium and grey-blue wild hyacinth may in a subsequent season, because of variations in blooming dates, become a mere fading shadow of its former self amid a strong stand of precocious white synandra. That year the "punch" in this same area may have to come instead from the red-pink tones of the pollinated *Trillium grandiflorum*, which heightens the geraniums' paler pink with bold bravura and brings out the hyacinths' subtones of lavender blue.

Then, too, the woods inevitably have physical as well as temporal limits and limitations, and from their boundaries liaison has to be made with less tractable acreage.

There is much to say about this casual, undemanding but infinitely subtle way of gardening—gardening in the wild. Join me as we walk around our eight acres, talking of the hows, the whats, the whens and the whys of my plantings, the relationships of the woods to its verges, and the respect for indigenous beauty I strive to maintain even among the more formalized transition plantings near the house.

As fall approaches I try to assess the growing season just past with help from the first black frost, which intensifies the autumn color to the point of pain and simultaneously thins the landscape so that its bones begin to show. Hills look steeper against the emerging ladderwork of trees; houses, hidden for months, seem to move closer; enduring groundcovers like honeysuckle, myrtle and ivy, previously part of the general greenery, reassert their presence.

By the end of October we become daily more grateful for a lingering autumn crocus, a lone cyclamen, a straggling clematis, a campion, a Korean chrysanthemum—even a reactivated violet. At winter's onset, weed and plant rosettes survive to console us for the brief but now absolute absence of native bloom. They run the gamut from the dark, glistening leaves of the evening primrose, *Oenothera biennis,* and the moth mullein, *Verbascum blattaria,* to the grey-felt forms of the common mullein, *V. thapsus* (303), or the tender greens of columbine (257).

If you are familiar with the mesophytic midland landscape (24), you know the sparseness of evergreen through it, even in the understory. You know in cold weather how it depends for character on somber-toned branches that turn the hills at dusk to a smoky purplish-brown, and bare twiggery that glows golden at sunrise and sunset. Its tree structure is further enlivened, where soils are hospitable, by the grey of beech, with its lovely ethereal dry foliage fluttering in the chill wind and restating the coppery leaf-fall against the sky; or, along the valley bottoms, by the white streaks of sycamore.

These sought-after touches, then, are the only relief "on high" in a winter landscape where evergreen—unless we count introduced varieties—is confined to an occasional native cedar (227). But when we turn our eyes downward we find on the floor of our late autumn woods and fields any amount of greenery which will last through the winter.

In the woods an astonishing number of wildlings that we usually associate only with spring peer out from under the drifts of leaves: the now dark-green, smooth foliage of *Phlox divaricata* (130), so unlike, as the name implies, its paler, downier spring form; the purplish-backed leaves of the foamflower (103); the soft, pale picoted hearts of *Synandra hispidula* (245), that "rare" biennial which, if it finds just the right moisture and shade, can become as overpowering as an army on the march; and two invaders always to be avoided near less vigorous growth: the appendaged waterleaf and the creeping buttercup (153). All these are outstanding on crisp mornings when their pubescent surfaces attract the frost rime.

Here, too, the pale lettucy fronds of the Jacob's-ladder (105) and the less pale leaves of valeriana (180) contrast with the leathery dark greenery of the Christmas fern (142), the spiral whorls of the Allegheny pachysandra (57), the elegantly structured hepatica (57), and the reddish embroidered clumps of the leathery grape fern (42). Fond recollection and promise lie in the myriad tiny

Winter Surprises

cotyledons of blue-eyed Mary (130, 223), the sylvan chickweed, the delicate translucent foliage of isopyrum (249), and meadow rue (151), which remains uncurled and relaxed during the lowest temperatures.

These natives are reinforced in my woods by a group of introduced plants that provide untold pleasure later, during the grey days between November and mid-March. Not only the leaves but the flowers of these aliens defy cold dry winds and frozen earth, resist ice glazes, turn up miraculously refreshed after a blanketing of snow—and, even when picked in a congealed condition, respond to arranging indoors.

The earliest and most persistent are the hellebores (53, 58, 60); the rarest, the winter cyclamen (181); the most rewarding, foolproof and prolific, winter aconites and snowdrops (54, 55, 308). Often before mid-February, thanks to these enterprising exotics, the woods delight me by being aglow with copius bloom, vocal with the humming of my neighbor's bees, and sweet with honeyed fragrance.

How does one acquire masses of these winter-blooming plants? Look at the ads in the horticultural magazines or consult the *Plant Buyer's Guide* for sources. Should you not find what you want, the Bailey Hortorium at Cornell University and the National Arboretum in Washington, D. C., will send you commercial listings.

As for snowdrops, the common *Galanthus nivalis* multiply rapidly from bulb offsets. Because their bulbs dry out so rapidly, the recommended time to separate any of the snowdrops is at the end of their blooming period. If you plant them in rough, lightly wooded areas, you don't even have to bother to divide them; the stronger bulbs push the unwanted ones to the surface in the fall, and there they lie exposed to their fate unless someone who wants a "start" gathers them up.

The earlier blooming and bolder *G. elwesii*, followed by *G. plicatus*, which grows up to 15 inches, and *G. nivalis* 'S. Arnott,' are among my handsomest interbred varieties. Doubles are chiefly valuable for their long blooming period. Their interesting centers are best seen if used as shown (225).

Snowdrops—all of them, of course, with predominantly white blooms—are often differentiated from one another by the green or yellow floral markings on their three smaller, closely overlapping segments. Identification by leaf characteristics as they unfold was adopted by the English specialist Sir Frederick Stern, but his work on snowdrops and snowflakes has just been challenged by Russian investigators who claim he lacked access to sufficient live material. Whatever the right or wrong of this controversy, I have always realized how essential for accuracy in writing about gardens is the study of living plants, and I hasten to point out that all groupings pictured in these pages were simultaneous combinations drawn from life, and were checked for attribution against many sources.

The so-called yellow and green snowdrop varieties I grow are not noticeably superior in whiteness of petal or distinction of stance, and their propagation is

One of the most satisfactory aspects of the woods between mid-November and mid-March is certain greens, highlighted with a surprising volume of color, that weave through the hillside, contrasting with leaf-fall or snow. The white bloom of the Christmas rose, Helleborus niger*—yes,* niger *means black, but here it refers to the root—is so intense that a few clumps stand out against expanses of leaves in the fall or, toward spring, against the restless paler white snowdrop bells,* Galanthus nivalis.

Scattered about among the hellebores are the highly variable variegated leaves belonging to Cyclamen neapolitanum. *Those of C.* coum, *which blooms during the winter, are rounder and a duller green. Cyclamens and hellebores are titans of hardiness.*

amazingly slow. This being so, they really give me less pleasure than the more available types. In this connection I think all gardeners should look at their plantings from time to time with a highly critical eye, to counteract that "collector's bias" which so often assigns rarity too high a place in the scheme of things. I do not mean to discourage acquiring new varieties, but simply to suggest discrimination. An enormous help in making choices, I have found, is *Collin's Guide to Bulbs*, edited by Patrick Synge, in which you will find illustrated in color many desirable species, all proportionately scaled.

Aconites are only slightly more difficult to grow than snowdrops, and they naturalize only a little less rapidly. Because they bloom so early, the tubers sent us from abroad are pretty well dried up and nubbly by the fall sale season. Soak them for a few hours, put them in pressed peat pots filled with loamy soil, group them where you can water them during dry spells, and sink the pots until the foliage dies down the following spring. There will still be enough of the pot edges visible to find them easily for transplanting, pot and all, into a permanent location. Aconites self-sow heavily in my woods, especially in well-drained sites. *Eranthis hyemalis* is the commonest, but no hardier than *E. cilicica*. This latter variety (70) has a slightly deeper and narrower cut leaf on a reddish stem, and blooms ten days later. It also self-sows. *E. X tubergenii* and *E. X tubergenii* 'Guinea Gold' are larger and a deeper shade of golden yellow. Being hybrids they increase mainly through bulblets.

As to the hellebores, perhaps because natural grooming is one of my major personal frustrations, I look on them with envy. For of all the plants I know, except the yew, they have one of the tidiest life cycles. And like the yew they are long-lived—fifty to seventy-five years.

Buy a few hellebore plants to acquire fresh seed. The *orientalis* hybrids will self-sow copiously, and seedlings may be transplanted successfully to almost any woodsy site. But *H. niger* needs a little help. I put sandy loam in a clay pot, sow the seed as soon as ripe, put the pot to soak until moisture rises to the top, sink the pot in some out-of-the-way place on a north-facing slope in the woods, and cover the top with a piece of glass. I forget about it for nine months and then find the pot full of sturdy cotyledons. When the seedlings have made their true leaves, I remove the glass for about a week and plant the seedlings individually in pressed peat pots. By early summer when they have become established in a lightly shaded seed bed, I put them, still in the pots, out in the woods, preferably in a north-facing site, and water them in well. From that point on they flourish untended. It is about three to four years from seed to bloom, almost as long as it takes for a divided established bloomer to recover and start again.

If you must divide hellebore clumps, choose late spring. The thick fleshy roots, if pulled into very small pieces with a portion of the tough rhizomatous crown attached, establish faster than if left in large pieces.

The so-called *H. orientalis* hybrids rise to twenty inches, carrying their prolific bloom high. Their nodding habit makes them ideal for planting near steps or

First to break the grip of the frozen winter soil are the aconites, *Eranthis hyemalis,* our New Year's greeting. Their super-strong necks emerge first as thick green-gold hoops. Gradually they release one side, pulling the leaf-enveloped bud aloft. Then within a day or two the yellow chalices, centered against glossy dark indented discs, cover the ground in fragrant clusters. Who is happier to see them—we or the nectar-starved bees?

And who could find fault with a flower that always shows its white buds by Valentine's Day? Whether the temperature is freezing or as balmy as spring, the snowdrop, *Galanthus nivalis,* opens its delicately balanced bells to the sunlight and gives off a honeyed fragrance for more than six weeks. If you want small-bulbed plants like this to multiply with abandon, site them on a hillside where the leaf-fall does not accumulate too heavily.

on slopes above a path where you can look into the richly encrusted centers of the varicolored cups. These range in color from dark red wine through purply-pink to creamy white. While some have sepals that are solid in color, others show greenish or reddish speckling.

Even when not in bloom the hellebores attract interest because of their foliage. The leaves of *H. niger* are thicker than those of *orientalis*, with fewer and coarser undulations at the edging of their matte silver-and-green surfaces. Those of the *orientalis* hybrids are almost metallic in their firmness and reflective power, and finely saw-toothed, as shown on the endpapers. The foliage of both these hellebores is cantilevered from a handsome arched stem and remains in good form except for a short period in late February when the new growth arises from the, by then, flattened and bronzed circle of the old. The strong, full-budded new growth of the *orientalis* hybrids, complexly convoluted, allows glimpses of bud color. The leaves of *H. foetidus* (60), which when crushed give the plant its name, die down in summer but are almost immediately replaced.

Among the neglected but rewarding winter-blooming plants are *Viburnum farreri*, sometimes listed as *fragrans* (225), that opens its spicy florets—fragile counterparts of *V. carlesii*—intermittently from November through March; the witch-hazels (50); and a large genus of hardy bulbs, the crocuses, that, if protected from rodents, can undauntedly add color from late October through March.

There is one thing I envy my urban gardening friends—the coarser palates of their mice. No other inhabitants at Cockaigne have been served with more expensive or recherché food than these predators. So devastating are their inroads among certain bulbs that I take the liberty of showing a small group of mouse-impervious crocus substitutes (62). I can grow crocuses in the open for a number of years by providing protective custody for them in lidded chests of ¼-inch wire mesh, but making and installing such irregularly shaped boxes takes great patience. I also retain a few patches of crocuses by planting bulbs in hard-packed, gravelly areas near rock-lined paths. This latter triumph led me to try a combination of wire mesh and sharp gravel for lilies (161) and Oriental poppies; and I have had some success with a plant deterrent scheme for crocuses and wild tulips (86).

If your resident rodents, like mine, deny you a range of crocuses, and you are too impatient to force the bulbs in those enchanting crocus pots the Dutch invented, find yourself a copy of Maw's monograph in some botanical library, or read Bowles' *Crocus and Colchicum* to realize vicariously what you are missing. I managed to grow the dramatic saffron crocus, *C. sativus*, in a rock-bordered bed for a few years. In the end, when the few bulbs the mice didn't find sprouted, they promptly fell victim to rabbits who, the instant it appeared, sheared off the dark green, silver-ribbed leafage which precedes the fall bloom. The lambent lavender flowers of *sativus* have gaudy red-orange stigmas blatantly protruding

If you look at the brilliant winter sky through a pattern of bare branches, you become aware of the symmetry that allows each leaf, when it emerges, its place in the sun. On no groundcover is this so-called phyllotaxy more clearly revealed than on the Allegheny spurge, Pachysandra procumbens, whose leaf structures form a series of perfect spirals. It is seen here dominating the winter form of Jacob's-ladder and the bronzed decumbent leaves of the sharp-lobed hepatica.

—but not nearly so far as the redder antlered ones of *C. tournefortii*. I had admired this spectacular bloom in Maw but never dreamed I would see it in life. My good fortune was the result of taking a flyer on a fall crocus mixture. Against the strictures of many garden writers who advocate one-variety plantings in solid color blocks, I was originally lured to the "mixture" category in catalogs by the greatly reduced prices. What not infrequently happens in such circumstances is that odd groups of rarities, highly desirable but too limited in quantity to be advertised separately, find their way into "bargain" catalog offerings.

Although true cold-weather bloomers, and some that appear in late February and early March, know how to take care of themselves, one's mind naturally turns in winter to the whole problem of hardiness.

Helpful lists are available for many shrubby plants classified as to their inherent genetic capacity and more or less proven limits of endurance in the various climatic zones throughout the United States (20). But gardeners seem fatefully attracted to plants that may be too tender for their surroundings. To some extent their optimism is not misplaced. What amazing microclimates one finds when comparing notes with friends a few miles or even a few blocks away!

The flowers of Helleborus niger *(below), the Christmas rose, rise on a single scape and show only a small protective bract barely noticeable when the flower opens. The irregularly cut pedate leaves often remain low-lying, but sometimes overtop the blooming stem. 'Potters Wheel,' one of the largest hybrids, is said, because of the bluish cast of its leaves, to be related to the* niger *subspecies from Yugoslavia,* H. macranthus. *The* orientalis *hybrids (opposite page and on the endpapers) are identified by a cockade of three enveloping leaves that frame the bloom.*

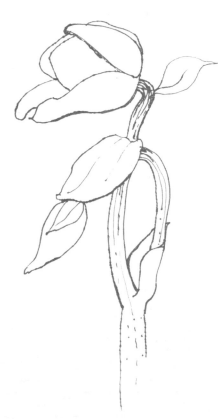

In fact, I've discovered very different responses from the same species within a quite limited acreage.

Is extra hardiness due to the added humidity a small creek provides or to its modification of frost effects? Is it caused by the presence of a moisture-stabilizing mulch or a temperature-stabilizing groundcover? Maybe less sturdy material has succumbed to frost damage at the bottom of a valley where cold air has pocketed, for air moves in a drainage pattern almost as rigid as that which controls water. Towering windbreaks often exert a beneficial effect on the lee side for as much as twenty times their height, with a disproportionate turbulence beyond. If kept approximately as high as the protected plant, they will accomplish the desired effect less erratically. Again, perhaps the shelter of a north-facing wall away from prevailing winds will give an even-tempered advantage to certain broad-leaved evergreens and, further, shield them from exposure to sun while their leaves are frosted.

Only under extremely adverse conditions of temperature, drought, insect attack, blight or air pollution does one have to worry about the hardiness of natives. It is true that some mutant forms are more fleeting than the type, *Phlox divaricata* forma *albiflora* (130), for example. And plants with variegated leaves, because of their reduced green surface, also tend to be weaker. Some doubles, too, in which the extra petals are produced at the expense of reproductive organs, must be increased through clone divisions, as in *Sanguinaria canadensis* forma *multiplex*, the double bloodroot.

By and large, though, natives can be counted on to flourish. With exotic introductions it is helpful to buy hardy strains of seeds and plants and to patronize nurseries as much as two zones to the north of you. If the plants I want are not available there, then I try hardening off material I buy from farther south in a controlled growing area where I can afford it good soil, needed watering and protection while it adjusts.

My surest test for warm planting areas is to watch where snow first melts or where winter aconite first shows color. These are definitely not the best sites for magnolias or other shrubs whose early flowers may be nipped by the frost, but are just right for the more tender bulbs that winter over their green leaves, like *Lycoris radiata, L. sprengeri* and *Lilium candidum.* Another predictably warm area is in front of a south-facing wall; but here heat radiation in summer may prove too great unless considerable watering is done. I have such a spot, and found that even my most sun-tolerant herbs could not withstand the reflection from a high white wall, and I was finally reduced to using it for summering out my cactus collection. Experimenting with a single species in varying locations can become not only a test for hardiness but, should a plant flourish in a number of different exposures, a way to extend its blooming period, sometimes for as much as ten days.

Just as there are microclimates within an acreage, so there may be microhabitats where soil variations can encourage unusual growth. In the Cincinnati area the soil, so largely alkaline in reaction, has some small acid soil pockets. Here the lucky landowners can boast the rhododendrons and azaleas for which we envy our neighbors in the more northern reaches of Ohio. Success with things ericaceous, as I learned the long hard way, depends on a good deal more than skill (122).

As I have indicated, the survival factor often has to do with proper siting. If a plant is in its element in shade and needs wind protection—our prevailing winter winds come from the southwest—placing it to the north of a boulder or large tree trunk can sometimes ensure success. Once you get to know conditions on your own grounds and the requirements of certain plant families, you are forever finding nooks and crannies into which to tuck a plant under a duffy mulch or expose it to a baking summer sun, depending on its needs.

I have seen certain borderline bulbs such as *Zephyranthes candida* flourish and multiply here in the blazing sun of a clayey border, although I have never been able to hold them outdoors myself. Yet I have one open, northwest-facing area where certain others, notably *Lycoris radiata* (170) and *L. sprengeri*, naturalize without protection; and their leafage, up all winter, survives exposure in as good condition as these same bulbs set out in a frame. *Lycoris aurea*, on the other hand, bought under the brash slogan "guaranteed hardy," could be certified hardy only in the most perfunctory sense of the word; it managed to pull through, but never developed enough foliage to produce bloom.

Hardiness has its mysteries, but there are a few commonsense procedures that help solve them. After having chosen basically hardy strains, establish the

As the ornate centers of Helleborus niger, *which are the true flowers, are pollinated, the white sepals turn pink and the centers develop plump to bursting seed pods. When the pods of these and other hellebores ripen, they twist and whorl along the seams to cast shiny seeds—varying from gunmetal to black with an ivory base—from a flaring, diaphanous beige-gold pinwheel. Even when empty, the hulls remain decorative against the faded color but firm texture of the sepals, as seen in the detail of* Helleborus orientalis *below.*

Helleborus foetidus, *the bear's-foot hellebore, a native of England and southern Europe, tends to be short-lived, but does self-sow. Taller than* H. niger *and the* H. orientalis *hybrids,* H. foetidus, *like the more sun-tolerant, wind-shy, prickly-leaved* H. corsicus, *has no basal leaves, but rises directly from the ground on a stem that carries both its palmate foliage and tall panicles of bloom. A welcome sight in January are the pale green buds (below) of* H. foetidus, *which top the leaves by 5 inches. In early March these expand into foot-high sprays of dark red-tipped ¾-inch chartreuse bells (right).*

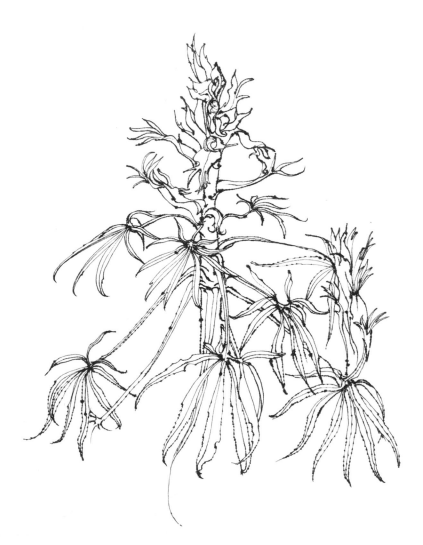

plants well before frost. Don't stimulate soft growth by feeding fertilizers high in phosphorus or nitrogen after July. This admonition does not hold for composts, which act slowly and can be lightly applied at any time provided there is moisture in the soil. Prolonged artificial shading of plants should be avoided in late summer and fall because acclimatization to cold is an energy-demanding process requiring all possible sunlight. Plants should also have access when days are short to the red rays which are predominant in sunlight at such periods, these rays being stimulators of root growth. In the late winter, however, partial shading of newly established material may prove of value against desiccation, especially from bright sunlight, and the stress of sudden temperature changes. What quite confounds all gardeners is not cold *per se* but the unpredictable, uncontrollable temperature drops and random rises that attack before a plant has naturally hardened off—a process induced by shortening periods of daylight or, as days lengthen in spring, before it has time to acclimatize its emerging buds and leaves.

On one prescription everybody seems agreed, especially for evergreens, even such small ones as thymes and savories. Thorough fall soaking before the temperature drops is highly beneficial against drying and consequent winter loss. We know that the greatest winter damage takes place in plants where ice crystallization occurs in the intracellular fluid or, less often, when the intercellular ice crystals become large enough to fracture the cells. But we also know that watering does not contribute to this process, since the moisture content within the cells is internally regulated. Sudden and swift temperature drops, then, in fall and spring are to be dreaded more than excessive cold, which, if it comes on gradually, plants usually withstand without harm. You may have observed yourself that the bulbs you protected by planting out flourished, but that the few you forgot in a paper bag in the toolhouse turned, after a sudden cold spell, into a mushy mass.

There is general consensus, too, that a properly nourished plant has greater potential for survival. It is true that individuals knowledgeable and adept at the addition and control of chemical fertilizers and moisture can produce more profuse bloom, heavier roots and greater greenery; but in a naturalizing situation such as I advocate, the slower but constant feeding which results from the use of compost (98) has started my plants off well and established them later with lower risk and minimal loss.

Ability to withstand drought is another vital consideration if one cannot water plants during periods of low rainfall. When watering is undertaken it should be repeated at least once a week, and to a depth of 6 to 8 inches. Less penetrating moisture brings roots up to the surface, where they are more vulnerable to the effects of drought. Incorporating compost with the soil, and dressing with compost, are moisture-retentive additions which encourage strong roots and very definitely promote hardiness. In fact, should I be asked for the single factor that has made my gardening pleasurably successful, I would attribute it to continual soil enrichment with compost. I stress the importance of periodic enrichment again because in our furiously hot and often dry summers organic material is constantly being burned out of the soil, especially exposed soil. As I have implied, there are ways of slowing this burning-up process with mulches (168) and with groundcovers (111). But both of these moisture-preserving methods have to be carefully employed so that they in turn do not take for themselves moisture and nutrients needed by plants nearby.

Commonsense procedures in siting, watering, transplanting (101), and proper pruning after bloom has passed may help plants survive winter kill, frost injury or outright freezing. What still needs more laboratory study is the relationship between flowering and seasonal changes of light and darkness. We are aware, at least, that species can be divided into those that bloom during short days, those that bloom during long days, and still others that are more or less indifferent to seasonal light variations. Some plants, like cacti and poinsettias, when moved to a new latitude, even under the best greenhouse conditions, fail to bloom unless light adjustments are made to simulate conditions in the latitude from which they came. Curiously, this kind of behavior is not limited to different species. It is found also within genotypes of the same species, as experiments with grasses that range from Texas to the Dakotas have shown.

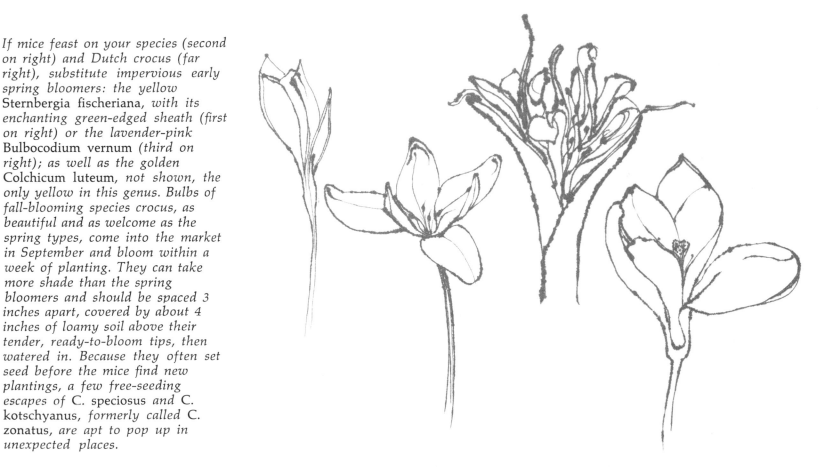

If mice feast on your species (second on right) and Dutch crocus (far right), substitute impervious early spring bloomers: the yellow Sternbergia fischeriana, *with its enchanting green-edged sheath (first on right) or the lavender-pink* Bulbocodium vernum *(third on right); as well as the golden* Colchicum luteum, *not shown, the only yellow in this genus. Bulbs of fall-blooming species crocus, as beautiful and as welcome as the spring types, come into the market in September and bloom within a week of planting. They can take more shade than the spring bloomers and should be spaced 3 inches apart, covered by about 4 inches of loamy soil above their tender, ready-to-bloom tips, then watered in. Because they often set seed before the mice find new plantings, a few free-seeding escapes of* C. speciosus *and* C. kotschyanus, *formerly called* C. zonatus, *are apt to pop up in unexpected places.*

As for those plants of borderline hardiness, which present to so many of us a perverse but irresistible challenge, many survive best if planted in early spring so they have time to become well established. The real heartbreakers are those "iffy" shrubs or trees that lure one into experimentation, and then leave such dreadful gaps when they fail. But if they are nonstructural in the design of the garden, trying them out is often worth the gamble.

Lucky is the year when, after the glorious color of the earliest introduced winter-flowering bulbs and hellebores, there is no hiatus in bloom. For often a period of dark days and very low temperatures returns the woods almost to the evergreen distribution of early winter, and you can hardly believe you have already experienced before Washington's birthday such a wonderfully floriferous prelude.

If these disruptive cold spells, sometimes plunging below zero, have occurred, it is then not until late February or early March that a fresh relay of aliens on bold sortie challenges your own hardihood and tempts you out again into the blustery weather.

Some years by mid-February you will find the first of the reticulate irises, so-called because their bulbs have a netted brown coating. Usually leading off is another of this species, the chubby 4-inch yellow *Iris danfordiae*. After blooming, it divides into many tiny bulblets, and flowers in subsequent years are rare except under ideal conditions. My own conditions are obviously something less than that. Nevertheless, for the excitement of having such early response from this species, I have occasionally planted *danfordiae*, as well as the even earlier white *I. vartanii*, or Christmas iris, but I must simply regard them as annuals. I now substitute a slightly later but quite hardy creamy yellow, *I. winogradowii*.

By the first of March a great mass of reticulates can be counted on. They return year after year and multiply, so that I have showy patches ranging from the light ice-blue of *I. reticulata* 'Cantab,' through the delft of *I. reticulata* 'Clairette,' to the purple-blue of *I. reticulata*—the type, and the easiest in cultivation—to the reddish purple-brown of 'Krelagei.' These last grow to a height of about 6 inches and have slight but distinctive variations in form and in the markings on their flower-falls. See *I. r.* 'Clairette,' both when just opening (next page) and arranged (219). Reticulates all have the same glaucous leaves, rigid and often very low at the time of bloom but lengthening out to 18 inches later. While the temptation to use these flowers to border a path is great when one considers their charm at blooming time, one regrets such placement shortly after, when the reedlike leaves collapse over the path and persist at least six weeks as lank greenery, with another week of yellowing, before they disappear until the following spring.

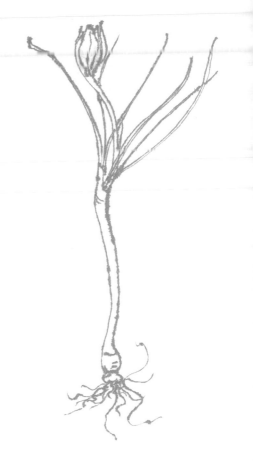

Recommended depth of planting for crocuses is usually given as only a few inches. This spring species, dug and drawn at blooming time, shows its ability to pull itself down to its preferred depth, and indicates that in our climate spring-blooming crocus corms grow best covered from 5 to 8 inches, at which levels they are found when collected in the Near East and Spain, regions where summers are as hot as ours. Many species seed freely, but the hybrid types multiply better through corm separation. The corms increase best in well-drained sunny situations. See the new one here forming on top of the old. It will resume its brown-webbed, flat, bulging appearance when it has absorbed all the nourishment it can before its leafy food factory dries off, and will then wait to bloom again the following spring.

Among early February bloomers, Adonis volgensis, like a spectacular double buttercup as it unfolds above its compressed, bronzed, ferny foliage, contrasts with the rich purple of Iris reticulata 'Clairette' and the lavender-pink Bulbocodium vernum. This almost sessile, funnel-shaped flower is valuable for its pinky color, rare at this season when yellows, blues and whites are in the ascendancy. But don't count on it for arranging, as it falls apart when picked. The petals are separate until well under the ground, where they finally converge into a tube. Below the adonis are shown a few fragile, intensely blue Scilla bifolia amid a groundcover of dark green tiny rosettes with many offsets—Arabis procurrens. Later the airy, small but strongly drawn white blooms of arabis, cruciform in shape, carried about a foot high, make an effective veil-like foil above the dying bulb foliage.

Just as aconite usually provides the earliest instance of massive bloom, pepper-and-salts (66) and the glistening brown sheaths of the trout lily (66) presage the arrival of our natives around mid-March. Once we see the first mottled leaf of these white lilies, also called dog's-tooth violets, we know the next shower will begin to color the entire woods floor. Day after day, as the bird chorus becomes more insistent, the sodden leaf-fall begins everywhere to burgeon. The movement of spring refuses to be held back another moment, and old acquaintances are hourly renewed, each in as pristine glory as the first time they flashed upon the eye.

So far, in looking at the drawings in this section, which must of necessity be highly selective, you may get the impression that color and form in my woods are built on a series of small-scale mosaics or choice vignettes. There are, however, much broader effects. Let's turn for a moment from particular floral groupings to the overall picture.

From mid-March on, in the woods of southwestern Ohio, wherever the terrain has been too steep for cows or is today too impractical for the bulldozer, you are bound to come on dappled rifts of wildlings. I never cease to thrill before the miracle of their spring resurgence: lacy Dutchman's breeches (end-papers), toad trillium with its watered-silk leaves (231), hepatica foliage (57), emerging Solomon's-seals (99), and bellworts (105). These are joined by many thousands of spring beauties (42) and anemonellas, tender twinleaf and aggressive May apples (see endpapers and 247), tremulous toothwort and wild ginger—all bound by an underlay of the fragile fern (endpapers). Each one imprints its oh, so definite characteristics on the retina, yet each accommodates to the whole. April is the time when nine-tenths of our native species choose to show their colors, and a single footfall can crush over a dozen blooming varieties.

On cold grey days, these ephemerals seem to go into hiding, their buds and closed blooms hardly differentiated from the leaves. But with each gust of warmth they become bolder.

The endpapers of this book represent a small patch of ground in my woods in early April, showing a typical combination of natives and sturdy exotics. How foolhardy it is, I suppose, to try to convey in words or pictures the true impression of such choice, complex and tender beauty. Only confrontation—direct experience—can elicit the total inherent response. Yet I persist, in the fond hope first of lighting up even in print an answering gleam in the collective multi-faceted eye, and—more ambitiously still—of sending you out to discover on your own the millefleur joy of wild-gardening.

Consider for a moment the actual fabric of the woods floor on which you will be embroidering. It has a close pile, with occasional cushiony patches where leaf-fall is heavy—all under a canopy of trees. The trees will remain dominant, and certain among them may prove inimical or favorable to your plans. Beeches will harbor beechdrops and trout lilies (66), hepatica (57), bloodroot (225),

Spring Madness

and twinleaf (see endpapers), celandine poppies (105), even shooting stars (235) —which like to be protected by the beech roots from the competition of other plants—as well as the tall grey-blue finials of camassia (245) and the grey-green blooms of *Ornithogalum nutans* (130). These two latter varieties are subtly set off by the grey of the tree trunks, while the tortuous exposed roots keep *O. nutans* from becoming objectionally invasive.

Oaks, whose roots go deep into the hillsides, are tolerant of a good many varieties, among them *Iris cristata*, winter aconites and hellebores. But maples, hackberries, elms and sycamores discourage company. Their surface-feeding roots tend to deny other growth both moisture and nutrients. The plantings you envision close in under them had better be discarded in favor of fallen leaf coverage; or, perhaps, if the location is prominent, you will be driven, as we were under one maple, to semi-formalize the area with an irregular coarse gravel mulch. The only plants I have found that live congenially under maples are *Duchesnea* (275) and the appendaged waterleaf, *Hydrophyllum appendiculatum*.

Walnuts are a law unto themselves, for their roots produce a substance called juglone which is credited with the power to wither, stunt, or deter some plants. I have a group of three magnificent old walnuts on an upland meadow influencing a circle with a 100-foot diameter. For twenty years, unaware of their inhibiting character, I casually set out under my three-tree walnut grove whatever I thought would look well, including some of my rarest daffodils. And, as luck would have it, they flourished. Violets, gill-over-the-ground, Virginia creeper, several kinds of corydalis, rue, hostas, myrtle and lush grass all abound here as well.

It is hard for me, out of my own experience, to come up with a true tally of just which plant species do fail under walnuts. Aside from an injunction against planting tomatoes—not exactly relevant in this context—the literature I have seen on the subject contents itself with vague warnings. Questions abound. Did hardy digitalis "go out" because of walnuts, or because of a too-limey soil? Were the lilies eaten by those notorious rodents? Was the humus in the walnut area too friable for squills and muscari, which seed freely in the hard turf path just beyond? Or do they simply get more sun there? For a time I thought my cyclamen losses were due to juglone until I found cyclamen cheerfully increasing under a walnut in the woods.

Then one day when I was reconnoitering in a downpour I realized what a violent drenching the shallow-rooted corms close to any tall tree—walnut or other —are subjected to as a cloudburst courses down the trunks, and how disruptive a drip they must be enduring from high branches even during normal rains. All in all, I find it hard to be precise or dogmatic about plant cultivation under walnuts, and suggest that only small trial plantings be made at first if you are in any doubt about the transplant's susceptibility to juglone.

As an example of really welcoming woods shelter, I cite in contrast a common tall native shrub in the understory, the spice bush, *Lindera benzoin*

By mid-March the minute Erigenia bulbosa, *harbinger-of-spring or pepper-and-salt, our first-flowering native bulb, is found in expanded bloom. That bloom often lasts until the appearance of the grey-white* Erythronium albidum, *the trout lily or dog's-tooth-violet, whose grey-green leaves, mottled with brown, bind it with the suede tones of the beechdrops,* Epifagus virginiana. *The perfect flowers of beechdrops bear a saphrophytic relation to the tree from which they take their name. Note the leaves of emerging* Viola canadensis, *the Canadian violet, as a groundcover near the large dried juvenile beech leaf from stump shoots. I have tried many western erythroniums and European forms of* E. dens-canis—*the term dog's-tooth refers to the root shape—but find that the bloom persists only a few years, after which the bulb sends up only sterile leafage. The proliferation seems to occur when the tubers become too shallowly rooted.*

No one could possibly guess that Petasites japonicus, the Japanese butter-bur, or fuki, shown emerging here in April, near the creek, would grow into our most impressive foliage plant—each leaf at maturity measuring over 2 feet across and rising to 3½ to 4 feet (opposite). The blooms, which start out as a dense red thyrse with small white stars, rush to keep up with the swiftly growing leaves, then collapse over them like a limp strand of jewels. Butter-bur never seems to set seed here, but then there is small need, because the roots creep invasively. You may control them by cutting the stalks. You may even cook the stalks, as the Japanese do.

Seen right is another sought-after food delicacy, the fiddleheads, or crosiers, of the ostrich fern, Pteretis pensylvanica. Fern eating has hazards for the uninitiated. (See page 109.)

Ranunculus ficaria, the lesser celandine (seen first), with its perky lustrous golden flowers and glistening leaves, will disappear within a few weeks after blooming and a very short period of yellowing. But don't be fooled. Next year it will spread farther than ever. Endowed with both fibrous and bulbous roots, plus axillary bulblets in the stems, this charming-looking plant can become one of the most menacing of weeds. The group here is growing on rich alluvial soil near a semishaded stream.

(225). Its tiny, aromatic blooms form a pointillist gold screen over the still stark spring woods. And under its thin brittle branches wildflowers group themselves as though the *benzoin* had as tonic an influence on plants as its extract has on people. An equally receptive and slightly showier alien is *Cornus mas*, the cornelian cherry.

All trees carry with them built-in patterning, not only in the vertical accents of their trunks but in the network of ever changing shadows they cast. In observing wildflower groupings you will often note surging pools of color below the trees with an ebbing toward the trunks—a rhythm that can be repeated effectively in subsequent similar plantings. Sometimes species like wild ginger (84), with adequate rhizome storage, will even choose closeup tree root sites and make an unforgettable picture as the downy leaves unfold, catching the light in showy triangulations.

It is by watching natural groupings that you can learn most about developing your woods to your own tastes and achieving new effects in harmony with what is already there. How often in placing exotic material I have simply ripped out sequences of some coarse undesirable plant that had already established an attractive pattern. Somehow, no matter how subtly random I think I am making the holes for new plantings at the time, or how bold a splash of color I anticipate, I am nearly always disappointed, when bloom comes along the following year, to find how stilted and ungenerous a gesture I actually made. I have learned, too, in projecting plantings—especially if the plant supply is limited—to keep the approaches to them in mind and to work for color display across rather than parallel to the view.

The value of such transverse placement was never brought home to me more amusingly than one day, when driving past a trailer poised on a grassy knoll, I saw twelve zinnia plants lined out in a long straggling sequence, apparently to permit multiple views of the highway. Sometimes, when colored material is scare, I clump it in a few strategic places. Or, if I have just one of two very bold plants, I find that they add a tremendous fillip if placed against tall green at a focal spot along a path. For further suggestions, see page 160.

After the winter months there is nothing more rewarding than the sequence of carefree naturalized spring bulbs. They nearly all bloom during the period of the vernal native ephemerals, whose foliage, like that of the bulbs, can similarly be covered during the dying-off period by the rising stature of the woods groundcover. Further details for the culture of rodent-proof, problem-proof bulbs appear in the text that follows. But first a slight pause while I discuss their less-than-candid sponsors—the catalogs.

How dependent we are on these pages of vainglorious presentation! And yet how deceptive they are! The overenthusiasm of the seller is only a small part of their deceit. Naturally enough, dealers put forth their best lure—the promise of gay color. But how many things they fail to reveal to the new gardener! Most particularly is this true of bulbs, when illustrations show huge

Spring Bulbs

All the bulbs shown on the following charts can take some shade because they die back well before the leaf canopy becomes too dense to allow them to ripen. Planting depths are indicated by the color block, which ends at ground level. All species are shown at the peak of bloom.

Endymion hispanicus, *the campanulate squill or Spanish bluebell;* Tulipa sylvestris, *the Florentine tulip; and* Ornithogalum nutans, *the nodding star-of-Bethlehem (73), prefer more sun, since they are the last to bloom and therefore to ripen. But you will find endymion growing well on a shaded south-facing hill (129). These pearly-textured bulbs flourish in either clay or loam. Related to the English bluebell,* E. non-scriptus, *with which they hybridize freely, the campanulate squills come in light, dark and purplish blues, and in pinks and white.*

Tulipa sylvestris *is never happier than when bound in the coarse roots of some shrub like* Magnolia glauca. *If grown in sod and sun, where it also flourishes, it has a tendency to go to leafage rather than bloom. Of the three forms I have grown—*T. sylvestris *'Tabriz' is the finest—all are delightful in their lovely fragrance and their starlike 3- to 5-inch yellow blooms on curving foot-high stems. One reason why* T. sylvestris *appears on this chart is that it is one of the few tulips I know that, along with the species* T. turkestanica, *and a large red with a dark center,* T. eichleri, *seem to have mouse-resistant capabilities. For more about tulips, be sure to consult A. D. Hall's* The Genus Tulipa.

There are a number of ornithogalums that are well worth planting. O. nutans, *the nodding star-of-Bethlehem, the most dramatic (73), can take partial shade. Its madly prolific relative,* O. umbellatum, *the common star-of-Bethlehem, is charming, but it is a bad field pest and highly poisonous to stock.* O. narbonense,

Eranthis cilicica

Bulbocodium vernum

Galanthus nivalis

Narcissus triandrus albus

in late May, and O. pyramidale, *a more vigorous June bloomer, have rangier triangular spires with small white florets that do well here, although their native habitat is the Mediterranean. They rise 1½ to 2 feet.*

The leucojums have a long blooming period, especially L. vernum, *the spring snowflake. My favorite, because of the beautiful proportion of its double flower to its 10-inch scape and the richness of its white bells against its dark green markings, turning yellow later, is the Hungarian snowflake,* L. vernum *var.* vagneri *(below).* L. v. *var.* carpathicum, *the Carpathian snowflake, like* vernum *an early bloomer but with a single bell, has lasting yellowish-green markings on its tips. Although the summer snowflake,* L. aestivum, *grows to 2 feet in May, the flower, even in the best form, 'Gravetye,' seems too small for its foliage. One cannot mention Gravetye, the name of William Robinson's garden, without obeisance to* The Wild Garden, *his germinal work on naturalizing that reads as well today as when it was written in 1870. The autumn snowflake, Leucojum* autumnale, *a tiny, pinkish, profusely blooming flower, will survive in full sun. I for one find it not impressive enough to warrant keeping its locale clear of otherwise overpowering summer growth.*

For the culture of Iris reticulata, the netted iris, see page 63; for more of Bulbocodium vernum, Parkinson's "Meadowe saffrone," see page 64; and for the species narcissus, of which N. triandrus var. concolor is shown here, see page 86.

On sunny spring days the woods are alive with the varying blues of anemones. The 6-inch-high Greek anemone, A. blanda, *with its scarcer pink and white forms, is a 2-inch daisylike flower. It is slightly taller and its blossom somewhat smaller than the blue wood anemone,* A. apennina, *which likes more open*

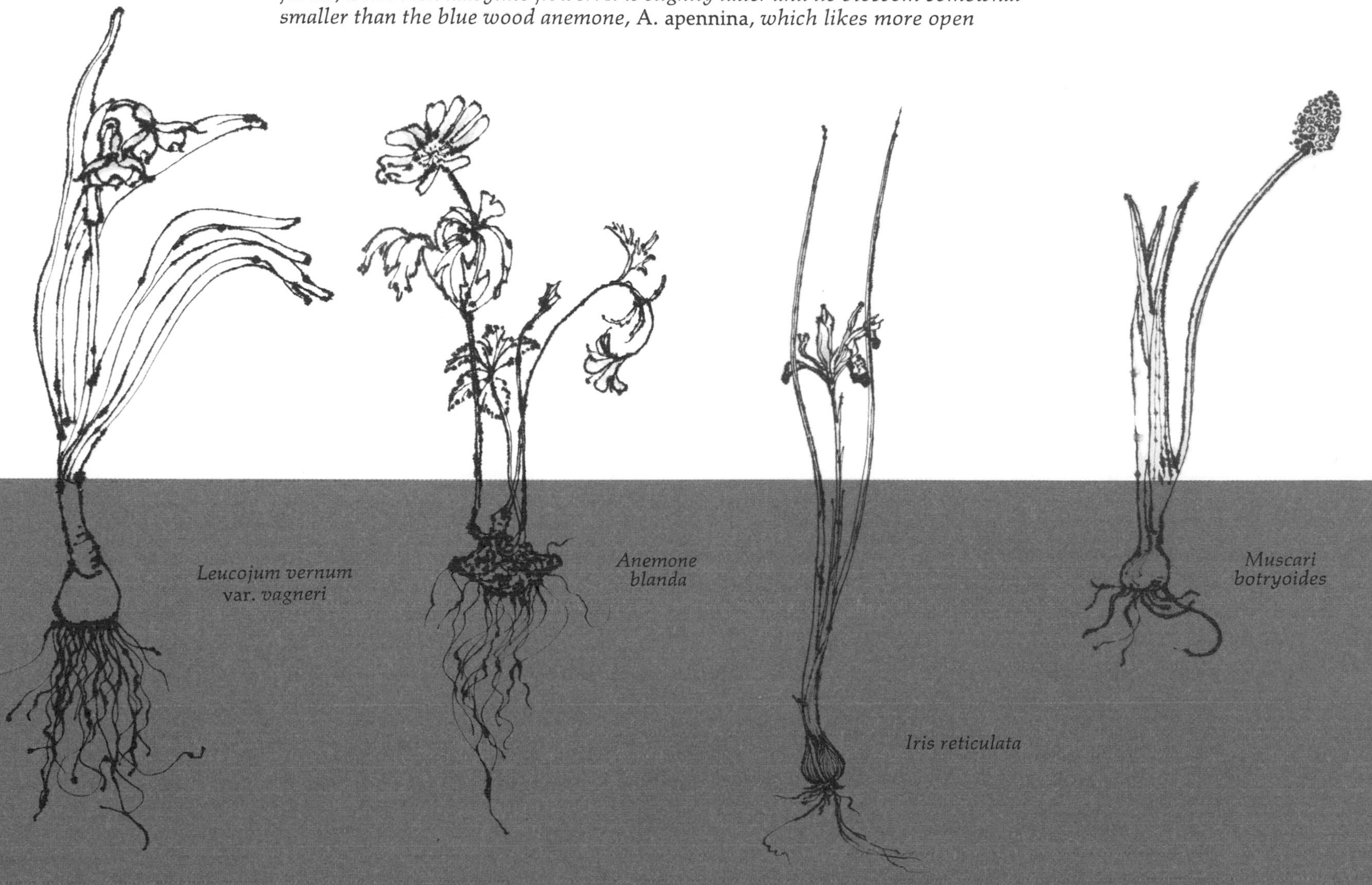

Leucojum vernum
var. *vagneri*

Anemone blanda

Iris reticulata

Muscari botryoides

exposure. Anemone rhizomes, blackish, with thickened projections that seem to overhang the central element and show tiny bristled remains of stems, are planted with the top of these projections up. They profit by as long as 2 days of presoaking. The European wood anemone, A. nemorosa, and its beautiful hybrid, 'Allenii,' are more difficult to come by, for their sticklike rhizomes must not be allowed to dry out. 'Allenii' likes a dampish site, as does the later A. sylvestris, the snowdrop anemone, with its free-running roots and 1½- to 2-inch white flowers.

The intensely blue squills, especially Scilla sibirica, and the delicate, very early, very prolific twinleaf squill, S. bifolia (64), present no problems and will even bloom in well-drained sod. S. tubergeniana, which produces its 4-inch blue-white panicles in earliest March, greatly resembles its later-blooming relative, Puschkinia scilloides, often called the striped squill. Puschkinia prefers more moisture and has proved more prolific for me than S. tubergeniana.

The grape hyacinths, carrying a raceme of many small bells constricted at the base and often fluted with greenish or white edges, show their channeled leaves in autumn. They all have stout, often stiff stems, and all relish full sun and heavy soil. The blues range from the all-turquoise of Muscari armeniacum through the particolored M. tubergenianum, the Oxford and Cambridge grape hyacinth, with its light flowers at the apex and darker ones below, to the deeper-hued particolored M. latifolium and the sturdy all-purplish-blue M. paradoxum (231). M. botryoides, a China-blue dwarf, and its white form called pearls-of-Spain do not persist for me.

The so-called florists' hyacinths are normally very hardy border bulbs. Their heavy heads are best seen in raised beds, but they are not particularly congenial with woodland plants. Sometimes one finds spindlier forms in old

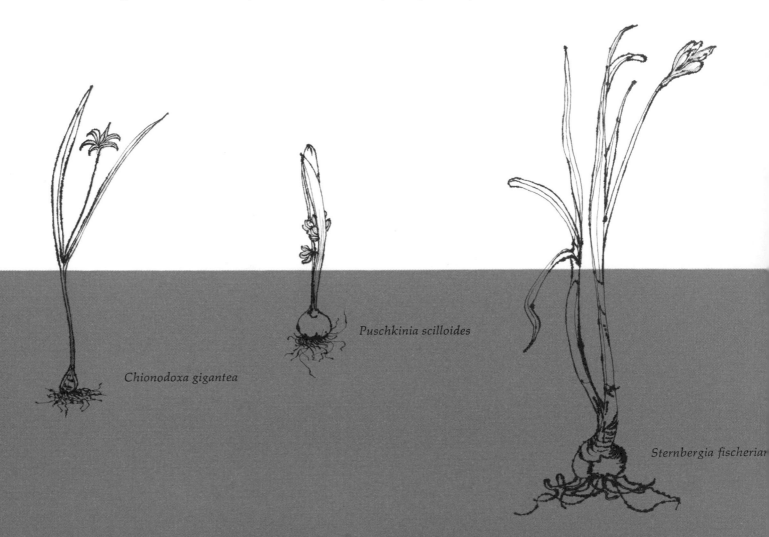

Chionodoxa gigantea

Puschkinia scilloides

Sternbergia fischeriana

gardens that look more suitable in the wild and at the same time extend the spring-bulb blooming season. The more delicately formed Hyacinthus azureus, sometimes called Hyacinthella, is very like Muscari in size and form except that its bells flare. Our wild hyacinth, Camassia scilloides (245), presents no problem, but with western forms I have been unsuccessful.

Sternbergia fischeriana, a charming spring form of this yellow, preponderantly fall-blooming family, should be better known (see page 62). For more about the spring-blooming fritillaries, see page 139. And for daffodils, other than N. triandrus, see the following pages.

You may wonder why Ipheion uniflorum, the spring star flower, fails to appear on the chart. I had had only failures with it, but just recently I discovered this charming pale-blue 6-inch-high starry bloom growing like a weed at a neighbor's. She plants it 4 inches deep and gives it plenty of sun and protection from wind. Microhabitat again!

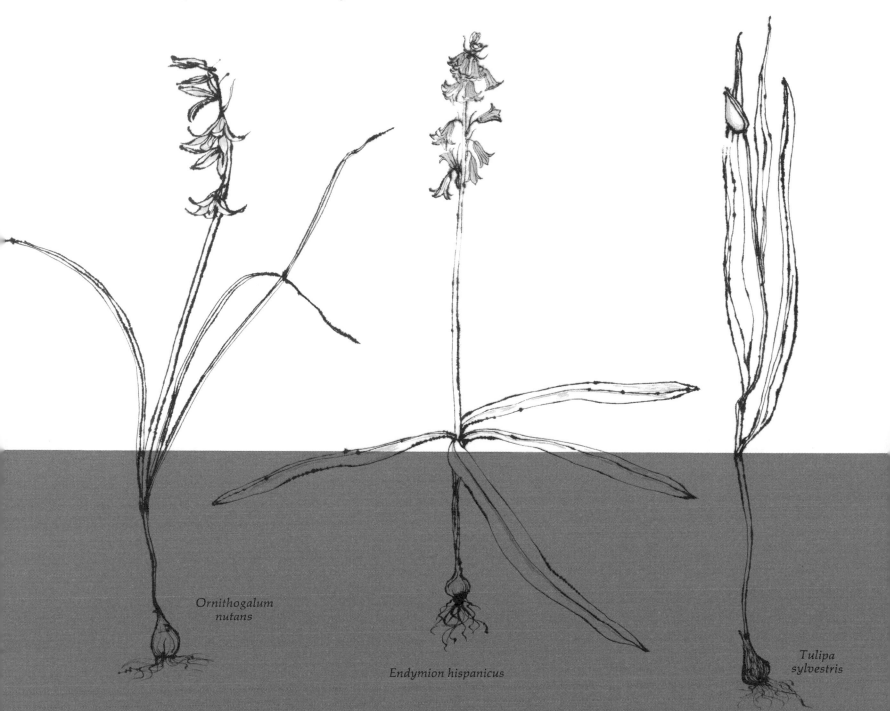

Ornithogalum
nutans

Endymion hispanicus

Tulipa
sylvestris

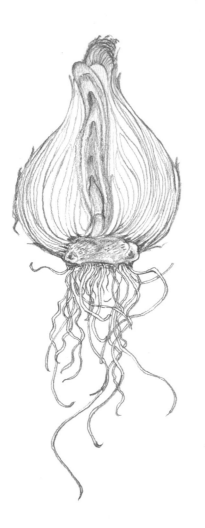

fields of lilies or tulips all even in height, breadth and hue. The more practiced gardener's eye knows that top-class stock has been given uniform rich soil, clean cultivation and care, and what's more, that the pictures were snapped at the peak of perfection. How did that same field look even the week before? Full of promise perhaps, but utterly glamorless. And how will it look two weeks from now? Really quite devastated, with all its blooms picked before they shatter, and foliage that is left to die back awkwardly in its continuously cultivated rows.

Take any of the shots of mixed bulb plantings crowded close together so that the "sea of color" can make its sales impact, and apply the before-and-after test above. Again, if you have done any growing, you recognize the promotional value of heavily planted sunk pots with skillfully inserted tufts of well-mulched groundcover. What you may not realize is that, after blooming, the bulbs will make huge clumps of leaves which, again, must be allowed to remain undisturbed if bloom is to appear the following year. If you grow mixed bulbs in borders, you can be as deceitful as the catalogers. You need only grow them in pots, lift the pots when the glory is over and let the foliage ripen out of sight, replacing the holes in your border or plot with annuals. Naturalizing bulbs in woods reduces your post-bloom problems in large part by the phenomenal push of spring and early summer growth, if you marshal it to conceal the inevitable masses of yellowing leaves.

Redbud weather, with penetrating winds and threatening skies, brings to the landscape—along with the greatest rush of wildlings—drifts of daffodils. There is no single genus so perfectly suited to our area, nor one whose versatility is so generally unappreciated.

Grown in rows like any other crop, "Easter lilies," as they used to be called in our valley, are picked in full bud, tightly bunched and stored in the potato cellar if that wandering holy day doesn't closely follow their flowering. Valley "lilies" are always as yellow as the valley butter and are confined to one variety: *Narcissus pseudo-narcissus*, the Lent lily.

But I was blessed enough, early on, to surmount such local restrictions. During my first spring in Ohio I made the acquaintance, among the Krippendorf beeches, of literally hundreds of varieties of this same branch of the amaryllis family, flung like golden brocade on the forest floor—from the first tiny beginners in February to the lean, latter-day poets and great flashy doubles of early May. The daffodil quest was a pilgrimage which during the intervening years I never failed to undertake, either at Lob's Wood or, as my own plantings became established, in the far smaller precincts of Cockaigne. For nothing I have grown has given me the long-lasting pleasure and return for effort expended as have my daffodils.

I never pin back the ears of these grateful blooms with paper clips, nor trap the pollen from their petals on a cotton swab, nor "iron out" their papery bracts, nor hold them over in my refrigerator in preparation for showing. But I must confess that I learned a lot from the ladies who do. An intensive review of any regional daffodil show is the quickest way to decide how you want to invest your daffodil dollar. For catalogs, no matter how profusely illustrated, can't give you an adequate idea of texture. This climactic attribute—texture—so understandably overstressed by daffodilians, varies greatly with both type and season. Prolonged cool temperatures at blooming time; rain immediately afterwards—even a man-made soaking where the situation permits—to simulate the spring subsoil moisture of their original mountain habitats; a thorough summer baking; a return of moisture during the winter months—these are the ingredients for near-perfect results. Despite the vagaries of weather, however, there is still no believing the invariable richness of form and fragrance of these absolutely rodent-proof, undemanding bulbs, which manage to find themselves at home in both meadow and open woods—as long as one remembers that, like all bulbs, their leaves must ripen to the point of disappearance without being disturbed, to ensure nourishment for the year following.

My first daffodil bulbs came in Aladdin-like quantity—several bushels from Carl Krippendorf. Because his stocks were healthy I didn't know that daffodils had enemies until about ten years ago, when my brother told me that his West Coast plantings had been completely decimated by narcissus flies. Rather than using chemicals against such disasters, the best procedures for the home gardener are preventive. First, patronize reliable dealers. They are even more interested than you in keeping bulbs healthy. Always burn at once any bulb not firm, or not free of black sclerotic spots, bruises, cuts, mushiness from frost damage, or decay. If there is "wool" at the base of the bulb, or if there are elongated protuberances on the leaves at blooming time, you can be sure your bulbs have parasitic stem and bulb nematodes—the so-called eelworms. Any affected plants should be dug up at once and burned. So should plants that show root nematode symptoms—leaves that brown at the tips and whose foliage dies back more quickly than normal—or plants whose roots are discolored. Healthy roots are white for their full length. I panicked when some leaves showed early browning and a rapid vitiation. However, no less an expert than Mrs. Lionel Richardson herself diagnosed the trouble as frost damage after I assured her that digging had shown firm bulbs and good white roots.

Daffodils are also subject to various virus infestations. One, said to be carried by aphids, results in yellowish-white stripes that appear vertically down the leaves. They can be seen, however, only by holding the leaves up to the light, and a roughness can be felt when the leaves are slid between the fingers. When the infestation is intense, a frosted line appears along the midribs of the perianth. This virus can be detected soon after the leaves first appear. Narcissus mosaic develops usually after flowering and shows up as a faint yellow mottling of the lower parts of the leaves. All infected plants should be rogued and burned as soon as such symptoms are noted. In fact, it is well to

Cut vertically, bulbs reveal their organic functionalism. In the daffodil bulb (opposite) the embryonic flower is sheltered in the enveloping leaves, all still within the hard pointed leaf capsule. In many bulbs the tip of this sheath forms the tool that drives up through frozen or dry earth and later becomes a papery thin husk (upper right, page 77). With some flowers, notably Sternbergia clusiana, *also listed as* macrantha, *whose tip penetrates the hard-baked autumn soil before its leaves, a tough, interlocking awl-like mechanism can be seen at the apex of the three major petals. In other sternbergias and colchicums where no leaves pave the way, no such reinforcement is visible.*

Below a cross-section of a hyacinth bulb shows the budded inflorescence fully formed. In both bulbs the overlapping tissue-layers give protection and nourishment.

look with suspicion on any clumps whose leaves are not sturdy or which die back more quickly than normal. Do not replant for at least three seasons in those areas where you have removed suspicious material.

Another preventive measure is to choose daffodils that have proven stamina. The oversize yellow trumpet types and those in Division 1c (77) and particularly 2c (77) are notably susceptible to virus, and the latter to basal rot as well.

In planting daffodil bulbs—or any bulbs, in fact—there is a tendency to dig holes so carelessly that the bulb may have an air pocket beneath it. See that the bottom of the hole is flat. Daffodil bulbs should be covered at the tip by at least 4 inches of soil. Planting as deep as 12 inches, especially in sandy or light soils, while somewhat delaying the moment of bloom, will both postpone dividing and prove a deterrent to basal rot. Given a good start, bulbs in time propel themselves up or down to their own preferred depth. Large bulbs should be sited at least 12 inches apart. All bulbs need well-drained locations and sand at the base if drainage is poor.

In woodland and meadow the addition of fertilizers is seldom necessary. Fertilizers and manure, even if well rotted, should never be used where they come in contact with the bulb. Potash, hoof and horn, green sand, raw rock phosphate and—with one reservation—bone meal (100) are good additions. Buy and plant bulbs as early as you can get them in order to develop full root systems. The first year you can expect a better flower from full-sized bought bulbs than you can the second year, for bulbs come to us from most commercial sources plump and well fed. Because of transplantation and the effort of reestablishing, you may be without any bloom the second year while the bulb recovers. Also, it may take several years to get a showing from the small divisions of bulbs you replant from overcrowded clumps.

Even though it may be repetitive, let me emphasize again this injunction: in growing any spring bulbs, choose a site you can leave unmowed until about mid-July, so that the foliage may ripen fully and enrich the flowers for the following year. Experts advise the removal of all seed pods to keep bulbs from exhaustion, but they recommend leaving the green flower stem, which feeds the bulb just as the leaf does. This procedure is well worth adopting for bulbs that are slow to increase or rare. But lack of time and energy has forced me to a modified approach. When bulbs are in bloom I pick generously for the house and for friends, but I pick in patterns, being sure to leave behind enough flowers to carry the color as I planned it. Frequently, too, I find that if an area is heavy in yellow, say, I can pick some clumps clean and the "stumps" of these thoroughly cut-over groupings give me a clue to thinning later, when bloom is over and I wonder where that area was that needed toning down in color intensity.

You may read about piling spring-dug bulbs into a V-shaped trench to let the foliage ripen off. There are usually engaging drawings showing them

Daffodil Classification Chart

I. TRUMPET NARCISSUS OF GARDEN ORIGIN

One flower to a stem; corona as long as or longer than the perianth segments.

1a, the yellow trumpets, with corona and perianth colored, corona not paler than perianth, stem from the species N. hispanicus. Examples are 'Slieveboy,' 'Kingscourt' and 'Bayard,' 'Golden Harvest,' 'Magnificence' and 'Rembrandt'—all good for naturalizing.

1b, with perianth white and corona colored, probably is a cross between the species N. pseudo-narcissus, the Lent lily, and N. pseudo-narcissus bicolor. 1b's are rather scarce because of genetic difficulties, but 'Preamble,' 'Trousseau' and 'Bambi' are examples of available breakthroughs.

1c, with perianth white, corona white—not paler than the perianth—traces back to the N. pseudo-narcissus subspecies: N. moschatus, with its forward-leaning perianth (80), N. alpestris and N. albescens. 1c's like 'Cantatrice,' 'Vigil,' and 'Rashee' are nearly always a creamy white. The still costly 'Panache' is a glorious pure white exception.

1d, any color combination not falling into the above, includes the reverse bicolors 'Lunar Sea' and 'Nampa.'

II. LARGE-CUPPED NARCISSUS OF GARDEN ORIGIN

One flower to a stem: cup or corona more than one-third but less than equal to the length of the perianth segment. Color distribution is same as I. All flowers in II, derived from crosses between the species N. poeticus and trumpets, account for half the registered varieties.

Typical 2a's are 'Galway,' 'Air Marshal,' 'Ceylon,' 'Vulcan,' 'Camelot.'

White and yellow 2b's are 'Festivity,' 'Polindra,' 'Daviot' and 'Tudor Minstrel.' There are also 2b's with orange, red and pink in their cups. Pink daffodils (82) are classified as to dimensions, and most of them come under 2b. Some are highly variable as to color. The following are steadfastly pink: 'Rose Caprice,' 'Rose of Tralee,' 'Accent' and 'Radiation.'

2c's include 'Ludlow,' 'Easter Moon,' and 'Arctic Doric.'

2d's include 'Daydream,' 'Limeade,' 'Bethany' and 'Binkie.'

III. SMALL-CUPPED NARCISSUS OF GARDEN ORIGIN

One flower to a stem; cup or corona not more than one-third the length of the perianth segments. Cups in III are called small. In many varieties the cup is better described as "disc," "saucer" or "eye." Color distribution is the same as for I. All flowers in Division III are crosses between the large-cupped varieties of II and forms of the species N. poeticus. Many of the newer hybrids tend to burn in the sun.

Typical of 3a's are 'Mangosteen' and 'Doubtful,' which does not burn.

Some of the most delicate colors and subtle shapes are to be found in Division 3b. As a consequence, forms like 'Aircastle,' 'Irish Splendour,' 'Mahmoud,' 'Impala,' 'Merlin,' 'Sunstar,' 'Syracuse' and 'Matapan' are better as subjects for arrangement than as massed outdoor groupings.

3c's are among the purest whites and include the large 'Chinese White,' 'Frigid,' 'Verona' and 'Polar Sea.' 'April Clouds' and the smaller 'Dallas' and 'Cushendall,' due to their poeticus heritage, often have a green eye.

So far no uncontested 3d's have been officially accepted.

IV. ALL DOUBLE FORMS, WHETHER OF GARDEN OR SPECIES ORIGIN

In doubles the corona may be completely replaced with perianth segments, as in 'White Lion'; or the perianth may be normal but the stamens take on proliferating frills that fill the cup, as in 'Hollandia,' 'White Marvel' and 'Swansdown.' One of the handsomest old doubles is 'Eystettensis,' the Austrian Queen Anne's double daffodil, with four or five stars-of-David superimposed on a common center but diminishing in size, each layer showing a margin of the one beneath it. A 1929 "miffy" version is 'Pencrebar.' Popular doubles include 'Sweet Music,' 'Golden Ducat,' 'Acropolis,' 'Candida,' 'Cheerfulness' and 'Double Event.' If the catalog emphasis is significant, doubles are evidently popular, but few experts deign to discuss their merits.

V. TRIANDRUS NARCISSUS OF GARDEN ORIGIN

V usually has less color and more fragrance than preceding divisions, and the foliage is apt to be slender. The bulbs are also choosier as to site and growing conditions, doing best in poor gritty soil with sharp drainage and exposure to summer baking. Varieties on the market are relatively scarce, and due to the preference of connoisseurs for these white and light sulphur-yellow forms, prices are on the rise.

5a, cup or corona not less than two-thirds the length of the perianth segments. These include 'Tresamble,' 'Lemon Drops' and 'Tiara.'

5b, cup or corona less than two-thirds the length of the perianth segments. Flowers usually late blooming and smaller than those in the preceding division, frequently with several more or less pendant bell-shaped florets to a stem. Some 5b's are 'Samba,' 'Hawera,' 'Sidhe' and the rare 'Arish Mell.'

VI. CYCLAMINEUS NARCISSUS OF GARDEN ORIGIN

6a, cup or corona not less than two-thirds the length of the perianth segment.
6b, cup or corona less than two-thirds the length of the perianth segment.
Due to its cyclamineus heritage, the perianth is often dramatically and attractively turned back from the forward-thrusting action of the trumpet. In these cases exposure of the trumpet's base makes it seem even longer than it actually is. Such VI's belong botanically in Division I, despite their separate official placement here.

Many of these hybrids are yellow, like the 6a 'Peeping Tom,' whose flower lasts three weeks, and 'Charity May,' a shorter-lived bloomer. Equally charming and also 6a are 'Dove Wings,' a bicolor, and 'Jenny,' a creamy white. The last three are all from the cross of 'Mitylene' and N. cyclamineus.

The long-trumpet ancestry of cyclamineus has produced some 6b forms of great quality. One is 'Beryl,' another 'Andalusia.'

VII. JONQUILLA NARCISSUS OF GARDEN ORIGIN

7a, cup or corona not less than two-thirds of the perianth segment. 7b, cup or corona less than two-thirds of the perianth segment.

This is probably the place to clear up the popular confusion about the name "Jonquil." All jonquils belong to the narcissus or, in common parlance, the daffodil family. But all daffodils or narcissus are not jonquils. VII's often have distinctively rushlike, hollow dark green leaves and tall slender stalks, with from two to six very durable and very fragrant florets. Those with glaucous foliage prefer gritty soil.

7a's include 'Golden Sceptre,' 'White Wedgewood,' 'Sweetness' and 'Alpine.'

7b's are 'Golden Perfection' and 'Trevithian,' old but hard to beat, and 'Bunting,' and 'Pipit,' a reverse bicolor.

VIII. TAZETTA NARCISSUS OF GARDEN ORIGIN

The tender clustered thick-stemmed blooms in VIII derive from a species literally translated as a small cup or "tazetta." The best known tazetta variety is probably the "paper white" we force indoors. **Tazettas** have the longest history and the widest distribution of any daffodil type. They were prized by the Romans and appear in Egyptian, Hindu and Chinese wall paintings. Tazettas have naturalized in the South, where many other daffodil types are not persistent or can only be grown from precooled bulbs. Hardiest in the North are the poetaz types, tazettas crossed with poets' narcissus. Examples are 'Cragford,' 'Laurens Koster,' 'Martha Washington,' 'Geranium' and 'Silver Chimes.' Their hardiness can be somewhat increased by planting them deep down and in sod.

IX. POETICUS NARCISSUS OF GARDEN ORIGIN

Poet characteristics are: very flat perianth, a small eye for a corona, wiry stems, remarkable whiteness, sharp fragrance, great durability and long season of bloom, with an accent on very lateness. Wild **poeticus** forms from Division X have yielded rather minor improvement in garden hybrids in IX. But three subspecies of the wild N. **poeticus** have generously enhanced the color and form of hybrids in other divisions: **radiflorus** *var.* **exertus** has contributed earliness, and variety recurvus, the Pheasant's Eye (85), radiant whiteness, a very flat perianth, a very green eye and pungent scent; and **radiflorus** *var.* **poetarum** is the key to the sought-after and increasing reds and pinks in other divisions.

Popular **poeticus** types of garden origin are 'Actaea' and 'Cantabile.'

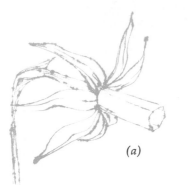

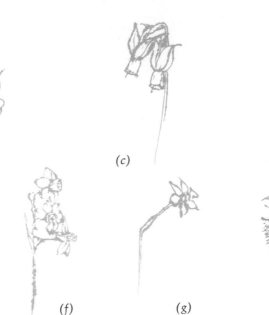

(a) (b) (c) (d)

(e) (f) (g) (h)

X. SPECIES, WILD FORMS AND WILD HYBRIDS

In this Division are listed a few of the over forty-odd wild species and wild hybrids from which countless garden hybrids have been developed: yellow trumpets from N. asturiensis *(217) and the Lent lily,* N. pseudo-narcissus *(74); white ones from* N. moschatus *with its drooping perianth (h); garden triandrus hybrids from* N. triandrus, *of which var.* albus *or Angel's tears is highly coveted (c); the cyclamineus-blooded bulbs from* N. cyclamineus *(d); and the wild hybrid known officially as* N. X johnstonii, *Queen of Spain (a). This almost legendary pale-sulphurish form is practically extinct in its highly localized native haunts, a victim of the plow during the Spanish Civil War. A very fine form grows in some Ohio gardens through the generosity of Carl Krippendorf, who bought the* **bulbs from Peter Barr in the early 1890s.** N. tenuoir *(b) and* N. watieri *(g) are related to poet and jonquil hybrids. From such species as* N. calcicola *(f), jonquilla hybrids have evolved; and from hoop-petticoat daffodils like* N. bulbocodium *var.* conspicuus *(e), hybrids like 'Taffeta' in* XII *(below).*

XI. COLLAR DAFFODILS

Since early times daffodils with six-lobed coronas have been observed, but it is only in the last decades that such mutations were made persistent through cross-breeding. Effective mainly for arranging, this most recently recognized division, with the corona split for at least one-third its length, includes 'Baccarat,' 'Modesta,' 'Canasta,' 'Orangery' and 'Estella de Mol,' seen left.

XII. NARCISSUS NOT FALLING INTO THE FOREGOING DIVISIONS

Here are such oddities as the bulbocodium *garden hybrids like 'Tarlatan,' 'Taffeta,' or 'Jessamy' and 'Kenellis,' which tend to bloom in very late fall.*

stacked diagonally. Always lured by diagrams, and prone to believe what I read, I tried this method. I found it amazingly difficult to cover the bulbs adequately with soil so that air didn't get to them; and the leaves, rather than ripening and enriching the bulb, simply dried. But then people who draw diagrams are seldom the ones who do the actual work! Although I had marked the trench with stakes, locating the bulbs after months of weathering was a major job. Should I try this technique another time I would line the trench with wire mesh and let the top edges project as markers.

Many suggestions are made for ensuring plantings with a natural look, such as casually throwing out a handful of bulbs and digging them in where they fall. The trouble with this happy-go-lucky practice is the difficulty of finding the bulbs again in a woods or on a meadow floor. I prefer instead to plant daffodils as if I were casting a coarse and wholly imaginary fishnet over a fair-sized terrain. The seine would probably crumple in the hollows, where I would plant more heavily, thinning out the bulbs toward the edges. The big jacquards, irregularly thickened at the junctures, might also reflect the dominant shadows of the great tree branches above. The tendency I find in my placements is always toward too meager and too short a planting, and one that doesn't overlap or thicken up enough against another with which it contrasts.

I do advise keeping daffodils separate from the more fragile natives, since most daffodils, as I have pointed out, need coarser plants coming up among them to hide their prolific dying leafage. *Hesperis matronalis*, the tall phloxlike dame's rocket, which is fragrant and blooms white through reddish-purple, is one good solution. Although biennial, it reseeds well, even though the seeds are great favorites of the goldfinches. Rocket seeds ripen just before the woods need clearing in anticipation of the fall bulb sequence. More as to how to handle this show on page 170.

Connoisseurs are adamant, I know, about keeping each variety of daffodil in its own drift. Since my first bulbs came to me by the undifferentiated bushel for planting in a relatively small area, I had to reverse this practice and instead achieve balance within variegation. I am not unhappy with the results.

As to transplanting time: if you wait until mid-July, as is recommended for our area, you usually encounter cementlike soil. My most favorable, if un-conventional, practice, when I rearrange my own planting or get a start from local friends, is to dig daffodils in bloom, transfer them at once in closed plastic bags and replant immediately. This way desirable groupings as to variety and color are assured. The soil, too, is usually fine for digging. If it happens to be dry I water the bulbs in.

The Classification Chart (77) can only reflect broad color indications. Weather and growing conditions may produce marked variations in brilliance of color. Certain flowers during their span of bloom may run through a varied palette, as with the pioneer famous pink, 'Mrs. R. O. Backhouse.' Its trumpet appears first as a creamy orange, only to turn, as it develops, into a clear, soft, deep rose which slowly fades to a delicious pink.

There is a marked difference among daffodils in their ability to withstand sun-scorch, warm dry winds or the often frequent icy spring blasts, as well as in floriferousness and, over the years, persistence of bloom. In many plants that reproduce once each season a 2n or diploid series of chromosomes is normal. Some plants have been found in the wild and some produced by breeding in which, due to cell wounds, heat treatments, X ray or the use of certain alkaloids —notably colchicine (178)—mutations have occurred to produce a 3n or triploidal—more frequently a 4n or tetraploidal—series of chromosomes.

What, do you ask, has all this rarefied genetics to do with dirt gardening? Just this: polyploidy may result in plants that have larger cells, stems, leaves, flowers and seeds than their ancestors. But these same plants may also be less persistent, have longer vegetative periods before blooming and show a marked incidence of sterility. Many breeders have observed that triploids seem to be longer lived and tend to naturalize more readily than do tetraploids.

Shown on the daffodil chart mainly are examples of proved stamina in our area, for both the garden and the show table. Some of these, deeply planted, have been down ten to twenty years. Among the ten thousand-odd listings in the *International Register of Daffodil Names*, where graceless blooms are relatively scarce, each daffodil cultivar represents from ten to fifteen years of some devoted soul's labor. The pleasure of choice is ultimately yours. Don't let the occasionally sky-high prices in the catalogs intimidate you. When you develop your own daffodil tastes you'll find that some of the best flower forms, and many highly satisfactory performers, are among the reasonably priced bulbs.

There is no more helpfully articulate an organization than the American Daffodil Society. Its devoted members reveal their preferences in national and regional publications, where you can also find discussions of such controversial topics as the plump Dutch bulbs versus the firmer English and Irish types, the worth of allegedly mosaic-prone novelties from Down Under, and whether the mounting enthusiasm for American hybrids is truly justified. And if you really want the lowdown on strength of stem, durability of bloom in the field or vase life, see *Narcissus Variety Trials* published by the British Ministry of Agriculture.

Whether choosing for naturalization or for showing, daffodil fanciers adhere to the classification adopted by the Royal Horticultural Society, on pages 77 through 80. If the following detailed discussion of the classifications and the chart bores you, skip to the growing of miniatures (86), whose charm softens the most hardened heart. For those who want to play the field, Divisions I through IX take care of daffodils of garden origin, Division X of species. Division XI is now reserved for the "collar" or split-corona types. Division XII is a miscellaneous classification.

To trace the development of narcissus cultivars look at Division X, which embraces the species, or wild, daffodils. Their diversity of form tends to hide a characteristic common to all the daffodil family, a perianth of six petals related to a cup or corona. The size and configuration of these two elements and the number of florets on a stem often furnish the best clues to the other eleven divisions.

Divisions I, II and III are all single-stemmed trumpets of garden origin. Extensive breeding in these three classes has gone on for the last hundred years. Their four subdivisions are identical as to color distribution: 1a: Perianth colored; corona colored, not paler than the perianth. 1b: Perianth white; corona colored. 1c: Perianth white; corona white, not paler than the perianth. 1d: Any color combination not falling into a, b, or c.

Differences in these first three divisions lie in the proportion between depth of cup or trumpet and breadth of perianth. The length of the perianth segment is measured on the inside from its junction with the corona along the midrib to the extreme tip; that of the corona is computed from its junction with the perianth to the end of its farthest extension when the edge is flattened out. Determining the exact measurement of these inconstant forms is the doubtful privilege of the breeder. Division I is long-cupped, II is intermediate, and III is short-cupped. All derive from the species of Division X (80). The bulbs in I, II and III are usually large if placed in fertile soil away from deep competing roots and covered to a depth of 7 to 8 inches. Although they will increase more slowly, they can withstand shallow-rooted groundcovers and won't need separating to keep a full complement of bloom for at least fifteen years.

Division IV, in which the perianth segments are multiplied at the expense of the cup—or vice versa—comprises all doubles, whether cultivated or wild. Division V gets its reflexed perianth through hybridization with species *triandrus* (78). Division VI has as its forebear the tiny *cyclamineus*, with its narrow perianth segments lying back like rabbit ears (78). Division VII contains all jonquil hybrids of garden origin—and to understand the rise of the term "jonquil" see the text on the chart under Division VII (79). Breeding in classes V, VI and VII is so recent that only a few varieties in these groups are second-generation hybrids. Most of them have a species or wild form as one parent. Division VII, the *tazettas*, the least hardy of the classes, may have up to twenty clustered blooms. The origins of true *tazetta* species are lost in antiquity. Division IX, or the poets, has the flattest cups of all. So we come back to Division X, the species or wild forms and wild hybrids, having accounted for the easily distinguishable classifications descended from them. This leaves us with Division XI for the rather scorned newcomers, the so-called collar or split corona daffodils; and Division XII, into which to toss all the confusing leftovers.

Before turning to particulars of the charted divisions, more about changes in taste. A daffodil like 'Dick Wellband,' 2b, one of the first redcups, was met

Note how Mertensia virginica, *the Virginia bluebell, with its coarse storage roots;* *and wild ginger,* Asarum canadense, *with its surface-crisscrossed rhizomes, make* *for almost impenetrable coverage inimical to any fragile growth on an open* *wooded southeast-facing hillside. Daffodils, because of their tough sheath (74),* *are capable of thrusting through. Their deep-set roots draw on lower layers of* *nutrients. Try the late-blooming, very long-lasting N. recurvus, shown* *opposite, in such a planting. Because the yellowing period of the mertensia and* *daffodil foliage is unsightly until mid-July, you will prefer to site such a grouping* *in the distant view or along a remote path. While the maroon flower of wild ginger* *is best seen from a kneeling position, the leaf, acute, furry and folded when* *emerging, becomes until frost a dark satiny disc, valuable as groundcover or* *for arranging.*

when introduced with salvos of enthusiasm. Today the veriest tyro would discard it at once, although dealers still show it occasionally, full color, in catalogs. Its stringy thin texture reveals its lack of weather resistance, and its fussy frill is no longer in favor. Collectors at the moment stress thick, smooth, waxy segments like those of 'Kingscourt,' which can even withstand hail, and 'Cantatrice,' which remains perfect after two days of rain. They prefer reds and yellows that do not sunburn. They want flowers on stable stems with short necks that present well-poised, symmetrically overlapping petals—except in recurved types, when the segments are expected to be equal. They revel in recent breakthroughs among the reverse bicolors, and look forward to the introduction of "self-reds."

Miniatures begin blooming in early February and, like their giant cousins, run the gamut, with perianths broad and overlapping, pointed, twisted, recurved; with cups ruffled, pinched, flattened and even bulging, like the profile of an old-fashioned wedding ring. Some are difficult; all are darlings.

Because of their small size and tendency to bloom early, many miniature bulbs arrive in a rather desiccated condition and need kind attention. Grow them in pots the first season to fatten them up, and make sure their thin foliage isn't cut down with the grass the first year. Mine persist well if sited where they get a good summer baking and enjoy good drainage. I have finally found just the place for them in a small grassy enclave about 10 x 12 feet which was once completely shielded by a mammoth wild cherry on the slope below. After the cherry's demise, the area, hedged in on the north, was relegated to sunbathing. Because of its limited space and the fact that it was depressed, and so beneath eye level from the house terrace, I decided that the grass there could be allowed to remain uncut until mid-July. Actually, in so small an area, earlier high careful clipping of the grass with a hedge shears has not proved impractical.

In order to enjoy the flowers on this little terrace at close range, and to group them attractively, I checkerboarded it informally with a few large, thick creek stones—to give the daffodils some background and to allow me to hop-scotch from one to another in the spring, and move confidently about among the plants, which vary in height from 2 to 6 inches and include both species and tiny hybrids. Moreover, the daffodils are irregularly staggered in clumps that leave pockets close to the stones for the addition of small botanical tulips and the species crocuses I have always admired but have never before been able to protect from rodents. I had always read that rings of daffodils could give such protection against predators because both leaves and bulbs contain needle-shaped crystals of calcium oxalate. Never before, though, had I found an aesthetic solution. Now I hope that the tiny daffodil area has achieved its built-in deterrent to tulip and crocus enemies, as well as giving the assurance that all the foliage of these bulbs can ripen undisturbed. For the last five years I have, for the first time, enjoyed increasing miniature daffodil returns, even with *triandrus* species. As to *cyclamineus* species, even though they are reputed to remain in growth for the better part of the year and therefore need moisture, my stocks are also on the increase. From comparison with miniatures planted among thymes, I would say that sod seems to give better winter protection, and the grass does not attract slugs as readily as other groundcovers do. Grant E. Mitsch, our most famous American hybridizer, who is giving the English and Irish breeders stiff competition at the Chelsea Show, suggested to me that failure with miniatures may also be due to disease, which often goes on undetected in their grasslike foliage.

Perhaps before spring color begins to fade from the woods we should consider our attitudes toward this great garden resource.

Think back for a moment to the use of flower color in catalogs. Whether we realize it or not the impression of gaudy effects we find there carries over into the notion of the garden itself. In short, color in catalogs is treated as pigment, and as such implies permanence. But bloom that creates actual garden color is both dynamic and fleeting, and needs strong and continuing plant structure with and around it to be effective even when bloom is at its height. The only way to use garden color in any sense as one uses paints is with the tones of a green garden, where you have a more static situation and the contrast of seasonal values is muted. Yet, even here, anyone who has worked with a green garden knows how profoundly seasonal values change both the tone and the power of plant form, and how the enclosure of surrounding deciduous greenery alters scale and emphasis.

On the other hand, while effective use of garden color presents major problems even when deployed against a stable background, the question of just what colors is open to a broad range of choice. Don't be afraid of developing your own palette. Having learned from teaching art that everyone's color and form sense is as revealing and distinctive as his handwriting, I should hate to impose rigid criteria for landscaping. I would rather share a few reactions which, along with my plant-growing experiences, may encourage independent creation in this living medium.

How disappointing it often is to read about gardens and then to see these same gardens explicitly illustrated. Nowhere was this brought home to me more quaintly than in a book published in mid-nineteenth-century Cincinnati: Kern's *Practical Landscape Gardening*. The text made good sense in a conventional way—on the need for foliage contrast, textures and balance in the plantings, and in all the other classic remarks about composition. One immediately began to clothe the author's ideas with one's own vivid mental imagery, but the hackneyed, formless engravings scattered through the text gave the show away. Just recently, again, I dived into an article about a painter's garden in Eire. The text was pleasant, even inventive and stimulating. Color photographs, though, revealed fragmented effects, with masses of red-stemmed

dogwood and interrogative yellow poplars and yews disjointing the lush gentle slopes and vistas of blue water. In another view the harsh white benches, pots and lattices near the house were of an incredibly ugly fussiness, detracting from the luxuriant plant growth beyond. The scene had obviously been contrived by a person whose love of color was matched only by his insensitivity to form.

One of my first encounters with landscape art was in leafing through an early edition of Humphrey Repton, that great eighteenth-century practitioner. He used a highly ingenious method of illustration. Repton was evidently aware of his clients' inability to "realize" his two-dimensional drawings, so he devised the most explicit before-and-after effects in hand-colored "pop-ups." While today few of us have available the large areas that fell to his lot as a designer, it might prove most efficacious if we worked out for ourselves similar overlays.

Repton's solutions may impress us today as mild, but he always managed to blend structures and more formal elements into the view as a whole. And he never hesitated to exploit the obvious. Unity—or harmony—in diversity, now as then, is an essential objective in all gardening, formal or naturalized.

Respecting composition in general, another basic concept must always be kept in mind: how the garden is to be seen. My woods garden, as I have disclosed, is away from the house in a nearby valley. As a consequence, none of its massed effects are visible unless I walk through it. My best friend, on the contrary, can enjoy her beech woods from her living room and can even watch the development of particular treasures from an easy chair. Because she has blocked out near neighbors with "eye traps"—that piquant term which includes fences, hedges, evergreen clumps, gazebos or any other barrier that shuts out ugliness —her view is more like that of a framed canvas with fixed perspective. My vision, as I move about my woods, must cope with great and constantly changing variations of terrain. Very diverse handling of mass effects in color and texture is called for. What is most important, such effects have to be bound both to fields and more formal garden areas with all sorts of skillfully understated transition plantings.

Significantly placed floral groupings can emphasize the forking or intersecting of paths, their height or density shortening or lengthening the vista as desired. If you are using dark evergreens like hollies, yews, magnolias or pines in this process, make groupings generous, or repeat them. Too small a unit tends in the winter landscape to become more like an irritating blemish. Test out the need for consistency in planting-values on interstate highways, where it has been found that when traveling at sixty miles an hour the eye needs half-mile plantings of considerable uniformity for a satisfactory impact.

In a stroll-through garden, areas ripe for enrichment are those in which steps or grades induce slowdowns, where uphill paths allow one to appreciate decumbent or belled plants that can't be fully appraised from above, where rises in ground call for a seat from which to enjoy colorful vistas, or where a level stretch can be made more provocative by a disappearing path that holds a surprise beyond in the form of a pool or sculpture.

In fact if you don't have variations of level in a garden you almost have to create them to enjoy to the fullest the color and characteristics inherent in various types of growth. My approach, no matter what the nature of its contours, is to get to know a tract from all angles, considering how to enhance it by dramatizing existing features or developing new ones where the possibility suggests itself. However you plan your garden, establish enough basic form in its tree and shrub plantings to indicate overall structure, and choose plant

What to admire most about Cornus florida, *our native flowering dogwood: its winter-budded twigs; its brilliant red fruit (295) furiously scattered by migrating birds and lying red on the paths among its paler leaves; its glorious 3-inch bloom, with stylish bracts forming a setting for its beadlike gold-green flowers; or its stance as understory in the woods, stretching its light-hungry branches horizontally to tap every possible bit of solar energy for the widely spaced blossoms? Compare such branches with a clustered one like this taken from a specimen at the woods' edge, where sunlight is plentiful.*

material of constant enough attractiveness so that you don't have to come up with the gardener's classic alibi: "You should have seen it last week!"

Path placement is of primary importance. Paths are best plotted, of course, when the leaves die back and you can sense your real problems of grade and vista at a glance. If your place is large, stiff wires twisted at the top to hold bits of colored plastic can be stuck in the ground and, I might add, can be shifted easily as you try out alternate plans. If a path or border area is in open terrain, a hose or coarse rope makes an even more quickly adjusted definer. On grades, the problem of erosion must be faced at once, and no disturbance of existing growth should be undertaken until your plans for replanting or cutting and filling are solid.

If delays occur after work on the paths has begun, a temporary light covering of wheat straw or the use of erosion netting is worth considering. The final surfacing of paths depends on the gradient, the exposure, and how much use they are likely to get. All these factors should be carefully weighed before deciding among rock paving, treated log sections, a less costly—and less permanent—layer of wood chips, nut shells, bark fiber or—least permanent of all—compacted leaves; and in moist, densely shaded areas, moss, and in sunny ones, grass. Whatever you use, keep the value unobtrusive.

In sunny, fairly flat areas at Cockaigne we have simply plowed out 6-foot walkways where slopes are mild; these have quickly adapted to sod. We keep the grass mowed short, and feather out at the immediate edges with a grass whip. I might add that, not unnaturally, our sunny areas are the ones where all maintenance, on-path and off-path too, is most difficult.

This brings me to a seeming diversion, yet one integral with landscape planning. Looking back, I am sometimes glad we failed when we bought our acreage to gauge the full implications of maintenance in general. Our program was innocent, romantic and reckless. I knew that at least two-thirds of our acreage needed drastic treatment, but had no idea of the practicalities. The end result I had in mind was inspiration enough. Thank goodness I can say now, with the pride of survival, that we dreamed and carried out our plans without being inhibited by fears of upkeep. In our bold projections, we knew somehow that the humpbacked eroding old cornfield would be transformed into a pleasant sweep of meadow, parted by a rising, gently curving approach-drive, shielded from road and neighbors by clumps of shrubbery and evergreens. Above, firmly founded on our imagination, stood the house, dominating the view and surrounded by future gardens. From the living room, to the south, the mind's eye took in a series of descending grass panels, set off on either side by a succession of dogwood, pine, fringe tree and yucca, like a very deep stage setting; and terminated by a semicircular hedge and the horizon beyond—the crest of the valley, a mile away. Off the kitchen were herbs; off the porch, broad crude stairs of ledge stone leading down to rock and sunken gardens; across the cir-

Chionanthus virginicus, or fringe tree, a dioecious shrub with wonderfully fragrant 10-inch-long white panicles, can be grown from seed. In nurseries you are apt to get a clone from staminate plants like the one shown here, with broader-petaled, showy inflorescences. If your seedling turns out to be a pistillate plant, you may be compensated for the thinner-petaled bloom by having attractive pendulous dark blue seed clusters in the fall.

cular entrance court more stone stairs giving access to transitional borders and, farther along, to the magical, if then sadly overpastured, woodland glen about which so much of this section of this book is written. And lo! all these things happened; not all at once, of course, and sometimes with little assurance that the necessary resources lay ahead. But they happened.

Exactly what plants or trees, for the most part, would be suitable or happy growing around and in these features I didn't bother to formulate, for actually I didn't even know the vocabulary, let alone the language of gardening. The ways to learn both, I thought, were by looking at other people's plantings and making the round of nurseries. The former produced the more helpful results.

To drop in and see how the other fellow did it is not a new sport, I found, when I read *The Regency Visitor,* letters of the Baron Pückler-Muskau, edited by E. M. Butler. He describes the coachloads of the elite who invaded the great English estates in the early 1800s even as thousands of tourists do today. Here, in this Pomeranian nobleman, was a man so determined to further the development of his own estate that he persuaded his wife to stay at home while he sought out a rich heiress abroad, who would then constructively join them on their rolling Baltic acres in a *ménage-à-trois.* That he made enough money to satiate his "parko-mania" in quite another way was due to mere chance. The whole story, however, amply demonstrates to what lengths a dedicated gardener, intent on promotion and heedless of outlay, can—and will—go.

If you rely on nursery visits you see mainly the juvenile forms of plants. As

a rule, the spreading oak you have in mind is a 2-inch-caliper whip; the "foundation" evergreens, no larger than footstools or taller than whiskbrooms; the flowering shrubs and ornamental trees equally lacking in the distinctive personalities that maturity confers. To forecast the future of such material in a given landscape takes a measure of prophetic skill.

It took a few years for me to realize, too, that if I were growing plants it was a better policy over even the medium-long run to put my energies into propagation by cuttings (118) and seeding (121) of shrubs and distinctive perennials, rather than endlessly bringing along showy annuals like zinnias and sweet alyssum, late to bloom and annihilated each year by the first black frost.

As circumstances have forced me to devote much time to more immediate living demands, my gardening life has been a happy escape—precious hours in which to enjoy and marvel at my changing environment. I decided at the outset that I didn't want to be absorbed by a sort of outdoor housecleaning and dusting process. I wanted to find plants that could "take it," whose seedlings did not need the protection of frames, plants that were very hardy, with long bloom periods or with pronounced structural forms that would set off flowering vistas, plants that were more giving than demanding.

As a starter, after learning some of the Latin names used in designating the plant species I most admired, I watched neglected gardens for interesting and staunch survivors, and tried out, partly by guess, cataloged plants which seemed to meet "woodsy" specifications. Such first steps seem logical enough, but even they cannot be taken without the full consciousness that plants simply refuse to be coerced. They will cooperate and gratify only when they encounter conditions they happen to like. What are those basic conditions?

We have mentioned the importance of siting for protection from undue cold and wind, acquiring and conditioning healthy stock, and developing suitable soils. Now for some additional considerations.

There is, for one, the relation of plants to each other. Over the years you see at work the principles of succession, where, left to themselves, stronger plants begin to triumph over others, to preempt light and moisture, eventually establishing more stable and exclusive associations. There are, of course, inevitable and often rapid reversals set off by "outside" events as seemingly minor as the loss of a single tree.

Recently, succession studies in neglected fields showed that many plants appear to possess weaponlike exudates that ward off other plants temporarily, and that after a year or two may even poison the ground against their own survival. But thanks to the nitrogen their decay has furnished, still other plants that tolerate the new conditions move in, until a different dominant surface cover is established. The complexity of such relationships makes this gardener marvel at the numbers of aliens that willingly adapt to new environments. Exudate factors, incidentally, may in part explain some of the failures when transplanting aliens and natives alike (67).

As one watches the changing patterns of native annuals, heavy now in one place, now in another, one wonders whether they are merely seeking new mineral and nutrient sources or responding to toxic substances of their own creating. One plant particularly inclined to wander about, blue-eyed Mary (223), seems to reseed in new areas after several successive years in the same spot. The gardener, in the face of increasing scientific speculation, still remains highly dependent on trial and error to reconcile many factors. Don't scorn your hunches.

How often I have tried to recall in my plantings the simple generous effects one sometimes sees in veteran woods—a slope white with *Trillium grandiflorum* (237) and ferns, against another slope bright with celandine poppies (105). Had I but known, when I started my woodland garden, that my co-author, Frances Poetker, had written an ecological dissertation on *Vegetation and Habitat Contrasts of a North and South Slope in Southwestern Ohio,* my efforts would have been greatly eased and my transplanting losses minimized. Her daily records of insolation, temperature and relative humidity from December through April show a positive correlation of daytime temperature differences on north- and south-facing slopes. Depending on the amount of sunshine, the south-facing slope registered from 10 to 17% higher temperatures and maintained a 3.5% lower humidity. And on clear cold nights, because of inversion, the temperature of the

Usually the tailored blooms of Liriodendron tulipfera, *the tulip poplar, are sky high on these bare-trunked, excellent timber trees which flash into golden pyramids in the fall when the white oaks, so often their companions, are a greyed-lavender. Because a young tulip tree was mistakenly cut off as a weed for three successive years, it developed low-spreading branches which still, thirty years later, support quantities of big greenish cups at eye level. One can distinguish the yellow and orange markings around their peaked centers, against which the ripened pistils will later form imbricated cones (307).*

south-facing slope was always markedly lower. Snow lasted two days longer on the north-facing slopes, giving the groundcovers there greater protection and the soil a 14% greater amount of moisture. Although the soils of both slopes were almost identical as to mineral composition, the greater moisture retention and shade on the north-facing slope accounted for 11% more organic content.

For the gardener, the significance of these findings lies in the specific vegetational contrasts. The south-facing slope needs tough characters. The north-facing slope claims most ferns, many of the most horticulturally desirable plants, as well as the mosses, which peculiarly must absorb all their moisture through their leaves alone. Once plants begin to seed they find their own favored locale, but for the gardener with only one or a few specimens of a treasured item to experiment with, placement with the greatest combination of survival factors is of real importance.

Consider some survival factors other than exposure. If you have so much as tried to winter a pot of basil on your kitchen windowsill, you know you're involved in a succession of stratagems to preserve succulence and turgidity. Granted that you don't have a heat failure, and that you started off with an adequate amount of soil, hopefully of good quality, the most crucial factor would seem to be moisture, regularly but not too frequently administered.

In naturalizing plants, watering, except at transplanting time, is for me entirely impractical. Consequently, one thing becomes clear. The soil must be, or must be made, moisture retentive, but not waterlogged. Drainage is essential for all but bog or stream-side plants that possess built-in mechanisms to cope with "wet feet." Where heavy clay predominates, one way to assure quick runoff without losing adequate moisture retentiveness is to work for loamy soil. This poetic term has still to be scientifically defined, yet every born gardener recognizes at a glance this loose-textured, dark, rich-looking, pleasant-smelling, velvety substance which contains great growth potential and results from the tempering of raw mineral material by the presence of humus. For "humus" you must have a substance so structured that the particles are separated to retain soil-air and yet allow moisture to move by capillarity. These are the conditions which microbial and insect life, described on page 9, must have to coexist. And this is why so much garden advice consists of suggestions for sufficient drainage to keep rain and runoff water from backing up and clogging the interstices that make room for root growth.

Despite the favorable soil base of our acreage, the scarce water supply heightened the importance of loam as a planting resource. I learned early to fashion a soil supplement from compost. With a virtuous sense of "making something out of nearly nothing," I began to husband almost all the organic materials I could lay my hands on: weeds, non-greasy kitchen wastes, grass cuttings, leaves in variety, tender hedge clippings—but not heavy woody ones, for wood tends to slow the action. The inclusion of leaves in making up compost is especially valuable. They contribute rare trace elements brought from great depths by tree roots. In fact, sometimes prospectors rely on leaf analysis to learn about the potentials of mineral deposits far below the surface.

There seems to be reasonable proof that if you use compost extensively your garden is ensured greater resistance to insects and disease. There is recent evidence, too, that plants are able to absorb greater amounts of chemicals from composts than they can from soil treated with the so-called artificials, because humus is structured to slow down the leaching away of nutrients which supply a welcome environment for an active microbiological population. Quite apart from the theoretical arguments pro and con in the organic-chemical controversy, I am a compost convert on the basis of personal experience. My water shortage alone led me from the beginning to avoid fast-acting chemical fertilizers which, I quickly found, demand—if plants are to profit by their use—a much greater amount of moisture than our rainfall provides.

A pragmatic bias was, I confess, greatly reinforced by a study of Ehrenfried Pfeiffer's *Bio-Dynamic Farming and Gardening*. This book cites a source through which the reader might get in touch with local organic gardeners who use an agricultural system closely allied to certain tenets of Rudolph Steiner's anthroposophy. An adherent living in the neighborhood offered to induct a friend and me into the mysteries of compost-making. We tramped her Kentucky ridgeback land, marveled at the growth she achieved, and were impressed particularly by the flavor of her produce and fruits.

Since this initial experience I have found almost as many recipes for making compost as there are for making bread. I can't resist, however, describing my own method. No matter what the details advocated, the principle is constant. Fundamentally, it's a heating process in which a pile of organic refuse decays. "Feinschmeckers" suggest mixed animal manures and other more esoteric additives to assure the presence of necessary minerals and trace elements.

The ratio of green manures to animal manures and other additives such as wood ashes should be in balance, as described below, so that the pile may heat sufficiently to decompose weeds, seeds and thick weed roots. To decompose seeds, the pile must reach 130° to 160°F, and 40° higher if you include heavy roots. Should the heap exceed 160° it will need additional moisture.

The major stages in composting are two. First, in order to guarantee oxidation, there must be some way of introducing air into the pile. After about two months of heating, sufficient bacterial activity should have developed to enable the organisms to obtain their oxygen from the decomposition of the material itself.

A general rule of thumb is to construct the pile at ground level. Rows of bricks or bands of very coarse gravel form a kind of latticed foundation which helps to ensure adequate drainage and aeration. The heap is then further built around 4-inch-diameter vertical poles wrapped loosely with chicken wire and

Asimina triloba, our native pawpaw or custard-apple, has stolen its name from the tropic papaya. Both have elongated mellow aromatic fruits, though the papaya's is larger. The tree, to 35 feet, has 9- to 12-inch dull green, rather sparsely placed leaves when mature. The foliage is new-fledged and a tender green when the 2-inch maroon flowers reluctantly recurve to reveal their full green-gold centers, which can be glimpsed best by tipping the branch up.

covered with a layer of newspaper. Do withdraw the poles when the heap is finished. Allow two flues to a 5 x 5-foot heap. A pile at least 5 x 5 x 4 feet high is recommended for good heat retention. Should you build a solid pile, air may be introduced afterwards by forcing a crowbar down at intervals and swinging it around in circles to form the flues.

Once the above temperatures are achieved for as long as a four-day period, the pile can be left to ripen. Some authorities recommend turning the pile to mix unevenly heated areas. A greater number feel that the pile can be closed without turning after eight weeks by covering with a four-mil-thick polyethylene sheet, and left to final maturation.

The best shape for the pile is rectangular. Don't make it much over 5 feet wide to avoid having to walk on it while spreading the layers: trampling packs the pile too much. Build it up in the making in such a way that its edges remain higher than the center, creating a slight oval depression at the top of the finished pile. This will catch rainwater, and so help to keep the contents moist.

If you have made compost before, start your heap with a single thin layer of the old compost. Should green vegetable refuse and raw manure be used in the new pile, keep the general proportions of about one part animal manure to three parts vegetable. With wholly new material, put down first a 6- to 8-inch layer of green refuse. Some soil usually adheres to the weed roots. If there is none, a light sprinkling of soil should follow. You may then scatter about 8 ounces of wood ashes—a source of potash—for every square yard of exposed surface. Some composters use a dusting of rock phosphate and green sand—a source of potassium. If fresh manure is not available, dried manure or dried blood is suggested as a source of nitrogen.

Now add to these bottom-most layers a 2-inch layer of manure. From then on it's a "da capo" performance, beginning again with the garden greens until the 5- to 6-foot height is reached. In any case, finish with a double layer of manure and a final covering consisting of either sod, top side down, a crust of about 2 to 3 inches of earth, or 6 inches of straw. And don't forget to take out the poles, leaving the wire, or to punch in the "flues," since air is essential to the "burning" process.

As the pile heats it sinks, losing at least one-third of its volume by the time the presence of earthworms indicates that the compost is ready to use. Length of procedure depends on the nature of the ingredients, the season and the amount of rainfall. It can be as short as three spring or summer months if the material is shredded, or as long as a year if not. Should compost that includes manures be very slow to decay, or remain undecayed, the cause may be excessive woody or cellulose material. If the pile doesn't begin to sink within a few weeks, poor ventilation or too great dryness is indicated, as may also be the case should ants and wood lice be present. An ammoniac odor means that the heap is too tightly packed.

Meet the native buckeyes. Ohio, or Aesculus glabra, a tree to 40 feet, with its very early coarse unfolding 5-fingered leaves and greenish-yellow 12-inch panicles, is shown here. A. pavia, the red buckeye, is half as tall, with rose-red flowers half as long in June, and A. parviflora, the bottle-brush buckeye, suckers at the base to form 15-foot-high wavelike masses carrying 12-inch white candles on the irregular crests. It is particularly opulent when cascading down a north-facing hillside.

I was interested in the reactions of our county agent to an extensive trip he made abroad with the local market gardeners. He reported some amazingly productive vegetable gardens, and found in each instance that they were organically managed and that the compost heaps used were kept moist with an infusion of *Equisetum arvense* (261). This plant, which has a ninety percent silica base, is supposed to increase photosynthesis when the compost is finally applied.

My own composting locations are varied. The first and most important is along a work path just off the garage turnaround to which manure can be delivered by truck, and where the pile is hidden by hedges. On the upper side of the path, and shaded by a tree not too close by, are two long bins cut into a low bank and retained with cinder block piled up to two feet on three sides but open at ground level onto the path. In these bins composting goes on alternately twice a year, with manure trundled to them from the turnaround by wheelbarrow in early spring and late summer.

The manure is mixed with partially decayed vegetable matter that has been allowed to accumulate in a large heap opposite the bins on the downhill side of the path. These organic materials are retained on the down side by an informal framework of locust that resembles a Lincoln-log fence. The lower heap consists

of those "something-for-nothing" weeds, tender hedge clippings, leaves, and non-greasy kitchen refuse such as melon rinds and corn husks. If for no other reason than that they attract rodents and slow the action, avoid using greasy wastes. Much of my material has become partially dried by the time it is added to the heap, so I sprinkle it during incorporation to the consistency of a wrung-out sponge.

Aside from incorporating compost into the soil when transplanting, I have adopted a system of modified sheet composting at woods edges and in shrubbery borders whenever I start to naturalize coarse perennials. Here I add generous amounts of compost to the surface of the ground near the transplants and cover the compost with light organic mulches (168). The mulch should never be so heavy as to crust or so wet as to mold, for access of air is necessary to allow the plants to assimilate sufficient nitrogen. This is a good method not only of giving the plants slow-acting, long-range fertilization, but of achieving water retentiveness until they establish.

For another type of slow-acting fertilizer, I now and then collect, before seeding time, woods-weedings, and fill up depressions in the forest areas where I can cover them unobtrusively with leaves. As the depressions fill in they often encourage interesting new growth, because the densely packed quality of the leaffall in the depressions has been lessened. These deeper pits provide good places to rob when you need some richer mold for transplanting nearby. Of course the shrinkage in these piles is greater than in the manured heaps, and the value of such non-manurial compost is rather as a soil texturizer than as a fertilizer. There are various simple leaf piles too, of course, which form naturally, and if left alone long enough can be tapped for rich mold.

We all know that uncropped nature left to herself returns to the soil not only the mineral nutrients taken from it but a far greater bulk of stuff made from air and water. In fact plants manufacture 90% of their tissues from water and air. It is these compounds of carbon, hydrogen and oxygen that improve texture, converting raw mineral soils into loam. In any area, however, where planting for highly concentrated effects is practiced, the situation calls for supplementary nourishment to keep the soil properly enriched.

Watch the changing pattern of woodland annuals in their instinctive search for better habitat, or notice the ever widening circles of a plant like *Iris cristata* as it reaches out for fresh soil. While most colonies of naturalized plants—epimediums, hellebores and ferns are outstanding examples—persist in one location hale, hearty and untouched for many years, others soon go on aggressive campaigns for new environment.

The healthiest and most floriferous lime-soil garden I ever saw was in England, and it belonged to Margery Fish. She used 150 cubic feet of compost per acre each year. This amounted to an overall coating of over 1 inch—and she applied it in the late autumn wherever gaps occurred in her heavily planted borders and groundcover areas. Not all of us are energetic and dedicated enough to

On a typical south-facing slope in late April the delicate pinks of the wild geranium are reinforced by the blue-lavender to deep purple spires of the native Delphinium tricorne, *seen overshadowed here by the powerful unfolding stalks of* Polygonatum canaliculatum, *great Solomon's-seal, which will rise over 4 feet. For other Solomons'-seals, see pages 119 and 271.*

Graham Thomas describes twenty-three hardy geraniums that carpet well in his Plants for Ground-cover. *For many years in partial shade and sun I have modified the strong magentas of some of the introduced geraniums with whites like* G. pratense *and* sanguineum album, *that true pink* sanguineum lancastriense *and blues like* platypetalum *and the fine form* 'Johnson's Blue.'

be so lavish. As a casual and intermittent gardener myself, my deviations from such thoroughgoing methods are legion. But my respect for compost and my continuing efforts to create compost of sorts out of the things at hand are unwavering.

In addition to incorporating compost and other organic material in soils, I have used bone meal. Everyone agrees that bone meal gives long-lasting stamina and strength to non-ericaceous plants. An especially valuable property is its slow release of phosphorus. You will often read that it is good practice to dig out small plugs of soil at intervals in concentric circles around the base of trees and fill the holes with bone meal and other nutrients. Don't be surprised if, in following this advice, you discover neat excavations at these same spots a little later. Animals, it seems, like bone meal, too. I suspect raccoons, for the work is so precise and even. The digging doesn't all happen in one night, but by spring the job is complete. Often, again, when I've used spoonfuls of straight bone meal in bulb planting, it gets eaten along with the bulb; or if the bulbs deter rodents, as daffodils do, the bulb may be found intact but upheaved, unless the bone meal is at least 12 inches below the surface.

There is a never-ending fascination in the way plants cast their seed: the silken parachutes of milkweed, the rattle cases of the golden rain tree, Koelreuteria paniculata (275), the barbed points and corkscrews of the triple-awned grass, Aristida oligantha, that are fashioned to bore into moist soil—not to mention the all too familiar barbs, hooks and sticky gums that enable other fruits and seeds to anchor on passing animals, and thus be distributed. Cyclamen (222) spirals its precious burden close to the ground for release. And here the Gothic finials of the cranesbill, Geranium maculatum, split at the base and curl back to permit seed egress.

Because of such experiences, I use bone meal chiefly in making up compost. There, thoroughly diffused throughout the pile, it is totally available for my plants but too scattered to attract animals.

While compost is the most valuable of all-purpose soil additives, peats, those vegetal residues in glacial swamps arrested from full decay by the acids of the bog water, are mainly texturizers. There are two major types of peat. One is peat moss derived from sphagnum mosses; the other is "lowmoor" peat, derived from sedges, reeds, mosses and similar types of plants. Both are valued for their water-holding ability. Sphagnum peat has greater holding capacity than sedge peat, but is more acid. Sedge peats are about one-third higher in nitrogen than sphagnum peats and register a pH from 3.5 to 7.

Anything based on logarithms for expressing acidity or alkalinity of soil, as is the pH scale, frightens me. So I willingly accept without further inquiry the dictum that pH values above neutral 7 denote alkaline conditions, those below denote acid ones. Although the scale runs from 0 to 14, best growth conditions for very acid-loving plants are in the 4 to 6 range, for those slightly acid from 6 to 6.5. Most of the plants I grow flourish in the neutral to 7.5 range. pH readings that increase ten times between each degree are most valuable for diagnosis of soil problems, especially in gauging the availability of plant nutrients. As the pockets of acid soils in our area are very limited, most of our natives obviously prefer lime. Thus, using the lower acid Pennsylvania and Michigan peats with a pH of 6 is less likely to upset soil balances. Because the nutrients in peat are no greater than in average soils, peats cannot really be considered effective fertilizers. Their additive value, as with mica granules and sand, is mainly as soil conditioners. Twenty-five percent peat to soil volume is considered a heavy application.

The "don'ts" of peat are two. First, avoid using it as a surface mulch, partly because it will draw moisture to its under layer and in turn keep plant roots shallow as they try to share in this high-rise moisture level. Another disadvantage to surface application is that as the peat dries some of the surface layer blows off, and the rest of it packs too tightly, forming an impermeable crust. Incidentally, used in areas where cigarette throwers abound, peat is—as are many mulches—a fire hazard. Second, when incorporating peat with soil, be sure it has previously been soaked enough so that it won't draw moisture from the soil to the real detriment of the plants it surrounds. Tests show that peat used dry in incorporations does not function for several years. As a consequence, unless properly moistened, the purpose for which it has been used—to give transplants a moisture-retentive boost—is simply nullified.

Aside from seeing that soil conditions are structurally and nutritionally favorable, there is an old saw that probably has some bearing on establishing any bare-root plants: leave the transplant no more than three months or no less than three years before disturbing it again. Today's container-grown plants from nurseries, however, with their compact root systems, can probably survive the gardener's in-and-out vagaries with more than traditional aplomb. Another sensible rule is to move spring-blooming plants after seeding, summer and fall-blooming plants in early spring.

There are new techniques that help plants to establish, like the complete coverage of both the tops and bottoms of the leaves, especially for evergreens, with anti-desiccant sprays. In such applications, follow the manufacturer's directions. And there are old ones like muddling the bare roots of transplants and seedlings by dipping the roots in a cream-soup consistency of soil and water as a protection during transfer to new locales.

Then, too, even a short period of shading after transplanting greatly helps plants to establish. For individual plants, use an inverted basket. Or cut an unwanted leafy branch and stick it in at the sunny side: it will give considerable protection until it shrivels. For plantings covering several yards I use cane matting, available at garden centers, supported on reinforcing rods that have been bent ninety degrees at the ends to form a broad angular wicket. Tipped over, the short ends quickly pierce the hardest ground, and the straight backs support the matting. In windy weather the matting can quickly be tied to the supports with plastic-covered wire threaded around the reeds.

Don't drown transplants. Water just enough after transplanting to make sure that the water replaces air pockets and leaves the earth close to all roots. And one more warning: don't confuse these larger air pockets due to digging with the loose structure which inherently incorporates soil-air in a properly constituted loam.

If transplanting in the fall, use an organic or a sand mulch so that should heaving occur there will be an unincorporated element that can sift into the cracks and protect roots that might otherwise become exposed. I have found, though, that the best time to transplant, especially for shallow-rooted plants or plants difficult to establish, is before mid-April. The only drawback is that if you're casual about planting records you are apt to dig into heavily populated sites, should the plants already there be late risers. Near very precious bulbs that go into a dormant disappearing act, I try to place stones on the down side to warn me of a presence. Conversely, a sturdy weed rosette may tell me that nothing of value is near.

Where does one obtain wildlings to take the place of the unwanted weeds? The all too obvious answer is, of course, "where they grow." It is an answer that will not satisfy either the conservationist or the conscientious collector, especially if it is proposed to disturb natural plant communities in areas where they are already sufficiently thinned by "development" and road-building. Yet it is in just these areas that the collector can move without reproach, if he manages to anticipate such activities. In fact, by taking up wildflower turf in the path of the bulldozer, he can play a positive role in preservation and at the same time establish a new sanctuary under his own protection.

On a typical north-facing woods slope at the end of April you will find jack-in-the-pulpits in all sizes up to 3 feet. Arisaema atrorubens, the Indian turnip—but don't try to eat it uncooked (109)—is the commonest type in our woods. The ill-scented flowers on its almost clublike spadix attract insects that, trapped under the ribbed purplish-brown hood, add protein to the plant's diet. Here they grow compatibly in a 6-inch-high carpeting of frothy foamflower, Tiarella cordifolia, with its evergreen purple-backed leaves, and contrast in their understated boldness with the delicate purple-flecked white of Disporum maculatum, the spotted fairybell.

Farther afield, in more remote places, there are areas where certain types of wild plants may in fact be overabundant, and where the collector—if he observes strict precautions—may, in our view, legitimately venture to carry off a limited number of specimens. First of all, consult and get the approval of the owner of the tract on which they grow, and then keep the site as intact as possible, covering roots of any disturbed plants. Better still, grow wildflowers from seed (121).

We have watched spring growth from mid-March to late April as one throbbing expanding glory miraculously orchestrated, magically stimulating. The landscape has shown only its perfections. By the last week in April the redbuds are fading, dogwood bloom loses strength against its greenery, daffodils run heavily to leaf, edges become raggedy, hedges beg for trimming, weedy plants tend to dominate the seeding ephemerals.

Fortunately, during this transition, some of the hardy exotics such as you see on pages 129 and 140 show gratifying promise. In the woods a harmony of greens makes a dark-vaulted background for occasional but telling color accents such as the scarlet bloom of *Silene virginica*, the fire pink, which is striking at one hundred feet or more. Against a wealth of textures, bold fern fronds begin to emerge, contributing toward the richness of patterns.

Most of the ferns can be counted on to hold until frost. But the delicate fronds of *Cystopteris fragilis* var. *protusa*, seen emerging on the endpapers, carpet large areas only until early July. Their matted creeping rootstocks have sufficient interstices to allow this fern to live in peace with the spring ephemerals. But some ferns, because of the impenetrable toughness of their rootstocks, preclude other growth and can even become unwelcome. I have seen *Onoclea sensibilis*, the sun-loving sensitive fern, with its dashingly cut triangular blades, so dense at the edge of a field drainage ditch that its sods could hardly be pierced by a sharp spade. Relocated in greater shade, with more moisture and less good drainage, it has been slower to develop, but grows compatibly with still other ferns and with the yellow *Iris pseudacorus* (153), astilbes, the spotted Italian arum (257), and the gooseneck loosestrife (153). Here toward the fall the sensitive fern bears its furled brown spore cases on 1½-foot stems. This form of reproductive stalk is rare in ferns, as most of them carry their spores in small raised dots, or sori, on the backs of their fronds in patterns as easily identified as signatures.

All ferns pass from a spore stage to another distinctly different one. From within a transient transparent liverwort-like substance, a tiny flask containing an egg develops. After it is fertilized by a sperm cell a rootlet strikes toward the soil, and a leaf, true to its adult type, goes skyward. If you try growing ferns from spores, this intermediate substance—the prothallus—must be kept moist at all times. The saturated brick described on page 122 is the propagating method to try.

Many fern plants are vase-shaped, and these need to be carefully handled. I refer not only to their placement—which should take into account their rather emphatic flare—but to their handling during transplantation. All ferns that emerge bunched from a central nucleus should be transplanted only when dormant or just emerging. In contrast to varieties with creeping roots, like the fragile fern, a type that can make constant new growth and thereby ensure successful transplanting at any time, ferns that grow from a cluster usually make only one set of leaves a year. They are almost sure to die if planted when in full leaf, unless at least half of their fronds can be preserved unbroken and kept unwilted until the roots establish.

Ferns are also pretty particular about depth of planting. Those of the maidenhair family, like *Adiantum pedatum*, cherished for the lacy strength of its great cantilevered discs, can cut across and simultaneously shield other growths (180) and, because of their wiry stems, come through quite heavy leaf-fall. The almost indestructible evergreen Christmas fern, *Polystichum acrostichoides*, like

most vase-shaped ferns, even deciduous ones, needs only its own fronds for winter protection, leaving its high crown fairly well exposed.

Equally enduring, if frustrating, is the ebony spleenwort, *Asplenium platy neuron* (293). I want to tuck it, with its swirled lower maindenhair-like fronds and its upthrusting shafts, at the edge and base of steps, where its entire form can be seen to full advantage; but it refuses to let me enhance its charm, and prefers to snuggle down in sun-speckled weedy turfs under brambles. Perhaps the preference of the spleenwort for sods is due to the more constant temperature of such a milieu.

No group of plants is more sensitive to light intensity in relation to moisture. *Athyrium pycnocarpon*, the so-called narrow-leaved spleenwort, and interrupted fern, *Osmunda claytoniana*, I can grow only on north-facing slopes. Cinnamon fern, *Osmunda cinnamomea*, and the Christmas fern (142) will take more sun if the soil is moist. Of the many ferns I have tried, those mentioned have colonized well for me. Other types seem to need supplemental watering, except for bracken, *Pteridium aquilinum*, which, because of its invasiveness, I have avoided introducing.

At first when I transplanted ferns I thought I was doing them a favor by sinking them in solid leaf mold. But they need more minerals than leaf mold alone produces. While the top layer of soil, where one finds them growing in the wild, may seem duffy from the rotting of old fronds, ferns are actually dependent on the rather heavier denser soil just beneath their crowns.

This is true also for some fern allies, which at first glance look like true ferns. The botrychiums, *B. virginianum*, the rattlesnake fern, and *B. multifidum* (42), the leathery grape fern, with their deep-striking fleshy roots, are found as more or less isolated plants in both dry and moist woods, while the similarly rooted single-leaved *Ophioglossum vulgatum*, the adder's tongue, takes sun and likes rocky terrain. For other fern relatives, see pages 26 and 66.

In some epimediums or barrenworts— so named because their woody roots cluster close together to the exclusion of other growth—the structure of the florets is easily recognizable. In others like E. X rubrum *and* E. macranthum, *the floret takes on a confusing complexity, almost as though the blooms were lidded. There is an orchidaceous delicacy about these sprays of ⅜- to ½-inch flowers that are fully visible only when their leaves are emerging. Before the flowers are mature, the leaves, kitelike on wiry stems, have grown enough to hide the color beneath—except at the edges of the thick patches, as seen on the opposite page. The florets above are, moving clockwise from the top,* E. versicolor 'Sulphurem,' E. X rubrum, E. X warleyense, *an orange-red and buff combination, and* E. X youngianum 'Niveum'; *with* E. grandiflorum *in the center, which ranges from a pure white to deep rose. The varieties mentioned above have prospered, in contrast to* E. X youngianum 'Roseum,' *the* lilacinum *of the catalogs. Epimediums are easily propagated by divisions made just before new growth appears.*

Summer Vigor

By and large the gardening I do has a minimum of follow-up care. Until mid-May the midland landscape is fairly orderly, and pampered favorites have nothing to fear from weed invasion. Then, suddenly, one good rain plus a few hot days is enough to transform order into chaos. Areas where you know good things lurk are completely changed in character. The limp, low, controllable chickweeds and ground ivies are superseded in June by plants that show a frightening vigor, tallness and strength. Areas where lusty ferns or hostas have predominated become overspread with uninvited growth. Selective weeding helps. But, should pure laziness or a series of house guests absorb me until mid-June, I discover that the six weeks of heat and drought that have intervened have brought about a reaction, a kind of natural shrinkage in the woods.

By mid-July spring bulb leaves have vanished, ferns have grown stalwart, and underneath the weeds the good material somehow has managed to persist undaunted. The white boneset (302), sanicle, *Sanicula trifoliata*, and the large-leaved waterleaf, *Hydrophyllum macrophyllum*, may seem all-pervasive. Agile bedstraw (42) clambers weightily over low groundcovers like a pale crocheted afghan. But a number of these egregious intruders can be "harvested" with surprising ease: flail your arms in wide arcs and the sticky stems of bedstraw adhere, pulling more bedstraw with them, and in no time you can rid yourself of great muffs of it. Even after weeks of laissez-faire, the shallow-rooted touch-me-nots, *Impatiens pallida*, are easily yanked off the hellebores hidden beneath them. Certain weeds like snakeroot, sanicle and waterleaf, while highly tenacious during most of the year because of their multiple rootlets, can be dislodged without a struggle when they are in bloom. At other times grubbing may be necessary.

Dock and plantains, which in damp soil resist trowel and spade, will, if the soil is dry and the root has shrunk slightly, come up intact with one hearty twisting pull near the base of the plant. For weeds whose roots are brittle and break readily, allowing new shoots to form—such as goutweed (116) and gooseneck loosestrife (153)—a heavy prior mulching of the afflicted area with peat will bring roots to the surface and reward you with a nearly exposed root network when you go after them several weeks later. I have a special approach to field garlic, *Allium vineale*, and for its removal suggest you have handy a spud digger and a plastic bucket. Place the digger about 3 inches to one side of the clump and penetrate the soil on a slight diagonal that will cut well under the bulbous roots. Lift sod and bulbs to expose a deep divot such as you get with a very poor golf stroke. Reach down and clasp the bulbous mass, compressing it hard while pulling. The tops follow easily and intact, but more important, the offsets of the bulbs are imbedded with your handful of soil and go at once into the bucket, dirt and all, for discarding. Replace the divot!

Speaking of onions, let me digress for a moment. It is the in-thing these days to gather edible wild plants and to cook and garnish them with flowers. But a word of warning: should we give all the poisonous plants mentioned in this book a distinguishing mark, you would be amazed at their prevalence. Never eat any part of a plant you're not sure of—or not sure how to prepare for eating. Your mouth may water at the prospect of freshly culled poke greens, yet almost every bit of this plant—roots, leaves, blooms and berries—is poisonous. Only the budded tip of the growing shoot can be safely eaten, and preferably if cooked in three waters of which the first two are discarded.

When you're sampling even widely recommended wild plants, down them with discretion. You may be tempted to gobble up delicious fiddleheads, but before you do be mighty sure they are the unfolding shoots of ostrich fern (69), and not just any fern, or the ubiquitous weedy sprouts of bracken, *Pteridium aquilinum*. Most ferns have highly allergenic properties, and as for bracken, it has a B-vitamin-destroying factor that has proved deadly to animals.

There is a growing cult of mushroom hunting. For the unskilled mycologist, gourmet delights in this field may be reaped at too high a cost. The argument is frequently heard that Europeans and some primitive peoples habitually collect, so why shouldn't we? If the forms are distinctive, like morels or puffballs, and before the latter have reached a size greater than the similar-looking forms of some poisonous types that have not yet broken their caul-like veils, no danger may be involved. If you look at the specimens of the *Mycena* species (184), you become aware of how many sometimes deceptively confusing forms a single mushroom variety may take on from emergence to aging. These are quite unlike many more reassuring types that get their start on submerged old stumps and each year expand their web of mycelium into a larger and larger hollow circle, which may increase in diameter for over a half-century. It is frequently to well-established "fairy rings" of edible mushrooms like these that some country families return with a feeling of safety year after year.

Among the most poisonous mushrooms are some of the amanitas at whose base, provided they are not too faded, a cuplike portion of the volva or membrane which enclosed them remains, its upper edges in a tattered state still clinging to the stem beneath the cap.

Many quite explicit and enthusiastic books on mushrooms have been published. Yet in nearly all a spirit of caution is overriding, some experts suggesting that a clump of at least a dozen examples of a single species be observed for identification before any gathering takes place.

Stinging nettles, *Urtica dioica*, which will make you very uncomfortable for a short time if you brush even lightly against them, lose their sting in cooking and are considered a beneficial spring purge. But poison ivy (121), which, on the contrary, may make you miserable for a very long time just for the touching, has no compensatory advantage. Never take a cavalier attitude toward it. I was immune for years, but suddenly. . . .

Still another celebrated noxious plant is the poison hemlock of Socrates, *Conium maculatum.* Looking like a slightly puffy and more fragile Queen Anne's lace (29) but of shrub stature, it browns off during August. In both fresh and dried form it attracts flower arrangers, as do its almost equally poisonous relatives, the water hemlock, *Cicuta bulbifera,* and *C. maculata,* the spotted cowbane. Avoid them all. Watch out, too, for *Rhus vernix,* the poison sumac. The above plants are prime subjects for removal, but, I need hardly add, must be handled with extreme care.

When I don't feel equal to weeding on my own, and don't want precious material removed by mistake, I adopt managerial tactics. I cruise over an area looking for unwanted plants on the verge of bloom or seeding, pick a bouquet of them for the yard boy, and tell him to grub out every example he can spy. Another lazy man's gambit is to pick off and collect the flowered and seeded stalks for burning. This is a safe, easy and next-best weed deterrent: not only are you rid of seeds, but few plants can resist repeated loss of top growth. In fact farmers often carry out a time-tested weed-elimination and pasture-improvement program by clipping twice and fertilizing during the summer months.

These hints for weed removal are given not without a wry sense of gratitude for what I have learned about soil from the weeds it produces. For healthy weeds mean that other healthy plants will flourish in the same area. If, however, that sparsely spaced, handsomely colored broom-sedge, *Andropogon virginicus*, makes a contrasting golden bronze note in a winter pasture, you will find not only eroded soil but perhaps soil in which lateral drainage is poor. On the other hand, where a patch of nettles grows, you can count on rich moist soil. Smartweed indicates insufficient surface drainage. And where you find dandelions you can grow legumes.

If weeds aren't healthy they can also point up in yellowing or reddish-purple foliage any number of mineral and trace element deficiencies. There are many books on agricultural crops richly illustrated in color which can start you on a diagnostic career.

A city-bred person never forgets the packed quality of curb turfs, their ill-assorted greens worn to the nub by countless feet, their lusty, long-rooted dandelions, docks and lambs-quarters bursting through the cement expansion cracks. And every suburban dweller knows that these same gregarious ruffians are ready to spring to life with strangling vigor in sunny, newly disturbed soils. Undesirable plants will always be with us, and it becomes a fascinating game to outwit them. Logistics, we have learned to our sorrow, cannot be bought off the garden-center shelves. Many of us already rack up in our tool-sheds, because we don't know how to dispose of them, more than enough poisons to kill a regiment. Best policy over the long term is to choose those plants strong enough and in such harmony with one another as to form pervasive ground-covers, inhibiting all but casual intruders. Throughout this book we have tried to suggest such groupings, but beg you to keep your eyes open to the many other attractive and defensive combinations that exist.

As the knowledgeable, obliging old handyman becomes as extinct as the passenger pigeon, we all welcome shortcuts to garden housekeeping, and are apt to think of groundcovers—and more groundcovers—as the easy way out. Preemptive smother plantings are often the answer in rough areas. But there are several special considerations. First, you need to free the area of persistent weeds, and weeding has to continue until the new cover establishes. During

In late April, before the alternate pinnately compound leaves of Robinia pseudo-acacia, *the black locust, are fully formed, 9-inch-long clusters of pea-like white blooms deliciously scent the air. The dappled shade of a group of these trees, with their nitrogen-fixing roots, furnishes an advantageous place for a nursery in which to grow seedlings of woodland plants—if the suckers of the locust are kept grubbed.*

this latter procedure the roots of the more fragile groundcovers, just beginning to take hold, are easily damaged.

Whether you think of the more invasive evergreen groundcovers as friends or enemies depends a little on the point of view. "Lady, you'll have all of this stuff you'll want," the contract-farmer said in an amused and condescending tone when we first acquired our property. He waved his hand toward a mass of blooming honeysuckle nearby for whose life I was pleading. Its fragrance was intoxicating and it was "holding" the earth at the top of a raw cut. My reading on conservation had persuaded me to look on this enterprising vine as highly desirable. Hadn't it been, the previous winter, a cheerful contrast to the dried stalks of dog fennel, ragweed and bramble that surrounded it? Wouldn't it be a good thing to encourage?

The farmer, as it happened, was right. Had he done his very best to remove every shred of honeysuckle, *Lonicera japonica*, he would still have left me more than I eventually had any use for. Where he acceded to my plea, honeysuckle is now kept in bounds by two assiduous mowing operations, one along a path, the other along an adjoining field. Islanded, not only is the honeysuckle controlled, but its extraordinary density keeps out everything else under the trees set out in the same area. It is true, of course, that until these trees were established they had to be de-vined with annoying regularity.

Speaking further of climbers, certain nonstrangling types like trumpet creeper, ivy and clematis can be tolerated on deciduous trees. Where I have tried to gain a very lush effect of colorful vines clambering up and over evergreens—a trick so effective in English gardens—damage to the supporting tree was evident. Is this adverse effect due to the difference in climate?

Although desirable in arrangements, vines to watch out for as smotherers are the bittersweet (301), *Passiflora lutea* var. *glabriflora*, the passion flower, and the five-leaved *Akebia quinata*.

Honeysuckle and ivy which are already heavily entrenched can be trained temporarily to simulate low shrubbery masses. Roll chicken wire or old wire fencing in loose loops to form simulated mounds, draw the free ends of the vines over them and they soon thicken up and hide the wire—until, in a subsequent burst of energy, you are ready to redesign the area.

Rich, dark glossy-green accents, as we have observed, are rare in the Midwest winter landscape. One dependable, handsome, shade-loving old standby is myrtle, *Vinca minor* (132), with blue or white flowers. Of the latter, the most prolific in bloom is *V.* 'Miss Jekyll's.' To establish vinca coverage quickly, it is wiser to plant clumps with the spaces between well mulched so that they can vine out from strong centers, rather than putting in many small divisions. With small plantings the roots which need shielding from sun are too exposed and the losses too great. The same suggestion holds for the shade-loving *Pachysandra terminalis*, the Japanese spurge. But even when I follow the approved method I must confess to failure in naturalizing this plant, perhaps because my soil is insufficiently acid, perhaps because it needs supplementary watering, for I've seen it do well in this locality with special care. Its cousin, the Alleghany spurge, *P. procumbens* (57), which is supposed to be difficult in both its typical and maculate forms, grows all through my woods on north- and northwest-facing sites.

For years the kind of English ivy with which I was familiar simply spelled gloom for me in winter, seeming to stamp on its surroundings a seal of dull conformity. Then I became aware of many hardy types with variations in leaf form, size, veining and pattern—and in colors from gold to grey. And I started collecting.

Hedera helix has a broad, more or less five-lobed leaf (247); *H. h.* 'Digitata's' leaf is fan-fingered, *H. h.* 'Helvetica's' auriculate, and *H. h.* 'Pedata's' long-peaked

In June, the ornately frilled irregular blossoms of the northern catalpa or cigar tree, C. speciosa, *rising another 6 to 10 inches over 10-inch leaves, display their subtle yellow and white interiors, enlivened with purplish spots. The striped entrance petals furnish guidelines for the insects which pollinate them. If only some way could be found to make the bold blooms last more than a few hours in arrangements! Placing them under a glass bell helps.*

at its apex. These four, representing extremes of form, and the more than on hundred hardy hybrids in between, have one thing in common. Curiously enough as long as they lie low, sending out their pliant stems along the ground, they retain their individuality. When ivies climb high and reach their adult stage, producing fragrant green blooms, their highly characteristic leaves are transformed into almost interchangeably identical ovate ones (283). Cuttings taken from these thick-stalked, arborescent finials not only retain this ovate form but can be kept pruned as small shrubs. Since this book is mainly about naturalizing, I won't go into the many other formal ways ivies can be trained: these would form a chapter all by itself. To identify ivies, consult *Exotica* by Alfred B. Graf, where fifty hardy ivies are illustrated.

One winter I saw dense sheets of straplike liriope foliage at the Missouri Botanical Garden and was determined to find a place for this groundcover at home. Described as bearing small-scale white or lavender florets on rigid spikes in August, the liriopes seemed more than desirable. This group of plants, however, has not proved useful to me in prominent places, because just when my garden is at its height of April color and bloom these so-called lily turfs form dead brown mats. They can be sheared in March, and when they cover a large area can even be cut with a mower to remove the dead thatch. But the brown stubble around the new green shoots remains unsightly. Just fifty miles south of Cincinnati this browning cycle is obviated by planting liriopes in densely shaded areas. Liriope is sometimes confused with the *Ophiopogons*, also called "lily turfs" but fussier to grow. They are easily distinguished from one another, though, for *Ophiopogons* are not stoloniferous and their florets droop.

You may wonder why, in mentioning hardy evergreen groundcovers, I have failed to wax enthusiastic about the euonymus family. *E. fortunei* 'Colorata' is valuable for its sun tolerance, but unfortunately is highly subject to scale, as are some of the attractive low-growing silver-and-gold-splashed euonymus hybrids. Minutely leaved *E. kewensis* has proved scale resistant for me. Among the deciduous euonymuses, *E. obovata* shows charming orange and red fruits not unlike bittersweet on its foot-high vining branches in the woods.

In planting such densely rooted groundcovers as myrtle and liriope I was not fully aware of their octopuslike tendency to spread deeper and deeper into the woods. Now when I accept them as aids against maintenance and less desirable growth, I try at the same time to put in distinctive barrier plants like groups of Christmas ferns or clumps of epimedium to warn me of the limits of encroachment I will tolerate. Certain of the tougher bulbs will, in fact, survive for years among these invasive groundcovers, so splashes of seasonal color need not necessarily stop at groundcover demarcations.

From Shakespeare—and who ever looked at flowers more perceptively?—to Victoria Sackville-West, my choice as the most consummate garden artist and practitioner of recent years, the thymes have won high praise. Who wouldn't

Albizzia julibrissin, the silk tree, a native of Asia, with 1- to 2-inch strong pink feather-puff blooms, seeds copiously in its adopted home but must be placed with care in the wild garden so that its tropic quality at blooming time does not strike too exotic a note. This close relative of the mimosa also has less hardy white or lavender forms.

try for a bank "where the wild thyme blows," or for a thyme lawn such as Sackville-West describes at the entrance to the herb garden at Sissinghurst? But alas! even such a genius as she didn't achieve success with these particular evergreens. Their patchiness was painfully evident when I saw them on location. Francis Bacon, another inspired gardener, was more realistic five centuries ago when he projected for his wild-garden "little heaps in the nature of mole hills—such as in wild heaths—to be set some with thyme. . . ." The unmanageable character of this well-loved species is sensed in Canon Ellacombe's comment that should thyme "ever come naturally in turf it should be welcomed and cherished for its sweet scent." And this is what I philosophically do—cherish what remains of my efforts to establish areas with allover thyme coverage.

But at least one kind of thyme, *Thymus caespititius*, not the shrubby but the creeping or *serpyllum* type, has survived for me here and there, not always in fullest sun, for over twenty years, along with a tough contingent of winter savories and lavenders. These plants actually cover quite respectable areas near the tops of retaining walls, or near stepping-stones, where drainage is excellent. In fact, over thirty of the forty varieties of thyme we have tested out at the Cincinnati Nature Center persist in rock wall pockets. I have also learned to ignore the comment that herby, creeping, rock-loving plants thrive in poor soil.

This may be true in more stable climates, but under our extreme fluctuations of temperature I find that they last longer in garden loam. Too nitrogenous a soil does of course lessen their flavor and tends to make variegated forms revert.

A charming evergreen herb that spreads in very shaded places, as its German name, Waldmeister, implies, is a dark green shiny *Galium*, often listed as *Asperula odorata*, the sweet woodruff. With its whorled leaves and minuscule starry white blooms, it is similar in form but not in color or texture to the horrid bedstraw (42). Among the deciduous groundcovers, one that appears tardily in spring but makes up for it by the long-lasting quality of its intense blue and russet seedheads is *Ceratostigma plumbaginoides,* a leadwort (292). Flourishing even in the driest clay, it seems to persist best where not exposed to the direct rays of the western sun. Another deciduous matting plant that takes sun and drought-packed earth is *Lotus corniculatus,* the bird's-foot trefoil. Avoid the invasive forage types. Use, instead, the variety *L. c. flore-pleno.*

Much as I love the contrast afforded by grey-leaved plants, I have been able to keep only a few of them. Massed dwarf sage and rue and *Artemisia pontica,* Roman wormwood, are standouts. In fact the latter can make itself too much at home and become a pest.

If your planting locale is large, there are a number of equally aggressive deciduous groundcovers that can with reservations be used to good effect. Goutweed, for example *Aegopodium podagraria* 'Variegatum,' helps hold steep, shaded, dry slopes, and its lively variegation, especially when contrasted with the solid greens of ivy and myrtle, is not entirely to be disqualified. Again, the lamiums, or dead nettles, easier to control and more delicate in leafage, discourage much sturdier invaders and, because of a certain substance in their leaves, are practically pest-resistant. Most desirable is the evergreen form, L. *galeobdolon* 'Variegatum,' which, like L. *galeobdolon* 'Luteum' (129), blooms yellow and enjoys light-textured dry clay soils. *L. maculatum*, often with white blotches on the leaves, has lavender-pink flowers and prefers moist sites. All these lamiums take shade, as does the hardy *Begonia evansiana*. This large-leaved spreader transplants most readily when just emerging. If planted in fall be sure to mulch with compost.

Moisture loving, too, are *Ajuga pyramidalis* and *A. reptans*. *A. reptans*, with rich blue spikes to 6 inches, is stoloniferous, and forms green, bronzy-purple and multicolored variegations of matted foliage in dense soil. *Pyramidalis* has pink and white as well as blue forms, as does *A. genevensis*. Neither of these spreads so rapidly as *reptans*. *Genevensis* grows to 12 inches and needs plenty of sun. Last but not least acceptable as groundcovers are the violets. They, like the ivies, can even compete for moisture with hedges, and are always at hand for transplanting from fields, or when weeding borders.

Perhaps this advice may seem to you a quaint way to end a review of reliable groundcovers, but I proffer it just the same: do not scorn plain old sod for sun or shade. As a stage or arena on which to deploy more distinctive plants it is unsurpassed. Whether your grass plot is tiny or field size, it will, I need hardly say, require cropping. Our own meadow areas can get along with five mowings a season. The most critical of these is the last, which prevents the grass from being so tall as to mat under snow. It will then hold until the first week in May.

While a dissertation on lawns would be out of place here, I am tempted to make an observation or two on grass culture. For one thing, hard labor and high investment are no guarantees of sure-fire success. For another, the greatest hazards occur when new lawns are made. Erosion can set in rapidly at that time, especially if topsoil is scarce. Enrich the soil with a sowing of legumes that will, if the seeds have been inoculated, produce nitrogen-creating nodules. For small areas use Dutch white clover, now almost worth its weight in gold, or the self-seeding annual, Korean clover. This suggestion is valueless, however, if you plan using chemical or preemergent weed killers.

Because, once established, groundcovers are easy to maintain, many new books on this subject are appearing which include plants as tall as hemerocallis and hostas, and as diverse as the Italian arums (257), the bergenias and lily-of-the-valley (243). I should rather reserve the term "groundcovers" for plants that "spin," like moneywort, *Lysimachia nummularia*, with its golden flowers —there is even a golden-leaved form now listed—or form matted clusters like *Anthemis nobilis*, the chamomile, recently referred to abroad by a later name,

Undaunted by its ponderous name, Camptosorus rhizophyllus, *the walking fern, strides nimbly about north-facing outcrops by striking roots from the apexes of its mature 5-inch fronds, as they form hoops and touch the ground. As with most ferns, this peripatetic variety can be further identified by the sori or clusters of spore cases carried in a unique pattern on the underside of the leaf, as shown on the far left. Walking fern persists if grown on moss-covered chunks of dolomitic rubble which contain more magnesium than our local limestone. Although still under study, the successful reaction of some calcifuge plants to tufa, another form of calcium carbonate with a similar magnesium component, may be due to the fact that the presence of magnesium makes the lime less available.*

Chamaemelum nobile, with its tiny daisy heads. Chamomile is also available for open areas in a nonblooming form. I prefer to think of taller plants, such as epimedium (106), as accents, rising above but in harmony with whatever carpeting plants they are placed near, and to use the term groundcovers for low, more cohesively textured plantings.

My first ventures in propagation followed closely on the acquisition of Cockaigne. I had developed an immediate and terrific hunger for plants, and because our most urgent need was for groundcovers to help in maintenance, I determined to produce them in quantity. I remembered the busy ivy factories my mother had set up indoors on all north-facing windowsills. Cuttings, I felt, would present no problem. I simply took old ivy shearings and started them in water. Once they were rooted, I planted them out in the 3 x 8-foot beds I had outlined with asbestos siding and filled with good soil. After that, I kept them weeded, watered and shaded in these protected enclaves in the wilderness that was our new property. What I had not realized was that lush root growth, stimulated by water alone, adapted itself to the medium. When the plants found themselves transferred to soil, which normally has about twenty percent air enveloped in its structure, they suffered a real setback. The relatively dry medium, plus the drying breezes and more light intensity than they had previously been exposed to, demanded livelier metabolic response. The poor cuttings had short odds on adjustment with a correspondingly low rate of survival.

I turned to books on propagation and followed the explicit do-it-yourself photos: the meticulous diagonal cut above or below the node, the diagonal placement in sharp sterile sand, constant moisture vigilance. Constant "peeping" to see if anything was going on, I am sure, was not recommended. But potting up when rootlets were about ½ inch long was.

What really gave me best results came in the post-polyethylene period and was called at the time the Lipp propagator: a flat, a pot or an old coffee can with holes punched in the bottom, filled with sharp sand or fine mica granules, covered after the cuttings were inserted with a thin sheet of transparent plastic, so braced with twisted coat hangers that the plastic could not touch the cuttings at any point. The fully saturated, enveloped pot or flat, after draining for half an hour, was partially sunk in soil to seal the plastic housing. If placed in light shade, roots formed in time without any further attention. This method of propagation—a technique which lies halfway between that of the old mason jar inverted over a single treasured cutting and the modern automated "mister," in which cuttings can even be made from tender new growth, has given me the most carefree and constantly successful results.

Another casual but effective way to propagate is by layering—a method which, like increasing your stocks through cuttings, assures preservation of the plant's original characteristics—an outcome very different from growing from seed, where the widest variations are inevitable. Layering lends itself best to

One of the constant pleasures of a woods is the rhythm set up by the natural plant groupings such as the repeated low reverse curves in the false Solomon's-seals, Smilacina racemosa, *ending with mistlike plumes, contrasting with the tall arcs of the true Solomon's-seals, which show their bells in profile (271). The tall doilies of the maidenhair fern,* Adiantum pedatum, *are a foil for the spotted, swirled leaves of the native pachysandra which often grow near them.*

runnerlike plants such as strawberries. A small pressed-peat pot filled with good soil can be sunk below a runner at a point where proliferation indicates a favorable site for root development. The runner is then bound to the soil in the pot with a hairpin or an inverted Y-shaped peg. When well established, the cord to the mother plant is cut and the new plant, with its roots intact in the pot, is lifted ready for transplanting to a new locale.

With certain vining plants like clematis and Virginia creeper, where length of stem permits, the above procedure may be multiplied, a series of notches being cut and held pegged down on the underside at nodes where leaves are originating. Then, when rooted, the stems can be severed between the nodes.

Layering is also an ideal way to propagate shrubby plants which, as cuttings, may have difficulty in striking roots. Select a procumbent shoot, or one you can bend down to ground level, with about 10 inches of tip left over. Where the branch is to touch the ground, cut a slit on the underside through to the cambium, but on a slight slant, so as to arrest the flow of sap, and form a sort of tongue.

Bury the branch at the cut about 3 or 4 inches deep in good loamy soil. By staking the remaining tip in an upright position, the tongue is held open along the slit. A small stone or a forked stick will pin the branch firmly to the soil. Roots may begin to strike and be ready in as early as six weeks, when the new plant can be severed from the parent. Or, transplanting can be delayed for about a year.

Another amazingly fruitful way to propagate new stocks from things at hand is to save whatever seedlings you find and the rooted fragments that come off desirable plants while you are weeding. These may be put immediately into a plastic bag to prevent loss of turgidity; and this bag in turn into a brown paper one, to keep off the sun. The plastic bag must, of course, be sealed every time after an addition is made. The collected oddments will stay in good condition for several days, and you may plant them carefully at your convenience in the nursery beds described above. Always shade the new transplants at first, and keep them watered until they establish. They will form a surprisingly rich reservoir on which to draw for enlarging old or creating new plantings. And with such material at hand you will find yourself recombining colors or using these plants as a foil to set off new purchases. Added to the bulb offsets and divisions you come by, you will soon find yourself with quite a capital of new material.

I have been at some pains to describe methods of do-it-yourself propagation —and shall follow with some suggestions for culture from seeds—in large part because I have found that the plants I want so avidly are not always to be had for the buying. I have no quarrel with the scientifically managed and mechanized techniques of plant production as adopted by the larger commercial growers today. I only regret that they are so commonly used to exclude any but the most "popular" and run-of-the-mill varieties. And today mass merchandising, toward which such systems are geared, discourages the production of unusual slower-selling specialties.

When I started gardening thirty years ago, I knew in the Cincinnati area a score of growers who prided themselves on the rarities they managed to propagate, and found time to share their enthusiasm with their customers. Today, to cut costs and meet supermarket competition, this type of grower is obliged to concentrate more and more preemptively on those showier standard items which, now as always, make up the "bread and butter" of his business. The result has been that horticulturally minded laymen are forced to rely increasingly on the fewer and fewer remaining commercial specialists for purchases—and on each other for cutting and seed exchanges. The role of various plant societies, members of which furnish an appreciable market for specialty growers, is also of increasing importance. Joining one or another of these groups will uncover new sources of supply and increase your knowledge in specialized fields. And you undoubtedly know local amateurs, or meet them through their ex-

hibits at flower shows, who will trade rarities with you. Much can, of course, be done on your own that is not too arduous. This is especially true if you have some concept of seed growing.

Every year on our place maples and cherries sprout up in nooks and crannies, thicker than tended crops. Some seasons redbuds join them. Recently we had a bumper showing of baby tulip trees. What makes these differences in germination? Scientists say there are three critical factors, of which the most chancy is temperature. Another is moisture, for the embryo must be moist constantly until it sprouts. And, once sprouted, seedlings must rely on dew or a light spraying of water. Another more mysterious factor is dormancy, which has to wear off at its own respective pace in all species.

No one seems to know quite what triggers germination. In some varieties, when seed is fresh, sprouting follows quickly. Then a few seedlings from that same lot may appear intermittently, from three months to three years or much, much longer, after what is known as alternating dormancy. Accordingly, I keep a place where I dump my rarer seedpots after the first crop, and sometimes find a few tough survivors that have broken dormancy at a later period. Some seeds are slow to appear because of hard coatings that need nicking or breaking down by frost, organic action or unusually high moisture. Seeds with pulpy exteriors are best rubbed free, as this soft material is often a source of undesirable fungal attack. Some seeds that are immature when they drop from the pod may require temperatures as low as 42° to germinate. Gardeners may stratify hardy seeds in successive layers of moist sand over the winter in order to subject them to the alternating freezing and thawing they may require under natural conditions. If this procedure is neglected, an approximation can be achieved by intermittent storing and withdrawal of plastic-bagged seeds in the refrigerator before planting.

In this connection there are two rather recent discoveries which are significant, and which nullify a lot of past advice in outdoor seed growing. One is that in the Midwest, where the climate is wholly unlike that of England, whence we originally imported so much of our garden culture, we should seed not in the fall but in March and April, even if the seeds lie dormant until May. Another is that most seeds do not need darkness to sprout. Since many of the flowers and shrubs I grow are for woods, most of my seedbeds are in semi-shade.

Man has discovered over a hundred reasons why seeds fail to germinate, so it is not surprising, perhaps, that nature is profligate in tossing them to wind and weather. You too can simply broadcast in place seeds that are easily acquired, those of your established natives and hardy exotics. Rough up the surface of the woods soil slightly and put down a light covering of milled sphagnum, mica granules, or ground leaf mold on which to sow the seed. The prior raking or scratching will prove a help in bringing the seed in close contact with the soil,

"Leaflets three, let them be"—even though they have the most enticing oyster-shell-white berries and those vining clusters, often elaborated with aerial rootlets, that suggest such beautiful arrangements. Poison ivy may also take the form of a shrub, and its leaves then look very like the compound leaf of the box-elder, Acer negundo. Compare the harmless three-leaved box-elder on glabrous stems (below) with the fairly symmetrical leaves of poison ivy, Toxicodendron radicans (above). The poison ivy may show more random leaf outlines, and the leaves are always alternately positioned below the terminal three-leaved cluster. In older plants, the box-elder may take on two or more sets of opposite leaves below its tripartite terminals.

Another harmless fooler is Virginia creeper, Parthenocissus quinquefolia, whose juvenile leaves, also often in groups of three, have regularly and lightly saw-toothed edges. This plant climbs with adhesive discs at the end of coarse tendrils, and lower on the knobby stem, the mature leaves are always five-fingered (149).

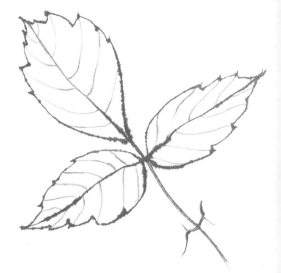

and the superimposed duffy material will provide a light mulch under which some moisture will condense. Another way to broadcast over a larger area is to enclose small quantities of seed in druggists' gelatine capsules with a sand and mica granule mixture to weight it. A good rain will melt the gelatine and moisten in the seed.

If you have a limited number of valuable quick-germinating seeds, scrub a porous old brick and soak it overnight. Put it in a 3-inch-deep pan about half full of water. Sprinkle the top of the brick with ½ inch of fine mica granules. Sow the seed in the mica, spacing it well. Cover the whole with a tightly bound thin plastic that is above and does not touch the planting surface. Keep the pan in strong light, but not in direct sunlight, until the seeds germinate. Then remove the plastic. When true leaves develop above the cotyledons, prick out the seedlings and plant them in sterile potting soil in pressed pots. Harden them off until the seedlings are strong enough to place permanently. If seeds are slow to germinate, like hellebores (54), or if the seed is very rare and you are worried about damping off, you can sterilize the soil by baking it in a 350° oven for as long as it takes a potato to bake at that temperature. Be prepared though, for unpleasant odors. A simpler way to discourage damping off is to use a ¾-inch topping of milled sphagnum combined with fine mica granules above an untreated potting mixture.

Using some of the suggestions above you can keep a small or large number of economical propagating projects under way with only a slight expenditure of time and effort all during the growing season. There is never a time when you can't profit by another glance at unusual catalog sources and garden literature in general. I need hardly say that my own eye is most apt to light on carefree hardy bulb and bulblike specialties. In recent years these have included the Araceae.

As a child, like all children, I thrilled to the homuncular jack-in-the-pulpit (103) with its protective green canopy. And who, regardless of age, can resist the arrestingly simple purity of a calla? Although a hardy strain of callas has been grown in our area I have had success only indoors, but have on occasion flowered their low small counterpart, *Calla palustris*, the bog arum, in my creek bottom. Even *palustris* does not, however, persist for me. Though I can meet its moisture requirements, it needs more acid conditions than I can give it. Another of the Araceae, *Acorus calamus*, the sweet flag, with aromatic leaves which are fun to nibble, has a spadix, but no spathe. It establishes easily. Northeasterners laugh when I tell them I treasure a few skunk cabbages, *Symplocarpus foetidus*; Northwesterners, in their turn, marvel that we so envy them their glorious *Lysichiton americanum*, the yellow skunk cabbage, ubiquitous in moist areas of western Oregon, with its great tough shiny-as-plastic yellow spathes. I am still trying to establish—but suspect of tenderness—*Arisarum proboscidium*, the mouse's-tail, whose spathe, as it lurks among the leaves, recalls my greatest garden enemy.

The beauty of its top-shaped crenelated buds makes one's every effort to grow Kalmia latifolia, *the mountain laurel, worthwhile. Although a lime-hater, it will persist under oaks on a ridge where the runoff from the alkaline soil is quick. Early fall or spring planting is advisable. Try partridge berry,* Mitchella repens, *and other calcifuges in similar locations. For surer survival, deal with a nursery that sells them in clumps, where enough sympathetic microbial material is incorporated to help give them a running start.*

The spotted-leaved, greenish-flowering *Arum italicum* 'Marmoratum' (257) clumps up well but never achieves for us the impenetrable masses one sees in its solid green **form** along shady paths in Sicily. Both are very similar to the English lords-and-ladies or cuckoo-pint, *Arum maculatum*, but are without their reddish-speckled stems. A smaller, even more spirited bloom I love is the green dragon; it is less well known, I am sure, because it is so hard to spy out and to photograph. It hides under its great cantilevered leaves (265), and its curious tightly hooded green spathe seems reluctant to release the long-soaring, reverse-curved finial of the spadix. See a smaller, less dramatic version of this bloom in *Pinellia ternata* on the same page.

After I discovered the arum described in the caption (126), interested friends rallied around to kibitz. "You must have it named." "You must have it photographed." "You must have a measured drawing made." Importunings continued. I listened with a growing sense of obligation, despite a spell of intense

heat and an imminent departure to visit children and a grandson on the West Coast. In the end, I set the recommended wheels in motion. Bettina Dalvé rushed out to make the measured drawing. The late Dr. E. Lucy Braun arrived and, after pronouncing the plant to be about ten years old, proceeded to gather data for a description. A friend of my son's found time to make a portrait photograph. Before I emplaned I sent the slides and drawing to Peter Hyypio in Ithaca. We left Ohio still mystified.

During our absence the plant was reported to have died back rather suddenly, and to have shown no inclination to set seed. Sober reassessment left its identity still an open question on our return. Peter Hyypio diligently searched the records in the Bailey Hortorium without finding any evidence that a cross had ever occurred between native jack-in-the-pulpits and green dragons. But he did find, significantly, in Ohwi's *Flora of Japan*, a description of an *Arisaema* similar to our "discovery." All is in abeyance while we wait now to see if the mystery plant returns, or if I can track down any purchase records. If it isn't a hybrid it may just turn out to be, indeed, *A. tosaense*—a rare unscheduled bonus in one of those mixed bargain assortments I have mentioned before.

Whatever the outcome, that apparition did bring forth all the excitement, scrutiny, analysis and mechanisms necessary to the identification, classification and naming of a new plant under the International Rules of Nomenclature. The binomial theory of classification we accept today goes back to 1753, when Carolus Linnaeus brought order out of the chaos then existing in the world of plants. Under the present code, precedence goes to the name first to appear in a reputable journal, provided the name is accompanied by sufficient description to identify it.

However, the issue of nomenclature—and that of classification, for that matter—is not so easily settled. For one thing, plant historians are constantly digging up earlier attributors. For another, there is the temptation among taxonomists to switch plants from one household to another. An example is the recent decision to remove onions and daffodils from the lily family, where they had lodged comfortably for years, to the Amaryllidaceae, because, like the amaryllis, these plants have a papery bract that subtends the floret, although they continue to resemble the lilies closely and basically in having all their parts in divisions of six.

In addition, improved scientific techniques—microscopic, statistical, experimental—now modify older intuitive judgments based on such external similarities and differences as the above, and bring about changing concepts in classification which may or may not necessitate changes in names as well.

If you are poisoned by it, you could not care less whether a plant goes by the name given it by Linnaeus, *Rhus radicans* (121), or if it now follows a commoner assignment to the genus *Toxicodendron*, as *T. radicans* (L.) Kuntze, thus separating it further from several harmless species of sumac or *Rhus*.

A surprising number of native orchids are earthbound, or terrestrial, like the stately 1½-foot yellow lady-slipper, or moccasin flower, Cypripedium calceolus *var.* pubescens, *growing on a rather dry hillside. The lichens on the dogwood branch in the foreground are* Parmelia caperata. *Their ancestors showed remarkable evolutionary adaptability by becoming two distinct forms of life in one. They have a tough fungal exterior and an interior of photosynthetic algae which the fungal coating stabilizes and protects, and from which it derives its nutrient sugars. But, ironically, they have been unable to cope with smog. Lichens are the miner's lamp of the upper air.*

This latter form, translated for the layman, tells him that poison ivy belongs to the genus *Toxicodendron*, and is of climbing habit; that it was listed first by Linnaeus and was given its classification by Kuntze. But some taxonomists fail to agree with Dr. Kuntze's assignment, and here, as elsewhere, the clash of expert opinion constantly threatens to modify or upset previous certification in the International Code.

What was my amazement one spring day to come upon, under a rather small pale green dragon leaf, the hood of an even paler jack-in-the-pulpit, green and white striated and ruffle-edged. Consternation ensued when the "roof" of the jack failed to terminate in the usual way, but extended downward instead as a very long tapering appendage. It reminded me, for all the world, of a more sacred simulacrum: a rustic crucifix we once saw on the wall of a provincial palace in Mexico. The Savior's forelock had been extended and allowed to fall to His knees, as if to give privacy to agony. Could this surrealist plant have been a hybrid of a jack and a green dragon? It had all the earmarks. For further discussion, see page 124.

Breeding and selection also produce changes in cultivated plants, giving rise to new varieties which must be cataloged. At the same time, confusingly, new material is constantly being produced for classification by the process of natural hybridization, which we continue to hope accounted for our problematic *Arisaema*; and further botanical exploration of the earth, which is far from complete, complicates things still more.

If, however, you want to track down a plant in the catalogs simply for the pleasure of growing it, you can get pretty desperate when you fail to find it under its popular name. We have tried, in every case where science and commerce have not caught up with one another, to give synonyms that will make locating the desired plant convenient for the dirt gardener.

If, like me, you are frustrated by "botanical English" and "keys," such as appear in *Gray's Manual of Botany*, there are many visual aids today that make identification of plants simple and pleasurable. For natives and escapes, Peterson and McKenny's *Field Guide to Wildflowers*, based on color of bloom, with the most idiosyncratic plant features highlighted by arrows, gives you instant confidence. Just leafing through the drawings in Dr. E. Lucy Braun's *The Monocotyledoneae* and her *Woody Plants of Ohio* introduces you unmistakably to grasses, all the desirable local native bulbs, trees, shrubs and vines. The condensed reprint of Homer House's great study, *Wild Flowers of New York*, simply known as *Wild Flowers*, is still valuable for its portrayal of flowers in actual color and at life size.

Much more complete, but less satisfactory for the beginner because of the inconsistent size and scale of its illustrations, is Harold William Rickett's *Wild Flowers of the United States*, of which the first volume applies to our area. Should plants you want to identify not be in bloom, Steyermark's *Flora of Missouri* is most helpful, for it gives roots and seed capsules as well as leaf and flower—as do the three comprehensive volumes of Gleason's *The New Britton & Brown Illustrated Flora*. Roy Hay and Patrick Synge's *Color Dictionary of Flowers and Plants for Home and Garden* does a superb visual identification job for garden plants, so many of which can be naturalized. And when you have satisfied yourself with these, go on an exploratory binge by consulting Sitwell, Blunt and Synge's beautifully presented botanical illustrations and bibliography of botanical literature called *Great Flower Books 1700–1900*. You will be amazed at how much painstaking and magnificent "floragraphica" our forebears brought into being. And you may even be inspired to collect plant literature, as well as the plants themselves.

As the searing, downright aggression of summer advances, reappraisal is in order, for landscape effects coarsen. The more delicate flowers and flowering trees, which have often been colorfully overwhelming against fragile greens, and the orderliness of tree structure tend to give way to larger individual blossoms and flower trusses that can hold their own against the more prevalent but less differentiated verdure. The middle ground closes in. As the eye roams, it may be diverted by the movement of cattle on a hillside pasture beyond the welcome accent of hedges, or seek distant masses of ferny locust (110), more greyed by bloom above a low screening of evergreens. It may alternately escape through gaps in the surrounding green shrubbery to explore the density of wooded landscape beyond, and come to rest with enjoyment on partially enclosed meadows in the foreground. The gardener wonders how to bring character and control to this summer vigor with the least effort, and how best to exploit wild and naturalized vistas.

No matter what the size of your property, don't be too proud to consult an imaginative landscape architect. The insight and experience that he can contribute may be invaluable, especially if you have some concepts of your own toward which you would like to work. It's easy to decide on the basis of the practitioner's local accomplishments whose style you prefer. Gardens by leading professionals, including their own, are often opened for public tours. Consultancy on an hourly basis may cost no more than a new dress. I was lucky to meet Henry Fletcher Kenney just after we acquired our place. Our first conference not only brought me a confirmation of how important it is to choose plant material that ensures easy maintenance, but set the framework for a bold horticultural device that has given our vistas a feeling of depth and perspective. I refer to the lavish use of hedging.

At Cockaigne hedges, high and low, link areas to each other—clipped in one vista to catch the light for a sweeping curve before a background of mixed scrub trees, billowing in another in front of clumps of evergreens. Other hedges which are themselves evergreen, neatly mounded or grown tall on either side of a curving path, are sited here at slight changes of grade to accentuate levels. Hedges not necessarily of great extent or continuity can also charm by their suggestion of change of pace as well as by their effectiveness as barriers or screening.

Think of hedges not as boundaries defining ownership, and as such nearly always at odds with the landscape, but as structural elements with positive values, to be lengthened, curved, angled, profiled, combined or broken at will. And always consider how they may relate to the natural contours or how they can be phased out with clumps of taller or lower growth, whether evergreen or deciduous.

Hedge plants are best moved between late September and late March in generous planting pockets. Break up the soil well at the base of the holes and see that some well-rotted organic material, as well as a handful of bone meal or hoof and horn, is incorporated before setting. Should the area be poorly drained, excavate a shallow trench along the projected hedgerow in such a way as to mound the earth where the hedge is to be lined out, so that its eventual level will be slightly above the surrounding area and surplus water will drain off rapidly.

Naturalized introductions on a partially shaded south-facing slope include, in late April, the 10-inch-high golden spikes of Lamium galeobdolon 'Luteum,' *a dead nettle; the blue and white spires of* Endymion hispanicus, *the campanulate squill; and the immature variegated leaves of* Hosta undulata. *Although rather fragile in form, the lamium manages to resist the invasion of coarse weeds, and forms a most satisfactory groundcover until frost. Could it be producing a chemical inhibitor that protects its territory? See page 67.*

Sturdy hedge plants, often disregarded because of their very familiarity and self-reliance, are those of the privet family, the *Ligustrums*. Granted that privets are "greedy feeders," and will rob nearby plants of moisture, they are not much worse in this respect than other hedging plants. Both Amur privet, *L. amurense,* and the smaller leaved *L. japonicum* have served me for thirty years without dying back or out, and recovering even after several snows so heavy that the branches were splayed out flat over the ground. The plants were put in on 18-inch center-to-center spacing and ruthlessly top pruned for low branching. The sides, as with most of our hedges, whether squared or rounded at the top, were always sheared on a plane sloping slightly outward from top to base, to furnish ample light to the lowest branches. Where any hedges abut lawns, great care was taken from the beginning never to let the mower brush against them; for lower branches, once destroyed, are practically irreplaceable. Preliminary careful clipping of a narrow swath of turf at the hedge bases with the hedge shears before beginning to mow adjacent grass areas creates a warning zone for the mower.

To keep hedges strong, trim them at regular intervals, especially deciduous hedges, so that the twiggery reveals itself uniformly spaced when the leaves drop. In all hedges, greater denseness and depth of green growth is maintained if, instead of simply shearing young growth to a given height across the entire surface, you take the time to clip down into the hedge at frequent intervals, making cuts on slightly lower twigs and side branches to force budding in all possible interstices. You really have to experiment to develop this skill. And be sure your shears are sharp!

The privets, relatively cheap to buy, are easy to establish from cuttings. See page 118, or Bailey's *Standard Cyclopedia of Horticulture,* for further details. When searching for all kinds of plant material, I never fail to consult this monumentally helpful work first. Even though it has not really been updated since the 1914–1917 period during which it first appeared, it never fails to enlighten me with its highly practical cultural information cross-referenced to common names and, except for recent cultivars, with its comprehensiveness. That horticultural giant, Liberty Hyde Bailey, still, through his Hortorium Memorial at Cornell, provides for the layman an available service for plant identification and source, as does our National Arboretum in Washington. For an authoritative answer, all you need do is to send a sample with a request. Heat-dry the sample between newspapers and tie it between cardboards, including both flower and leaves. Before inquiring about cultivars, though, consult the more recent Royal Horticultural Society's *Dictionary of Gardening* and its current supplement.

Among the privets, *Ligustrum amurense* and *japonicum* are more time-consuming to maintain than Regel's privet, *L. obtusifolium* var. *regelianum,* whose naturally horizontal downthrusting branches can be more or less casually

Another late April combination on a southeast-facing slope shows the foot-high umbels of the blue-purple and the white Phlox divaricata *and P.* divaricata *forma* albiflora, *respectively. The sharp color of the blue-eyed Mary,* Collinsia verna, *the last bloom of which can be seen on its seeded stalks, contrasts with that sophisticated escape, the lilylike* Ornithogalum nutans, *the nodding star-of-Bethlehem. Its grey-green and silver blossoms are one of the subtlest of color combinations. A rich green groundcover, not shown but often seen with this grouping, is the twinkling stars of* Stellaria silvatica, *the sylvan chickweed.*

131

trimmed. Regels are highly effective as a barrier at the top of a slope, where their decumbent line harmonizes with the grade.

Another privet, coarser in all respects than the plants just discussed, is *L. quihoui*. To enjoy its much larger showy white panicles in August, prune it sparingly. Both Regel's privet, with its dark blue berries, and *Ribes alpinum*, the alpine currant, with its intricate golden twiggery and naturally mounding profile, form relatively carefree hedging.

Hedges are often used to bound an area and screen off mixed weedy growth beyond. If one side of a hedge only will be seen, and in locales where dogs, raccoons or 'possums tend to establish paths, a light barrier can be erected on the far side of the hedge to thwart them. Cut 2-foot lengths of ⅛-inch wire and put a loop at one end of them; then cut an 18-inch-wide strand of coarse galvanized netting the length of your planting. Weave the stiff wire braces into the netting vertically at about 2½-foot intervals. Hook the netting at the top. Then insert the wire that projects at the base into the ground to a 6-inch depth. This barrier, even at first, is almost invisible and permits a strong interlocking hedge to develop impervious to holes and tunnels.

Yews, especially the very hardy *Taxus cuspidata*, furnish a practically indestructible evergreen hedging throughout Zone VI. A local garden wit, in fact, has observed that in this area only two things are, seemingly, inevitable—death and taxus. Massed in low clumps, and in a sort of short reverse curve, *Taxus X media* often forms enough of a barrier to frame a well-accented beginning to a path, as may also taller groupings of the vertical 'Hicksii' or 'Hatfieldii.'

Yews tend, when clipped, to be too formal in appearance near woods, and have to be watched wherever they are placed to avoid their adding too black or too spotty a winter value. Evergreens valuable because they can tolerate partial overhanging shade are spruce, broad-leaved *Mahonia aquifolium*, the Oregon grape, and hemlock—although the last may not prove long-lived.

Native cedars, *Juniperus virginiana*, mentioned before as the only evergreen indigenous to our area, should not be encouraged by anyone growing trees of the apple family. It plays the host during alternate years in the life cycle of juniper gall rust, an organism which causes an orangey deposit and gall formation (303) on apple leaves. Native cedars can usually be had for the digging, and will hedge satisfactorily. They are attractive near more formal areas when clipped, and when used as groups or clumps farther off in the open landscape their cone-shaped natural tidiness subtly recalls the same evergreen values.

Another plant suitable for clipped hedging is *Lonicera fragrantissima*, winter honeysuckle, which gives a pale, almost evergreen effect. It can also be allowed to reach its normal 20 feet of height. If it gets out of hand, it tolerates cutting back almost to the ground again. The fragrance of its inconspicuous mid-February bloom is not always pleasant if you are too close to it. Be sure your variety is *L. fragrantissima*, for *L. maackii*, the Amur honeysuckle, reaching

Whether seen in an old Dutch flower painting or along a stretch of the woodland's edge, protected from afternoon sun, Fritillaria imperialis, the crown imperial, one of the early summer bulbs (140), dominates its surroundings. The stately burnt-orange bells whorled under the tufted leaves exude a foxy odor that discourages intimacy. Be fearless at least once, though. Tilt a bell and enjoy inside its spectacular six crystals held in white nectaries on a black ground. My crown imperials grow to over 3 feet in a mass of Vinca minor, our common myrtle, and their dying stalks are hidden by the rising leafage of Jerusalem artichoke, Helianthus tuberosus, a late-summer bloomer which can also surmount this useful but invasive groundcover without apparent harm to itself or its regal neighbor.

about the same height, always stays basically vase-shaped. *Maackii's* translucent red berries, each and every one, seem to sprout, and seedlings will quickly take over large areas. We have an inadvertent south hillside of it which has proved a wonderful sponge for traffic noises from the road below, and through it we keep tunneled paths for walking which are lovely and dense on hot summer days and brilliant when glazed with ice against winter sunrises. *L. maackii* is very shallow-rooted, and wide bays are easily weeded out along the paths to allow for a variation of plantings. I thought as this area developed it would be ideal for birds, but they prefer to nest only at the edges. Within the mass you discern no vestigial nests whatever.

Speaking of traffic noises, it has been proved that bands, even of deciduous trees, in 30-foot-wide plantings reduce the noise by one-half. Establish evergreen buffers if you can, not only against noise but against oncoming traffic lights which, where a road curves, may prove very disagreeable.

Informal hedges of mixed shrubbery are often recommended as maintenance-free. But most shrubs need some pruning, and as these conglomerates grow they take on a densely weedy character. At woods edges, I prefer as binders our native spice bush (225), the wild hydrangea (278), the large widely spaced leaves of pawpaw (94), or the dark rose-panicled *Aesculus pavia*, for they allow many of the tall summer blooms more freedom to develop than do some of the denser heavier-feeding alien shrubs. Some exceptions are the single kerria, *K. japonica*, with its charming open yellow bloom in June, and *Rhodotypos scandens*, the jetbead, another equally rangy shrub. The latter shows simultaneously with kerria, and has large white four-petaled blossoms about the size of the large-flowered trillium. For a real treat, group these two shrubs at a path edge along the woods above a mat of bluets, *Houstonia caerulea*. And, incidentally, in transplanting bluets be sure you have both staminate and pistillate plants—use an enlarging glass to make sure.

A word of caution about very thorny hedges, which can be bothersome to weed or prune. Catalogs sing paeans of praise to the hedging rose, *R. multiflora*. But don't listen! Even hedges of a much less invasive shrub rose, which charmed us at first with demure blossoms looking as though they had been freshly strewn over the great mounds every morning, expanded in a few years to a 10-foot width so unruly, and with such a mass of inaccessible dead canes at the center, that a bulldozer became the only satisfactory final solution. Even in younger and narrower thorny hedges, weeding is so formidable a task as to rule them out of consideration.

Suitable for taller hedges in this locale are the European hornbeam, *Carpinus betulus*, and even the egregious rose-of-Sharon, *Hibiscus syriacus*, of which there are some interesting new cultivars. The latter leaf out late, but their prolonged mid- and late-summer bloom is most welcome. If your place is big

The trumpet creeper, Campsis radicans, *with its two-toned orange flowers darker within, climbs with aerial rootlets like ivy. Unlike wisteria, honeysuckle and other stranglers, these vines can be allowed to find their way high into trees. But if you want to remove them without harming the tree, clip them low and let them die before pulling them loose from the bark. This vine shows its colorfully exploding constellations in July. Note in the drawing how the stamens, impatient with the reluctance of the funnel to open, have forced their way through the side of the tube.*

enough you can resort to that old farm favorite, the osage orange, *Maclura pomifera*, as a road barrier, and enjoy its stylish green 5-inch-diameter fruits on the bare branches long after everything else is gone. Should you really need a stout thorny hedge, the hawthorn or *Crataegus* seedlings from an abandoned pasture or *Poncirus trifoliata* (136) can be used.

There is a great temptation to compile lists of hedge plants, groundcovers or creepers: in fact, to expand it to a comfortable categoried compendium of all sorts of plants suitable for sun or shade, bog, clay or sandy soil. This job has in fact been excellently done for woody plants, shrubs, vines and groundcovers in a series of books by Donald Wyman, and for horticulturally interesting natives and hardy exotics by Mabel Cabot Sedgwick in her completely reliable *The Garden Month by Month*.

Forsythias make the gaudiest of informal hedges in spring. The bright yellows of *F. suspensa* are well modified if draped against a grey wall. Where forsythia has no such modifier, it is well to choose a less intensely colored variety like the pale *F. primulina*.

The earlier-blooming so-called "white forsythia," *Abeliophyllum distichum*, has never proved fully hardy for me, and the August-blooming *Abelia X grandiflora* often kills back in winter, although it comes up again from the base. A much more beautiful shrub for shade, which kills back, like abelia, about every fifth year but is well worth planting in clumps at woods edges, is the sacred bamboo, *Nandina domestica*, with its June-cascading white panicles and its huge tresses of red berries that hold until the New Year.

The soil-exhausting and moisture-demanding characteristics of hedges, which might discourage their use in some critical places, can be avoided by exploiting partial barrier devices. Occasional posts with rope or chain between will garland an area if planted with something as restrained as ivy or as prolific as grapes or rambler roses. Some shrub, *rugosa* and rambler roses like 'Dr. W. Van Fleet' never get blackspot, and the only reason we gave up our own Van Fleet was that it grew so vigorously as to keep the back screen door from opening. Grapes are somewhat more tractable. Old, contorted wild ones with thick stalks can be pruned into mounds with a few overflowing lower shoots trained as groundcovers. Their winter form, without the large-scale leaves, prolongs a sketchy but characterful note, and is dramatic against a graveled base.

One of my favorite partial barriers can be seen in essence on page 145. Cedar fencing panels, a yard wide and 4 to 5 feet tall, are split and wired back to back like a sheath, and are slipped over two metal fence posts. They are diagonally set at about 4-foot intervals to form louvers in a long-drawn-out Hogarth curve behind clumps of hardy perennials in an informal border. Trained against each is a tall clematis. And, at the back of the matching border across the path, repeating the curve but only high enough to screen rough grass beyond, are shrubby clematis like *C. recta* and *C. heracleifolia* var. *davidiana*. These reflect a similar foliage in lower form, although they do not, of course, carry the color so high as those opposite.

This idea of bringing color high can be achieved in another, more formal, way by training shrubs in standard form. And when these materials themselves are not formal, interesting binding effects can be gained in transitional areas. I have seen this concept carried out with rose-of-Sharon, forsythias, *Poncirus trifoliata*, sometimes listed as *Aegle sepiaria*, and *Hydrangea paniculata*, not the usual *grandiflora* but the type that gives bloom through all of July and August, with anywhere from one to four shoots trained in a clump, clipped more or less hard, to conform to its placement and surroundings. Coarse rosetted plants like yuccas can also form low groups, with intermittent accents of tall evergreens introduced to achieve partial screening.

There are several shrubs and vines to be aware of and wary of: all the polygonums, the Indian currant, *Symphoricarpos orbiculatus*, and bamboos like cane (39)—unless you can contain them as suggested for honeysuckle (113).

Current styles in gardens are bound to influence our planting approaches, both formal and informal. At the moment, there are two quite strong trends, both popular because they lead to reduced maintenance. One is toward the wild garden; the other is inspired by the passageway and "room" gardens of Japan, with their small scale and their extensive use of boulders and dwarf shrubs. Most stateside imitations of Japanese gardening I've seen lack the cunning inadvertency of the originals, as well as their subtle interplay of texture between plants and structure. The replicas are not dictated by ritualism as are their Japanese prototypes—in which an exquisite preoccupation with detail even extends to the pruning of individual pine needles—and lack the dynamic character of the originals.

The determination to achieve minimal upkeep, with which I am sympathetic, sometimes leads to the extensive use of chemical herbicides. I find this development ominous. Even with the least persistent of herbicides, like the chlorophenoxy-based 2-4-D and 2-4-5-T, effects may be disastrous. We know, for example, that forbs—herbaceous nongrass or nongrasslike plants—are quickly killed by 2-4-5-T. Recent tests show that cuttings taken from stock plants in areas treated with herbicides have feebler power to strike roots, and those that survive are stunted in growth. I wish, in fact, that I had never been lured into the byways of chemical weed controls at all. But when I read that I could get rid of a well-established sapling in the heart of a hedge planting, I succumbed to temptation. The trick could be turned, I was informed, by using a type of herbicide which expanded the internal molecular structure of a plant until it ruptured the cells and caused self-destruction. With surgical care we incised the sapling, applied the herbicide as directed—only on the cut—and then stood back to watch the Borgian process. Sure enough, the sapling rather quickly died; but so, the following spring, did the hedge plants nearby.

Who wouldn't love to see a misplaced trumpet creeper vanish? For even if it is cut back deep annually it still produces shrublike greenery by fall. A friend recommended the rather desperate expedient of tying the vine-tip into a pop bottle with some of this same cell-bursting fluid. As luck would have it, though, my vines slipped their nooses, and in a frantic wind dance swept areas of the rock garden with their poisoned tips, with lethal effect. But the trumpet creeper roots, of which we found sturdy evidence 12 feet below grade when we dug our basement, continued to flourish undaunted.

Years ago we tried herbicides for broad-leaved weeds in our meadow when plantain seemed to be taking over. We lost some of the plantain but in its stead acquired some undesirable and wholly unexpected coarse grasses.

Recently, in the most reputable journals, excellent weed control from fall

Give birds a continuous supplemental lift during the months between November and May when their natural resources are lowest. You may prefer the rest of the year to let them earn their keep searching out insects, scales, weed seeds and the fruited shrubs you have planted for them. Squirrels and other rodents are foiled by the ceramic feeding station shown on the opposite page. English sparrows are annoyed by its movement and are discouraged if only sunflower seed is kept in the ten-pound-capacity copper-roofed platform type illustrated below.

137

Summer Bulbs

Though most impressive, Fritillaria imperialis, *the crown imperial, on pages 132 and 140, is by no means the tallest of the summer bulbs. This honor goes to* Cardiocrinum giganteum, *the giant Himalayan lily (161), and to the* Eremuri,

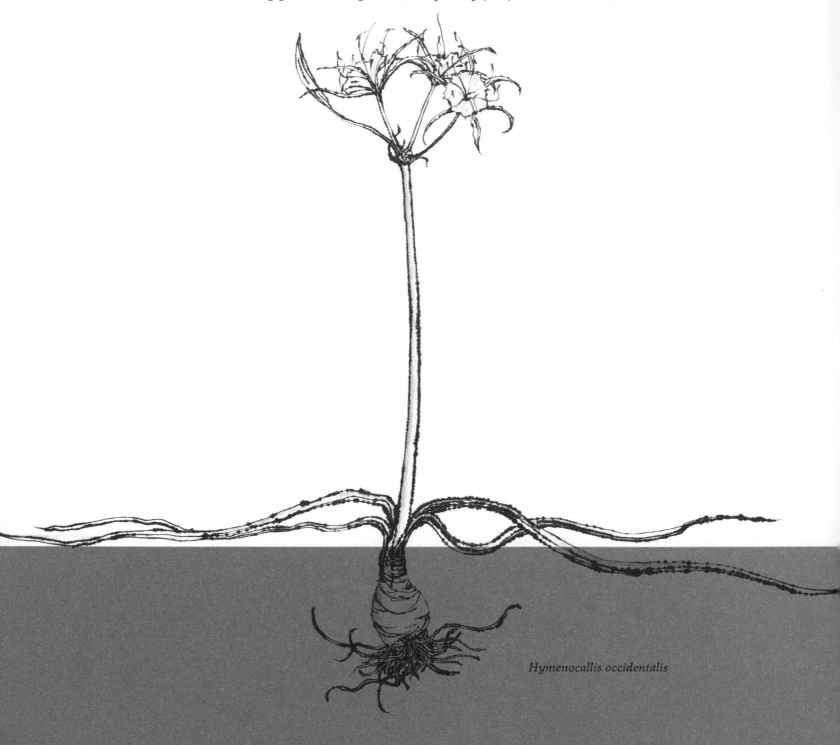

Hymenocallis occidentalis

or foxtail lilies. One of the latter produced for me a 28-inch white spike above a leafless 5-foot stalk. The leaves are a recumbent straplike star below. Because of the narrowness of their bloom, the foxtails must be planted in masses to be effective, as at Sissinghurst, where, like pink flares, they reach for the light diagonally in front of a 12-foot-high curve of clipped yew. In our climate the blooming period for this species is very short: the lower florets on the stalk deteriorate so rapidly as to make the infloresence quickly look ramshackle.

Great clumps of the imperial fritillary, if properly sited in partial high shade, need not be disturbed for years. F. imperialis grows to 36 inches, with red-orange 2-inch bells. There are also yellow and red hybrids, which I have been unable to establish—perhaps because of a mosaic they seem to have brought with them on arrival. Fritillary bulbs, like those of lilies, should not be allowed to dry out. Look, if possible, for a local source of mosaic-free bulbs.

Anther bushy but more delicate and sophisticated fritillary is F. verticillata, a Japanese type with smaller yellow-green bells and three narrow curled leaves whimsically placed above the blooms. See endpapers and page 239. If you are growing from seed, allow the bushy types of fritillary to remain in seed pans for several years before transplanting. I fail to hold the smaller, more solitary F. meleagris, the guinea-hen flower (233), more than a few seasons. It is said to persist in moist sunny meadows.

Thanks to an imaginative seedsman, I met the "alluring alliums." Relegated by most people to the kitchen as "mere" onions, many of their honeyed blooms can grace the living room, as Frances Poetker shows on page 269, with A. cepa, the common or garden onion, and 'Rocambole,' the giant or serpent garlic (198), often mistakenly called Allium scorodoprasum but actually a form of Allium sativum, with coiled scapes. A. porrum, the leek, the most decorative among the culinaries, is unfortunately biennial, but makes a striking accent plant. Have you ever seen it at Mount Vernon, clumped against box with nasturtiums at its feet? The tough persistent white flowers of A. tuberosum, Chinese or garlic chive, are always available for cutting in August.

Among the edible natives is the wide two-leaved white A. tricoccum, around which the spring "ramps" festival is celebrated in Appalachia. From its restrained elegance and distinguished black seeds held glistening in buff pods, no one could guess the rustic frenzy it induces.

My allium season begins with A. moly, the foot-high lily leek, holding aloft ½-inch bright yellow stars clustered in 3-inch umbels, and A. karataviense, the Turkestan onion, again 3 inches but producing a greyed-pink bloom less than 6 inches above one of the most beautiful of leaves—glaucous and striated with purplish-brown markings—for which I really grow it. But even when I don't pick the leaf, the plant seldom holds longer than three years. Later the shade-tolerant white, A. triquetrum, with its triangular 10-inch stem, and A. neapolitanum, the Naples onion, just barely hardy and therefore holding no threat of invasiveness, are worth having for cutting.

Some varieties of allium, like A. stellatum, the wild onion, should be avoided like the plague if you live farther south than southern Ohio, for it blankets the fields in autumn. Grown here in semishade with colchicum (177), whose color it matches, it becomes an asset. Another late bloomer, A. senescens, with a low rosette of swirled grey leaves beneath a pink foot-high 2-inch umbel, is never invasive either.

Alliums to treasure are the spectacular A. christophii, more commonly known as A. albopilosum, the star-of-Persia, shown on page 299, carrying its metallic 10-inch blue-lavender bloom on 20-inch stems, and the even bigger pinkish A. schubertii, which rises to 1 foot. For their dramatic dried state see page 299. Some violently magenta-purplish alliums like A. rosenbachianum and A. giganteum grow to almost 4 feet. So does the 'Green Eyed Dragon,' not yet formally classified, an equally tall sparkling-white green-centered cluster. As the globular blooms are only about 4 inches in diameter, these varieties need to be planted in large groups with, preferably, a complementary planting at their base. The list above is just a taster, for there are many more desirable alliums for your delectation.

Blooming with lycoris (170, 172) and colchicum (174, 177) is the overpoweringly fragrant white 2-foot-high spider lily, Hymenocallis occidentalis (138). This hardy plant recalls the form and fragrance of the June-blooming tender Hymenocallis calathina, also called Ismene calathina, of thicker substance and lower growth. Blooming at this time, too, but not shown, is the only crinum I have found to be hardy here: C. X powellii 'Album.' Although farther south only the rounded portion of the bulb is buried, in our area the entire bulb should be covered and winter-mulched. But its performance in the open is not comparable to those of its bulbs that are potted and wintered over.

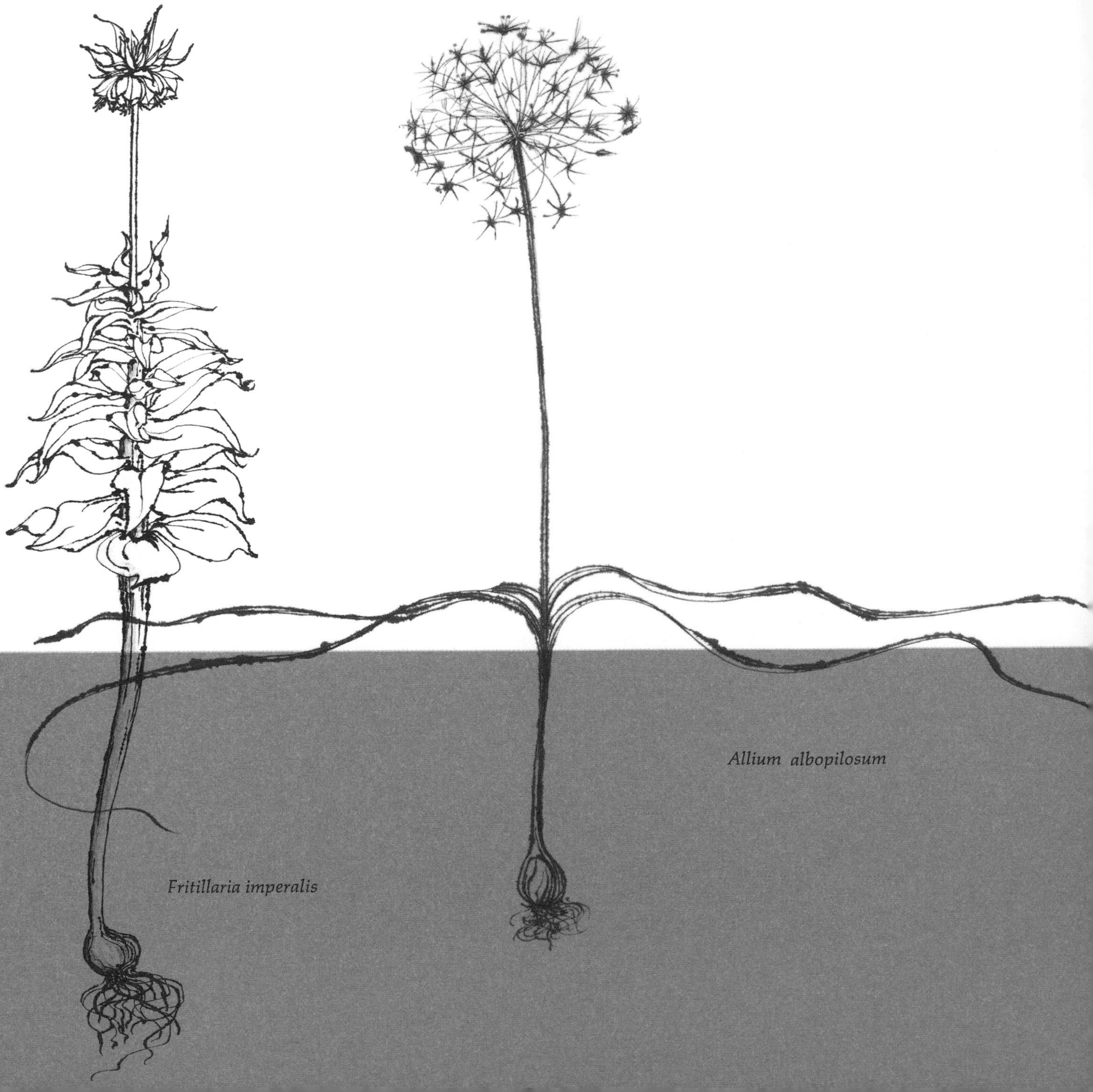

Allium albopilosum

Fritillaria imperalis

to fall is reported through the use of preemergent herbicides "with no cumulative effects unless"—and here comes the caveat—"the herbicide is incorporated into the soil." Then follows a list of exceptions, including hydrangeas, fir, hemlocks, three kinds of hollies and all tuberous-rooted plants.

In areas of mixed growth it is impossible to estimate, until too late, such perils as spray drift and the extent of water-borne damage through drainage. Controlled "laboratory" results are an open book compared to the countless dangers hidden in the web of interlocking dependencies we find in a garden. I much prefer, instead, sticking to old-fashioned garden practices like mowing in meadow areas and screening out weedy growth through shrub-clumps, hedges, barriers and smother plantings (111).

As summer advances you realize how crowded your garden is with guests, many of whom, like viruses, you recognize only by their injurious effects. Some, not unseen, you will pardon, and even be grateful to have met in passing: the agile tree frog sliding to elegant comfort down a daylily trumpet at dusk, or a crickety creature of such emerald opalescence that you wouldn't begrudge him a leaf or two of even your choicest specimen. You may resent the career of some silent undercover leaf miner even as you marvel that, like the most vocal and ambient of his neighbors, he never fouls his nest. You may enjoy the structured elegance of the cicada, even while you strickenly note the yellowed stripe down an iris leaf that reveals the passage of the borer into its heart.

Fortunately a wild-garden by its very nature is more resistant to many of the less welcome visitors. The indigenes are a tough lot on the whole and, given half a chance, seed and colonize where conditions are at all favorable. With the hardy aliens you introduce, try for pest- and disease-resistant varieties, and do all you can to keep them strong and in congenial exposure, soil and drainage. Put in many kinds of plants, for it is where monocultures dominate that the greatest trouble breeds.

For instance, myrtle has been hit in sections of my place by a disastrous browning. It has been worst where this groundcover not long before was too closely transplanted in an attempt to achieve an immediate overall effect. Soil and drainage happened to be less favorable in the affected areas, and sun exposure rather more than this groundcover likes. Thinning by removal of all afflicted stalks, thorough composting with the addition of iron—in chelate form, which makes that mineral more available to plants—and a scattering of powdered seaweed, which has trace elements and growth stimulators, has brought about complete restoration.

I urge you at least not to rush out for a pesticide or fungicide at the first yellowing or mottling of foliage. Some damage which you attribute in your innocence to insects and diseases may be the result of soil deficiencies. If you've already used sprays anywhere close by, the symptoms may well be a side effect

of that application itself. The trouble may also be caused simply by winter damage, sun scald, drought, or soil and air pollutants. That injuries have derived from air pollution is indicated unmistakably when browning or other distortions appear just where leaf surfaces are exposed, yet leaves shielded by others are free from symptoms. To familiarize yourself with more evidence of pollution damage, see the pictorial atlas on this subject called *Recognition of Air Pollution Injury to Vegetation* by Jacobson and Hill.

Don't disdain simple preventive practices like a fall cleanup of diseased material. Watch for harmful egg cases. Make carrying along a plastic bag a routine matter for disposing of diseased foliage, so that spores from it don't spread as you wander around your garden. Don't work when the foliage is wet. Disinfect tools with a liquid chlorine bleach when you move from one blighted plant to another that is disease-free. Remember that since wilts and browning are not always caused by viruses or insects, but may result from a lack of moisture, the preventive may lie in mulches (168).

Tolerate—within wide limits—all living creatures, whether they be birds, toads, snakes, skunks, moles, shrews or mice—yes, even mice—as well as indiscriminate predators like mantises, wasps and ants; or occasional disruptors like earthworms, who may leave castings on your lawn but are, with their deep delving ways, bringing minerals to levels where they become available to plants. Diminish the mosquito count by attracting purple martins into the kind of high-up, sweep-commanding apartment house they find congenial.

Learn specifically how to encourage, import and use beneficial insects. Introduce countermeasures like ladybugs for aphids or the milky spore disease treatment, which is fatal to the grub stage of Japanese beetle. A number of such individualized disease controls have been tested by the USDA to make sure that they are not transferable to man. Try insect sex lures and sterilants, baits and traps. You may even attain your objective by foiling the life cycle of a pest, as our neighbors have done in the Little Miami River bottoms. Here the ground stays wet, so that an obligatory late planting of the corn crop has always saved it from attack by the corn borer.

Try, too, companionate plantings. For added suggestions, read Beatrice Trum Hunter's *Gardening Without Poisons*. The theory behind such combinations is that the root exudates of one kind of plant are distasteful to the nematodes, eelworms or other underground predators of its neighbors. Sometimes results are delayed, as in the case of marigolds, where effectiveness will last over several seasons, but starts only after the marigold has stopped growing. Experiments are now going on in segregating these exudates as future substitutes for the actual growing of the plants themselves. A "reverse technique" is to put in deliberately small quantities of sacrificial "trap" plants, varieties that are highly insect-prone and will lure the creatures away from your treasured specimens. When periodic invasions occur and the use of sprays is imperative,

If you can find a densely shaded site, try as a groundcover Saxifraga stolonifera, *the strawberry geranium, with its subtle white and grey-green leaf markings and its incandescent irregular white flyaway blossoms in June. As with the bronze and variegated ajugas, this groundcover seems to like a heavy soil where drainage is not sharp. Seen here with the Christmas fern,* Polystichum acrostichoides, *and English yew,* Taxus baccata, *the strawberry geranium maintains lively year-round interest.*

The problem of transition from formal to native areas is eased by the use of daylilies, peonies, gas plant, oriental poppies, shasta daisies and other tough perennials that can be naturalized along informal paths. Here some widely spaced cedar sapling panels bring clematis color high, furnish a foil for the hemerocallis, and form a partial screen against rising untended summer growth in areas beyond. Shown is Clematis X jackmanii 'Henryi' *and a very fragrant pale yellow hemerocallis hybridized by Dr. Leonian. The latter has flowered every season for over six weeks after being in place more than twenty years. Its foliage is healthy, its blooming habit prolific. Because of these endearing traits, I'd hesitate to trade it in mass plantings for any of the something like twelve thousand registered cultivars developed in the past three decades. Be sure to choose hemerocallis types suited to your climate, for southerly ones, especially the evergreen types, while glorious in catalogs, may disappoint you in performance. Does the situation call for a tall-reaching spray or a denser lower accent? It's worth a trip to a trial garden, like Kingwood in Mansfield, Ohio, to determine your choices—not only for stance but also for color and texture. In lieu of such an opportunity, send to the American Horticultural Society for their superb "Daylily Handbook." It will make you an instant addict.*

employ botanicals such as rotenone and pyrethrum. The latter should not be used in aerosol form, as the mixture, with certain propellant chemicals, has been found to exert an adverse synergistic effect.

The following example of synergism—that "cooperative action of discrete agencies, such that the total effect is greater than the sum of two effects taken independently"—is instructive. The insecticide Heptachlor lies in the soil for two years, where, in combination with chemicals found in most soils, it weathers into heptachlor epoxide, a substance that is many times more lethal than the original. The outcome biologists fear is that residues which ultimately find their way into our bodies may make contact with other chemicals we ingest and go through similar transformations, and that for such reactions there may be no known antidotes. It is now clear that scientific advance is beset by ambush and booby trap, as well as by head-on hostility. We have already suffered enough from the unexpected side effects of promising shortcuts to put us on our guard.

Rotenone and pyrethrum—neither of which should be held over from one year to the next—last long enough after application to do their jobs, but they are not incorporated endlessly into the soil to poison beneficent organisms and earthworms, and so start the deadly cycle Rachel Carson fought in *Silent Spring*, and which we must continue to fight as valiantly today.

It is all too easy, though, to embrace biological and mechanical controls "on the rebound." A word of caution here. It is already being suggested that we breed plants lacking in B-vitamins or certain enzymes—plants that will starve out insects. The difficulty here is that when we eat these plants, or the animals that have fed on such deficient tissue, we not only lose valuable nutrients, but ourselves become subject to the resultant so-called metabolic toxins. Poisonous transference can also result from plants treated with "systemics." Train a wary eye on such esoteric devices as using radioactive isotopes in insect baits, or blanketing whole fields with radio or sound waves. These waves literally burst insects apart, good and bad alike. A method which is older and disappointingly prosaic—but far less alarmingly indiscriminate—is to spread a little bran.

If you strenuously disapprove of spraying in general, take comfort in the fact that pests and diseases have their own cycles and their own enemies. Fundamentally we must heed old Francis Bacon's advice that "We cannot command nature except by obeying her." And in order to obey her truly, far more sensitivity to her ways is required.

As we go to press amid the bans and counterbans, the loosening and tightening of regulations for organophosphate-persistent pesticides like DDT, we read of new "self-destruct" additives designed to make them harmless. As yet, since the effects of the self-destructs are not in any sense fully tested, let me sum up the situation in a succinct warning from an extremely authoritative, lengthy and current report, *Cleaning Our Environment* by the American Chemical Society, that every layman should ponder well: "The relationship of contaminants to the ecology is very nearly a total mystery."

A natural Delta hybrid, 'Dorothea K. Williamson,' shown here, is ideal for arranging. It blooms below the often sharply folded riffled leaf, presenting rich violet-blue 4-inch open flowers, horizontally and appealingly spaced on the zigzag stems so that each flower can be individually enjoyed. Taller is the interestingly rigid Iris fulva. The latter, with its hybrids, has extended the usual iris colors into tawny coppers, terra cotta and red.

It is not only to herbicides that we can attribute mysterious failures. Consider our native columbine. How many different vistas that name evokes! From the time I saw it swaying so airily in my mother's sandy Michigan garden and on the cliffs of my grandfather's place at Brickey's Mills in Missouri, I was determined someday to grow it myself. So when Freda Rosenfelder offered me flats of it from her exuberant plantation at Ryland, Kentucky, I was sure I could count *Aquilegia canadensis* (257) among my own treasures. Yet, try as I might these last thirty years, *A. canadensis* refuses to establish for me. On the other hand, at Lob's Wood, a few miles away, it seeds weedily along the clay paths; and at Old Man's Cave, situated among the picturesque tributaries of the Hocking River in south-central Ohio, it can be seen to its best advantage suspended against sky and hemlocks, its fragile elegance a perfect contrast to the monumental scale of the sandstone canyons.

My columbine-curse will, I begin to foresee, forever thwart my growing enough *canadensis* to crush the seeds to a paste for perfume, as the Ponca Indians do, let alone being able to cut a show of it for arrangements against our grey living-dining walls where its yellow and rosy-orange variations could be so gratefully enjoyed. Perhaps my soil is "too rich for its blood." A neighbor, ironically, has the greatest luck with the tall white *A. vulgaris* var. *nivea* 'Grandiflora,' which seeds in rifts through her light woodland. I have established this variety with difficulty, and only where I put down a rock at its roots. But, from a few plants of the squat deep blue variety 'Hensol Harebell,' I can count on persistent seeding in many places—a dry retaining wall, the borders and the woods edge.

Let me speak of another plant which evokes equally clear memories. During my elementary school life, the hot June days which signaled the end of the academic year were heralded by a recurrent still-life set-piece. As one monitor gave out battered enamel paintboxes with hard pellets of primary colors, and another distributed large sheets of rough manila paper, a third handed around water pans and tousled brushes. The teacher, meanwhile, busied herself choosing the least battered specimen from a bucket of German irises her pupils had proudly brought in. This favored stalk of "blue flags," with its noble, arching standards and mysteriously bearded falls, careened for a moment tippily in its milk bottle as the teacher placed it on a high stool for all to assault.

Inky blue tones ran uncontrolled down the wet manila sheets, standards swayed, falls drooped, the stalwart glaucous leaves, as we labored happily away, began to take on yellow-green tones not unlike those of the decals which here and there decorated the backs of our grubby hands.

Ever since those early frustrating attempts to immortalize a beauty that so clearly transcended its human surroundings, I have been grateful to the bearded, or Pogon, irises. As a gardener, however, I have found their glorious span over-brief for their demands on available space, and for the necessary work involved in keeping them in good condition by dividing, checking them against borers, and

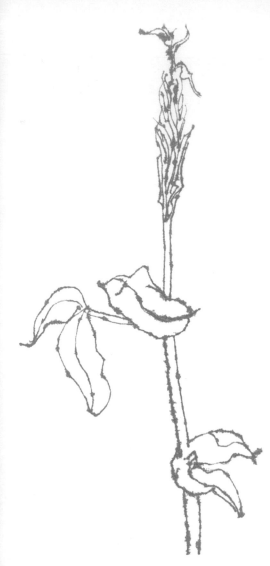

A Greek vase fragment shows a group of mariners loading bags onto a ship owned by Croesus. Do these laden bags furnish a clue to the king's wealth? No one really knows, but they might have contained psyllium seed, a prized product of the ancient world. Today, incidentally, colchicum seed oil sells at one hundred fifty dollars an ounce. Of more importance than the transient monetary value of seeds and their extracts is their strength and health, on which our very survival depends. But more of seeds, as well as some of the one hundred-odd known reasons why they won't germinate, on page 121. This complex furry grey-brown pod belongs to Thermopsis villosa, *the Aaron's-rod lupine. The beanlike shape, swirled into a rigid standard, is typical of legumes.*

resetting. Every year sees bearded garden hybrids multiplying, and their blooms everywhere becoming more flamboyant. Some of the tempting newcomers hide a weakness of stem and a greater susceptibility to borers that result from the use of Southern strains in breeding. But the most compelling reason why I've turned to other iris types is that I have yet to see bearded iris look well in a naturalized situation.

A word about iris classification as it affects their culture before turning to types that do effectively respond to colonizing. The roots of iris may be bulbous or rhizomatous. On pages 63 and 71 I have already referred to the early bulbous reticulates. Another large May-blooming section among the bulbous types, the Xiphions, which includes Spanish, Dutch and English varieties, is sometimes claimed as hardy here. The Xiphions barely hang on for me. One May-blooming bulbous iris in the otherwise reluctant Juno group, the 15-inch *bucharica*, has lasted for years. Its popular name, the cornstalk iris, warns one that its somewhat exotic bicolored yellow and white blooms, bunched in the leaf axils, make its convincing placement tricky. About the time it flowers you will find, too, in the wild, a blue irislike bloom only about ½-inch big, with fibrous roots. This is the blue-eyed grass, *Sisyrinchium angustifolium* of the Iridaceae, but it is not classified as a true iris.

Among true types, the rhizomatous that start blooming in late May are the bearded Pogons, or garden irises, discussed above, and the Regelias, Oncocyclus and Pseudoregelias. The latter trio does not like our growing conditions. Also rhizomatous are the Apogons or beardless irises. I wish I'd known earlier of the rhizomatous crested Evansia types, which are more disease and pest resistant, easier to grow once established, and more consonant with the informal landscape than are their commoner bearded cousins.

The Apogons should be planted, as the bearded types are, with their rhizomes almost exposed at the highest point and their long roots well anchored. They prefer richer more friable soil that stays moist. The ones listed below have grown well in lime soil, but many of the West Coast beardless, as well as the Japanese types, I am sure, have failed to persist in the naturalized areas of my garden due to their need for greater soil acidity, and because of our hot dry summers. Let me add, however, that with these and other one-act performers I never regret buying the ticket and attending the opening, even if it turns out to be a one-day stand.

In late April my first beardless but crested iris, the Chinese native, *Iris tectorum* (245), blooms in white and blue. The blue area is handsomely marked with darker blue as though by a skilled if carefree brush. This iris, also known as the Japanese roof iris, forms open-arced clumps that bloom well for five or six years before needing division. Transplanted into sun or partial shade, their wide-ribbed light green leaves achieve a 15-inch final height and stay in good decorative condition until frost. Due to the characteristic arching quality of the leaves,

Clambering up the stalks of
Thermopsis villosa, *which parades its*
yellow plumes 4 feet high against
woods edges in July, are the tendrilous
leaflets of Vicia americana, *the purple*
vetch, and the graceful five-fingered
forms of the Virginia creeper,
Parthenocissus quinquefolia. *The last-*
named will carry a deeper gold and
red against the woods' green at frost
time when the interlaced flattened
pods of the thermopsis become a rigid,
interlocked mass.

these irises look well cascading near rock stairs or slopes. *Tectorum's* lavender-blue and white forms grow out from under the bases of trees in partial shade and protected from western sun. In similar terrain our native low-growing *I. cristata* follows suit. But wherever you put *cristata,* it tends to work its way in great fanlike strides to fresh soils. Transplanting is best just as the floppy new fans reach out for anchorage. The small triangular rhizomes are very shallowly rooted and the interconnecting black cords between fans lie completely above ground.

A vision of Japanese iris played a large part in the color I planned for my creekside, especially masses of velvety flat-topped beardless *kaempferi* growing erect and solid like farflung embroidered kimonos. A monotone background here of water and greenery, like a sectional screen, would modify the color where needed. As these images flashed tantalizingly across my inner eye, it failed to occur to me that there were good reasons why I hadn't seen any such effects around. After managing to bloom a few feeble plants, I made the discovery that has so often since disqualified any number of captivating introductions to Cockaigne: Japanese irises need the acid soil my acres cannot provide, and withdrawal of water after blooming.

The cultural requirements of plants, like many of the most important things in life, are seldom discussed fully enough. In order to get the results you dream of, cultural demands must be adequately met. If you cannot furnish them for certain plants, look around for substitute material that carries the same general form or color. What would replace the Japanese at the streamside? Which irises could endure having their roots in water all of the time? The yellow iris, *I. pseudacorus* (153), for one. The *laevigatas,* similar in form to *kaempferi,* but differing in not having a heavy rib down the middle of the leaves, for another. So can irises from the Louisiana Delta, like *I. fulva,* the copper iris. Another Delta derivative, *I. brevicaulis,* formerly called *foliosa,* prefers upland wooded pastures. One of my favorites is a hybrid of *fulva* and *brevicaulis,* 'Dorothea K. Williamson' (146). I have better luck with all the Delta types when they have good drainage and rather more sun than they require in their native surroundings. In fact, to establish them, it is well to set out at once in good garden loam and in full sun the single rhizomes dealers send you. As soon as you have a sizable clump, transplant them after blooming to their permanent sites. Bloom comes only on those plants that remain evergreen over the winter.

Also beardless, and one of the most reliable iris types, are the Siberians. They are often thought of only as border plants, but they colonize satisfactorily in moist, well-drained spots, and their leaves create big 2½-foot spearlike clumps at the waterside. A persistent bloomer too, at this time, is a beardless grey-blue iris interesting for small arrangements, *I. ensata.* The 2-inch blooms of this sword-leaved iris nestle down among its prolific grasslike leaves. A giant group, some rising more than 5 feet, are the Spuria irises. They are sun-loving and apparently indifferent to poor dry soil. I have had blue, white and yellow masses thriving in the heaviest clay untouched, except as I share them with others, for

The sparklerlike white pistillate blooms of Thalictrum dasycarpum *var.* hypoglaucum, *the summer meadow rue, are carried ethereally to 8 feet along shady creeks, not so high on sunny ones. Shown opposite, the blooms rise to their full height with their glaucous ferny foliage 4 feet above the 30-inch leathery discs of the Japanese butter-bur,* Petasites japonicus *(69 and 235), which reflect light from their surfaces and exclude it below where only toads and their ilk can enjoy the beauty of the great stems with their frail but confidence-inspiring rib structure.*

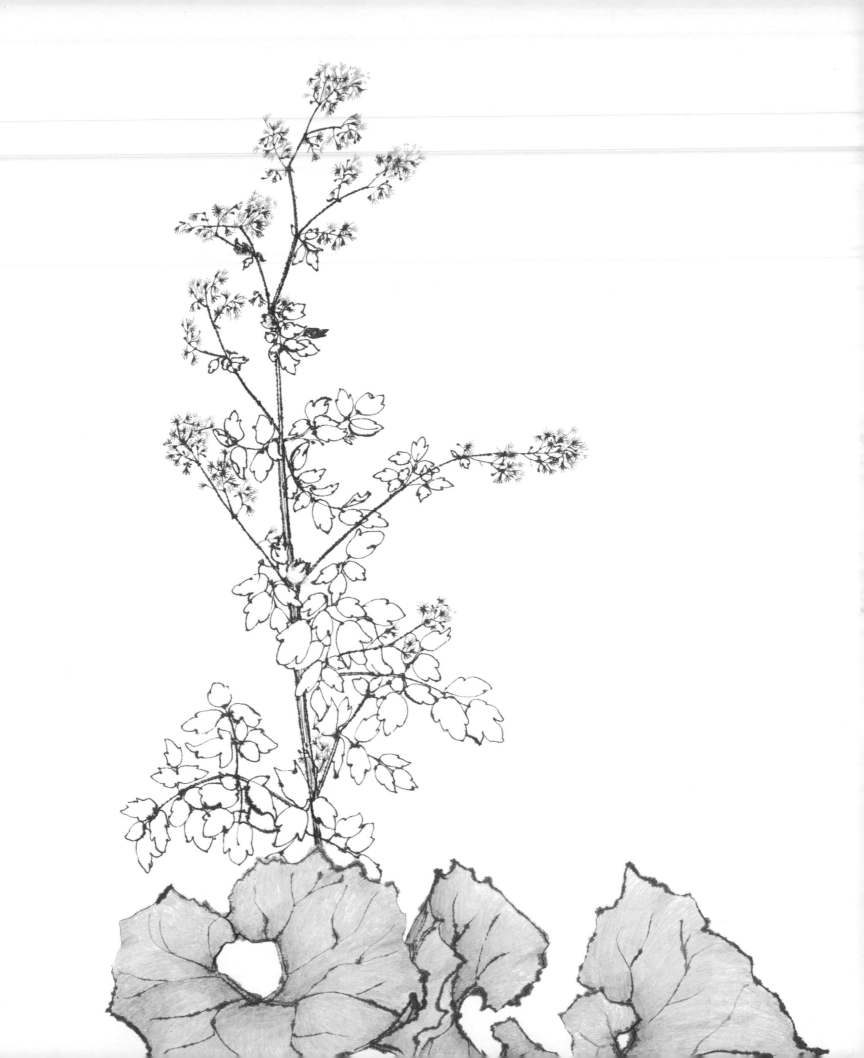

Stately at the waterside is Iris pseudacorus, *the yellow iris or water flag, and the prototype for the French fleur-de-lis. The leaves may rise to 5 feet, and in the paler variety,* I. p. strictum, *can go to 7 feet. The seed pods of this iris start upright and later swing down heavily, as though washed by the current. Then, in their final state, they straighten up again, like candelabra. These dramatic pods, as those of other irises, are welcome additions to the storehouse for dried arrangements. Panicles of* Lysimachia clethroides, *the gooseneck loosestrife, each floret as sharp as enameled French funeral flowers, reach rhythmically above the creek. The surprising thing about both these plants is their willingness to flourish in both dry and wet locales. But when in a drier environment this white loosestrife demands dense shade, and the iris is of much smaller stature. Creeping buttercup forms the groundcover.*

over thirty years. But more recently planted yellow hybrids have been very slow to increase either near them or in richer soils. Often called "the poor man's orchids" but quite capable of adorning a patrician parlor, the 5- to 6-inch Spuria blooms are grouped rigidly in overlapping fashion. Enveloped in rather bulky reduced leaves, the heads are heavy, the blooms themselves larger in scale but close in form to the Xiphions (148).

Tolerant of rather dry situations is the fall-blooming irid, *Belamcanda chinensis,* the leopard flower or blackberry-lily, so named for its charming orangey-yellow blooms spotted with purple-brown, and for its clustered blackberrylike seeds. On page 289 you can see *Belamcanda's* typical iris leaf fan still exhibiting a few last flowers before frost, and the partially husked pod disclosing the distinctive shiny black seeds that crest to 3 feet above the ground. Reputedly perennial is another fall-blooming but true iris, much like *Belamcanda* in general form, *I. dichotoma.* It is often called the vesper iris, because it opens its reddish-lavender blooms only in the late afternoon. Mine has never lasted more than one season.

You may wonder why I seem compelled to try out so many different irises. But each described above has its own niche in the landscape. Each inspires a particular mood for arranging. Each contributes in its turn to extending the exquisite form of iris bloom from February to late September.

Every morning, in spite of heat and drought, dew lies on the grass because of our proximity to the Little Miami River. Nowhere is the dew heavier or more evident than along our creekside, which becomes more inviting as the summer progresses. Dew streaks the grasses with rainbow light—grasses now tall enough so that the passage of a fox is like the sudden slipping of an orange scarf among the blooming heads—so swift and silent you wonder if you dreamed it. But no, the color flares again against a clump of yellow irises and competes with the regal blue of *I. brevicaulis* and the golden buttercups.

All three of these plants are happy choices for our small "run," where the flow alternates from torrent to trickle. There are only a few spots on the valley floor where seepage from hillside springs or small gravel beds in the watercourse itself encourages true water lovers. One of our first innocent errors was to think we could control this mischievous little watercourse of ours. "Streamside" sounds so romantic, but if you have ever tried to cooperate with a stream you know that the compromises are going to be all yours. At the very outset we built a low wall across the "thread" at its upper end to create a louder babble below a very small natural pool. Growing more ambitious, we decided that a sheet of water would greatly enhance the view, and found below, at a contraction of the valley, what seemed an ideal dam site.

There is no need to belabor you with the harrowing details of our ill-fated pond project, except to point out a few major frustrations. The blue clay we brought in as barrier material ruined the slope down which we lowered it on a crude

sheet metal sled: it took years to plant out that broad slick streak. We did not, of course, rely on the clay alone for retention. A friend, himself a former dam builder who had suffered repeated set-backs from "crawdads"—they are perfectly capable of tunneling through as much as twenty feet of hardpan—described for us his specifications for a really impenetrable core. It consisted of galvanized metal sheets bolted together and set in concrete; and he generously added some advice on how to confect spillways and overflow pipes. We followed instructions. The rains came. Water gathered; and so did algae, as the submerged foliage decayed. Finally the water cleared and I began to plant all the things I thought likely to succeed, many of which I fondly recalled from Frances Perry's authoritative *Water Gardening*.

Some of these plants, like the flowering rush, *Butomus umbellatus*, the bog arum, pickerelweed, cat-tails and arrowhead, survived long enough to bloom. But alas! The little pond proved a fleeting accomplishment—a brief respite from doom. Within a few months it had already begun to fill with silt from the tilled fields above us over which we had no control. In a few years even marsh marigolds and skunk cabbage dwindled. After that the pond simply disappeared. The more or less stabilized result of our hydrological effort is today a wider valley, U-shaped instead of V-shaped, its floor as high as the dam itself, with a creek that tends to cut deep into the silt. Eventually I had to substitute for the large-leaved native *Nelumbo* with their choice yellow lotus blooms, *Petasites japonicus*, the Japanese butter-bur (69). Creeping buttercup (153), taller and more aggressive than forget-me-not, took over the edges previously enameled with blue, but both these plants showed a remarkable readiness to come through repeated coverings of mud in just a few days. I had to content myself, too, with the gooseneck loosestrife (153), which fortunately lay out over the creek in the same kinds of rhythms as its predecessor, *Saururus cernuus*, the lizard's-tail. Later I altered my more aristocratic guest list even further, and welcomed Miami-mist, jewelweed, the tall meadow rue and spires of the blue lobelia, astilbes, and ferns—not, as it turned out, too bad a fate, really.

Thus, while my water plants may be second-guess and substitutes, my forms are authentically riverine. So is the atmosphere of the glen—cool, contributing a constant moisture that stimulates an unexpected luxuriance which is absent in a forked branch above us that becomes dismally dry by midsummer—the condition Mrs. Trollope generalized about. In fact, along the low banks above the creek, escaped white *Phlox paniculata*, the garden phlox, now blooms thickly, unattended, with perfect leafage—a condition I can never achieve in my borders, no matter how much I water.

Climbing the mossy stone stairs that lead back from the cool shade of the valley into the baking sunlit heat of the fields above, I find a guerrilla war being waged at the edges between the stabilized woods areas and the cropped grass of the fields. I often think, as I look on this contested milieu, of Reginald Farrer's

Little did the Tradescants, father and son, who introduced the spiderwort to Europe, realize how many favorite garden forms would be hybridized from it there and sent over to grace modern American gardens. Nor could they guess tradescantias would become the "fruit flies" of plant genetic studies because of their clear chromosomal content and ease of propagation. The finely wrought beauty of the flower's central element, with its tufted, intense blue "fuzz," is worth looking at under a hand glass. The glaucous form, T. ohiensis, *can be found wild in whites, and from pale pinks through deep purples.*
T. virginiana, *shown here with brome grass,* Bromus purgans, *like chicory, needs sun to stay awake.*

account of his journey to the Marches of Tibet, where he hoped to find unusual plants suited to the English climate. En route he traveled hundreds of miles through China in his palanquin, curtains drawn. Why should he bother to look? Along the roads where land for food raising was at such a premium, he felt certain that no inadvertent growth could survive, no interesting specimen light a gleam in his eye. Mary Moulton, who spent her early years in a remote part of China, understood his indifference, but told me of the horticultural wonders she had discovered in old temple grounds and monastery property, and wherever the natural wilderness contrasted to such great effect with the endless wide cut-stone stairways that ranged through the monastery's holdings. These two complementary observations prove, I hope, that you can abandon an orderly grass crop at the edge of a path or shrubbery in favor of an intervening zone with the random charm and statuesque bloom of certain old country road verges.

I've wrestled not altogether successfully for years between control and liberty in the no-man's-land between woods and fields, and my closest solution is the formation of "bays" in among the trees, shrubbery and hedge barriers—in other words, a compromise between attempted "landscaping" and the tumbled anarchy that comes with natural succession (36).

Along the edge of field areas I make occasional indentations—scallops in which striking accent plants, or a sequence of strongly colored flowers, can break the monotony of the shrubbery edgings. These "bays" must be "boy-controlled" with discreet grasswhipping and weed pulling. Correlated with the tree and shrubbery bloom, such informal field borders can pack quite a wallop. Attractive summer-flowering trees that withstand competition are the fragrant black locust (110) and the catalpas—both the native white (112) and the stunning blue princess tree, *Paulownia tomentosa*, that has naturalized along the Ohio as the result of a Johnny Appleseed-type river captain who brought back the seeds from his Far Eastern travels. Other Orientals effective in such locations are *Syringa reticulata*, the Japanese lilac tree, its bold leaves a background for dense creamy trusses like something out of a Persian miniature, and *Koelreuteria paniculata*, the sun-loving golden rain tree (275). Native to America are the *Halesias*, silver bell or snowdrop trees, of which *H. carolina* seeds freely in established plantings; the tulip (93) and the smaller fringe tree (91); *Aesculus pavia*, the red buckeye, much like our Ohio buckeye in flower form (97); and *Aesculus parviflora*, the bottlebrush buckeye, with its great white panicles above billowing foliage.

Consider some combinations that lend themselves to such rough terrain: a towering golden-studded *Koelreuteria* faced down with creamy discs of elderberry and spikes of yucca; or yucca (267), overhung by neighboring sumac (159), with orange-red clusters of trumpet creeper (135); or masses of yellow and orange hemerocallis (145) interspersed with the white spires of Spuria iris; or orange butterfly weed (275) against a backdrop of elderberry and blue baptisia. Or change the palette, starting with baptisia, to pink milkweed (23), and add the architectural strength of pale lavender teasel (297) or blue thistle-headed echinops and pink or brick-red monarda, relieved by the white casualness of the hardy pea, *Lathyrus latifolius* (273). For another combination with this same pea, see page 166. *Lathyrus* blooms from June through September and is magnificent in late summer contrasted with the incredibly blue spikes of *Salvia pitcheri*.

Think too of wild rose (275), Queen Anne's lace (29), and chicory (23) under the ethereal foliage or fragile pink pompoms of the silk tree (115), or pink, red and white hollyhocks with elderberry discs and yucca, and a nearby heavy carpet of pink crown vetch, *Coronilla varia*, or rosy-pink clover and, once more, the dense white of the Spuria iris. Again, in the orange and yellow tonalities, visualize the shrublike feathery wild senna, *Cassia marilandica*, its yellow axillary trusses speckled dark brown by its prominent stamens, combined with dynamic lower growing plants like the butterfly weed, and in deeper shade behind both, masses of lavender *Hosta ventricosa* (165)—and, if you are lucky, a purple clematis (145) on a fence nearby.

Look at the common milkweed (23), with its dull pink globes and bold leafage, and think of it with Queen Anne's lace and the sparkling blue of chicory with its long season of bloom. Mallows bask in some of my moister, less elevated

In August 1765 William Bartram described a previously unknown tree he had first seen along the Altamaha River when he traveled in Georgia with his father, John, during the autumn some ten or twelve years before. It had, he stated, "3 inch white flowers standing single and sessile in the bosom of the leaves and ornamented with a crown or tassel of gold-colored refulgent staminae in the center. . . . The inferior petal . . . hollow, formed with a cap or helmet entirely includes the other four until the moment of expansion." This member of the tea family, which the Bartrams named Franklinia in honor of you-know-whom, was "plentiful" over an area of two or three acres. Yet it is to the "dry, woody, cuneiform" seed they gathered that we owe all the Franklinia plants of today. For although the trees were again reported at this same location in 1790, they have never been found there, or elsewhere in the wild, since. Some sources attribute their disappearance at the site of the original discovery to flooding, some to a virus attack.

sunny bays. Still later rudbeckias, asters (287), Jerusalem artichokes and black-berry-lilies (289) vie for space with many varieties of goldenrod (287), while giant white morning glories (283) clamber tirelessly up majestic mulleins (303).

The trick in bringing out the best qualities of such bold summer blooms is to make certain, for one thing, that pinks cannot wage hand-to-hand combat with oranges and yellows. A red monarda will heighten the pink of wild roses, and a magenta one intensify the blue of chicory or the pinks of hollyhocks. But an adjacent clump of wild orange daylilies with its modifying tan tones can cancel out a previously brilliant color contrast. Remember, too, that unless you have great quantities of blue blooms, or can highlight the blues against yellows or pinks, it is often hard to make the blues carry.

Another approach, rather than trying to plant these informal shrubbery bays, is to use a selective weeding technique. Appraise growth already on the spot, encourage the coarse field weeds you want to retain, and supplement them with agreeably colored tough introductions. If you start from scratch with some of the field weeds mentioned above you may find them, however, surprisingly choosy as to soil conditions. There are also some roadside beauties which are better left in place and picked for drying directly from their native haunts, such as *Tragopogon* (303); the violently yellow tick-weed sunflowers such as *Bidens frondosa*; and the beautiful but smothering escape, *Polygonum orientale*, the prince's-feather. Before picking fragile pods, douse with lacquer-based hair spray.

I was never more cognizant of the patterning of foliage than on a trip in June across mid-Illinois. As we reached the rich fields where soybeans, corn and winter wheat stretch across the plain like a great patchwork quilt, we stopped for refreshment on a slight rise. The sky was clearest blue, filled with scudding white clouds. As the capricious wind passed over the level land, it undulated the round leaves of the soy plants like water-lilies on the surface of a pond; it riffled the young cornstalks standing pale against the rich brown earth; it stirred great and eccentric waves in the burnished gold of the ripening wheat in an unending variety of rhythms.

Our mesophytic landscape may not weave so hypnotic a spell, but it does reveal an even greater range of forms, from which the light glances in equally magic fashion. And it is against this—our wealth of green forms—that we must deploy our color accents as summer advances. In dry, sunny areas we can install *Asphodeline lutea* (255), the towering yellow Jacob's-rod, and recall its glaucous leaves with *Euphorbia myrsinites*, and its golden florets with the low-growing 4-inch discs of Missouri primroses (190). Later, accidentally or by contrivance, we may find the purplish liatris among the nearby yucca leaves. Our repertory, at all seasons, can be crowded with lovely, commonplace and grossly underestimated plants like these.

One often searches long and hard for material that will bring individuality without being bizarre, exciting forms that contrast with but won't distress the

From July all through the winter, the rhythmed upthrusting red-panicled fruits of Rhus typhina, *the staghorn sumac (159), one of the most popular bird-feeding shrubs, are strong, valuable features at dry woods edges where the suckering habit of this 15- to 30-foot tree can be controlled. The more shrublike smooth or scarlet sumac,* Rhus glabra, *can also be an asset in dry places. But beware of* Rhus vernix, *the equally handsome poison sumac with greyish berries that rise to 20 feet in moist places.*

view. The yuccas are one neglected answer, responding staunchly even in very poor soil. I have used them at the edge of an informal but long path, planting them in big clumps where they serve as modifying material for a pine and dogwood background.

Yucca lends itself best not to flat but to irregular sunny terrain. There the giant panicled spikes tower one above the other in bold masses. Try them clustered asymmetrically beside a short stair or toward the base of a long one. Or group them along a curving rising approach-drive, where they sweep up against tall old conifers. They can be useful on a sunny impoverished slope in random clumps, and in old age achieve a stature of 12 feet, as dramatic in effect coming out of an old rock wall as the spectacular agaves we so admire in Mexico. And yuccas are always useful for cutting, coming at a time when the spring surge is over. Both *Y. filamentosa*, sometimes called Adam's needle (267), and *Y. flaccida* 'Ivory Tower,' with less drooping florets, are perfectly hardy in the heartland. If you are interested in moths, you can see the small ghostly white ones yuccas attract for pollination by using your flashlight some night while the plants are in bloom.

The "varied elevation" principle recommended for yuccas holds also for daylilies, tritomas, lycoris or similar flowers which tend to carry their blooms at about equal stem height, and otherwise form bands rather than the rising color masses irregular topography affords. Even old vegetable garden rhubarb, *Rheum rhabarbarum*, with its outsize, long-lasting, handsome leaves and creamy bloom-stalk, makes a definitive dense accent for transitional areas. Ornamental varieties of *Rheum* are cherished in the best English gardens, and I always promise myself to try growing them from seed—notably the alluring *R. alexandrae* and the showy *R. palmatum* which likes moisture.

Don't forget peonies, which, once established, can become really magnificent hillocks of foliage, especially if you choose a spectacular single, like Clusius' great red peony of Constantinople, *Paeonia peregrina*, or a tree peony, *P. suffruticosa* 'Dr. Rock,' which has large dark red poppylike splotches at the base of fluted semi-double white petals. Investigate the distinctive forms hybridized by Dr. A. P. Saunders from the peony species, flowers which recently made a clean sweep of awards at the internationally famed Chelsea Show.

See, too, accent suggestions made under the summer bulbs. And if you are willing to put up with the short life of biennials, try the named tall *Verbascums*, mullein hybrids.

Nothing is more regally dramatic than a clump of lilies backed by shrubbery, or rising majestically at the edge of a woods. How surprised a local gardener was when I told her years ago I was going to specialize in lilies. "And where would you get your bulbs?" she asked, for in those days healthy sources were rare. She was even more surprised when I replied, "From seed."

I was confident of success, for I had read—and believed—all the authorities.

I dug deep to put in sand and gravel drainage. I prepared beds so loamy that I "could plunge the hand down as far as the wrist." Now, thirty-five years later, my true lilies are still few and far between, but the reasons for their scarcity are not those I had anticipated. Lily seeds are, in fact, easy to germinate, and other methods of propagation even easier. Planting scales which offshoot from the bulbs and the bulblets of those types that produce them in the axils of their leaves is surefire, not to mention the easiest way of all—to buy the glorious de Graaff hybrid bulbs available in different varieties for a long season of bloom.

The problem continues to be protecting bulbs, bulblets, scales or seeds from ants and mice and all the other creatures who find them so toothsome. My one quite effortless success with lilies involves Madonnas, a group of them growing in a clump of black locust trees. The bulbs developed from scales which must have been inadvertently shoveled out of an experimental bed nearby when soil was being renewed. For years and years these lilies have persisted, increasing slowly because I always cut them generously for arranging. But the nitrogen-enriching powers of the locust roots seem to help the lilies, and also in some way shield them from rodent damage.

Nowhere else on our place do lilies enjoy such natural immunity. My only other unalloyed lily triumphs result when I go to the trouble of making cages for them: 14-inch deep cubicles constructed of $\frac{1}{4}$-inch flexible wire mesh. Even then, when I simply planted the lily bulbs in these sunken protectors, my precautions failed, though I followed all the other requirements: the gravel and sand drainage at the base, the setting of the bulb slightly askew on its own sand area over good loam, and neatly filling in the enormous hole made to insert the wire box. Only when I covered the last 2 inches between box and ground level with sharp-cut gravel did I meet with success. That final addition proved the ultimate mouse-deterrent. The lilies have sufficient room to increase, and added surface composting seems to give them enough nourishment to develop until they need dividing.

Lily bulbs should never be allowed to dry out and, if bought, should be planted as soon as possible, especially *L. candidum*, which in August sends out basal leaves that survive the winter.

We all have our favorite lily types, and one that really "sends" me is the Canada lily. For it and *Cardiocrinum*, the prodigious Himalayan lily, I am willing to go to very great pains. *L. canadense* needs acid soil and moisture to attain real stature. I plant it where drainage is good, so that the runoff coming through lime soil will be swift. To assure even more rapid drainage, I put a slanted sand-covered rock under the bulb, and surround and cover the site with well-rotted oakleaf compost. My reward comes in late June, when the woods are almost solid green and the lilies' rich orange-yellow bells hang majestically from their candelabralike supports. *Cardiocrinum* needs only patience and a fat purse if you assign it a semishaded, deep, loamy location. I have bloomed it twice over the years. As it is monocarpic, it pays to purchase a few small bulbs that can grow on along with one of flowering size. In achieving a 3-inch-caliper stem to 8 feet from a base of large heart-shaped leaves, there may be as many as 20 foot-long down-thrusting trumpets altogether, the interior marked in maroon stripes. As the flowers fade beautiful pods form which, as they ripen, turn theatrically upward. From bud to seed is an inspiring progression worth rapt observation.

For a similar experience—this one from the depths of an armchair—nothing I know quite equals the wonderfully synchronized photographs that trace the career of a poppy from seed to bloom and back to seed again in *The Hidden Life of Flowers* by Jean Michel Guilcher.

Some of the labiates make fine accents. You can always identify members of this family—mints, sages, thymes and so many other herby plants—by their square stems, opposite leaves and two-lipped, five-parted flowers. Should you want to investigate further these and other flower-family relationships in general, and are baffled by the conventional approach, see Fischer and Harshbarger, *The Flower Family Album* or Anne Dowden's *Look at a Flower*, both of which make such unforgettable visual sense.

Sages are among the most satisfactory and dramatic of the labiates. Even the native *Salvia lyrata*, the lyre-leaved sage of the prairies, is effective. Good old *S. officinalis*, the garden sage with which you stuff the turkey, will make beautiful contrast plantings that last for years. But don't neglect its dwarf form or its purple variants, such as *S. o.* 'Purpurascens,' an evergreen used so effectively as border edgings in France. Sometime, too, I should like to grow pink-flowered cultivars like 'Inchmery,' the coppery, light crimson 'Emperor,' the dark, rich red 'Enid Anderson,' and others in tones ranging from white to deep pink with a maroon center in the 'Highlands' strain—varieties which as of now I know only through books.

Try the very hardy perennial sages like *S. superba*, also known as *virgata* or *nemerosa*, with its 3-foot-high purply-bluish spikes, which will continue to bloom over a two-month period; or the meadow sage, *pratensis* or *haematodes*, in a range of color tones; *przewalski*, with its almost bell-like flowers; or *glutinosa*, pale yellow. One of the toughest sages, a most heavenly blue, is *pitcheri*. It has rather thin leaves and stiff stems, but its synonym, *azurea* var. *grandiflora*, indicates that I am not the first to value its size and vividness. Grow the self-seeding biennial *S. argentea*, the silver sage, for its huge magnificent hoarfrosty leaves and tall branched white blooms, or *S. sclarea*, clary sage, distinguished by white and pale blue flower heads and reddish bracts. Actually, I prefer for style the similar but more interestingly colored *S. sclarea* var. *turkestanica*, but its leaves have from their odor earned it, not I fear unjustly, the epithet of "unwashed lady." These clarys self-sow freely, as does *S. pratensis*.

Other labiates suitable as accent plants are *Phlomis tuberosa*, Jerusalem sage, whose seemingly whorled leaves enhance its axil-clustered bloom, and *Physostegia virginiana*, the false dragon head, native to our Midwest prairies and so often seen in clumps in the sun next to country mailboxes. There is a beautiful white cultivar, 'Summer Snow.' And remember the labiate monardas, with their sharp color and structure, which charm hummingbirds and butterflies as well as ourselves.

When we hear katydids we know we can count on hostas in variety. The queen of them all, *H. plantaginea* 'Grandiflora' (below), the August lily, spans the frost-free days with its rhythmed, stylish heart-shaped leaves in perfect condition, and with pure white 4-inch blooms of rich fragrance the entire month for which it is named. This plant favors densely shaded places. Newer hybrids, also fragrant, such as 'Royal Standard,' white, and 'Honeybells,' slightly lavender, make claims to greater sun tolerance but will have to fight to replace the stable

old Chinese form which can still be found flourishing under many a fin-de-siècle porch railing. While the leaves of 'Grandiflora' are always handy for bouquets, its white blooms are somewhat more difficult to arrange, as each floret lasts only one day and they are so carried that one side of the stalk tends to be empty. Some of my friends complain that, when naturalized, *H. plantaginea* disappears. One says "mice," another "slugs." If you suspect slugs, tempt them with a little beer protected from the elements in a plastic bottle lying on its side. But first, cut a few holes in the side of the bottle above what will be the fluid line, fill, and slightly sink the container to make access easy. The slugs then crawl in and drown. These pests will also collect under old overturned citrus rinds or potato peelings, but if you use such bait you have to collect and destroy the catch each morning. It is a more constructive practice, perhaps, to encourage or import toads, one of the slugs' greatest natural enemies. Hosta damage often attributed to slugs may actually be caused by the taxus or black vine weevil, a nocturnal beetle. If this creature is the cause, you will also notice depredations on Japanese yew, other conifers and lilacs.

In any case, do find a congenial place for this hosta, a truly magnificent plant which has endured for me in one grouping for over thirty years, with occasional dollops of compost and separating every decade or so.

Other members of the hosta or plantain lily family are almost equally reward-ing. Distinguished for their fragrant bloom and disease-free, handsomely ribbed foliage in distinctive and often variegated greens, hostas are finally enjoying as much favor here as they have for centuries in Japan. Ambitious things are afoot in American hosta circles, and it's hard to keep up with introductions, especially since hostas hybridize easily and the nomenclature was and still is in a highly disordered state.

Well-known types (opposite) have the flowers scaled to the approximate height they rise on their own stalks above the jointure of the leaf and its stem. Leaves are shown cut at ground level.

Most hostas flourish in high shade. Those, however, with either waxy or frosted leaves bloom more profusely in sun—even noon sun. If they show a slight browning at the leaf edges, you can arrest it by watering the roots, which, because of the heavy canopy of leaves, may not be receiving enough moisture. Many hostas, if planted in loamy, well-drained soil, form hearty clumps that stand division if the clumps are sliced in pie shapes with a sharp spade. The crowns should be reset almost at the ground surface and, if separated in the fall, mulched against heaving. Those with variegated leaves may revert, after trans-planting, to a solid green. Should the variegation fail to return, try moving the plant to a location where it gets less light or a less nitrogenous soil.

You may enjoy a long season of bloom beginning in mid-June with *H. sieboldiana*, known too as *glauca*. Note (opposite) its densely flowered short white lavender-tinged bloom and great grey leaf blades up to a foot long on foot-high

Hosta ventricosa   *Hosta lancifolia*   *Hosta sieboldiana*

stems. The greyness of the foliage may be diminished if *sieboldiana* and its cultivars are too heavily fertilized or too deeply shaded.

By July *H. fortunei* flowers, and its forms, *H. fortunei* var. *gigantea* and *robusta glauca*, have blooms that reach from 3 to 5 feet. Late in the month the most prolific bloomer, spreader and seeder, the Chinese *H. ventricosa*, formerly known as *caerulea* (165), shows its long, dark, rather constricted purplish funnels, white striped, above deep green leaves. About the same time you can expect a generous burst of lavender bells from the old *H. lancifolia,* also called *lanceolata* or *japonica,* more delicate in form, with leaves about 1 foot tall, with a lustrous tender color. This is one of the better edging hostas, as is *H. minor* 'Alba,' which blooms a month later. In late July *H. decorata* 'Thomas Hogg' sends its lavender spikes above its rather blunt leaves, which are neatly edged in white, as does *H. undulata,* which can be seen emerging (129) with its eccentrically variegated foliage about 9 inches tall. *Undulata* comes in several leaf sizes and in a sturdy all-green form, *H. undulata* 'Erromena,' just as some of the green species already described have forms that are variegated, like *H. fortunei* 'Aureomarginata,' with a narrow yellow margin, or that very handsome *H. fortunei* 'Albopicta' which early in the season shows a chartreuse margin around a clear yellowish center. Later, the whole leaf turns dark green. Last of the hostas to bloom, as its name implies, is *H. tardiflora,* which shows its 12-inch stem of purplish to white bells and its lanceolate leaf well into October.

By the first week in August the hardy or everlasting pea, Lathyrus latifolius, *in its lovely white form has become rampant and strikes a clear note against the sophisticated muddy-pink petals and somber orange-brown cones of a towering composite,* Echinacea purpurea, *the purple coneflower. Through the airy blue stars and pale green foliage of* Campanula americana, *the tall bellflower, one sees, in the woods beyond, masses of ethereal autumn lycoris,* Lycoris squamigera *(172), which dramatically reiterate the tones of the coneflower petals.*

Fall Enchantment

By the end of summer there are, even in the woods, brown patches where the soil has been baked clean of its old leaf cover to reveal its readiness and need for renewal. A mixed cover begins to accumulate late in the season with a few dogwood leaves, followed shortly by the larger, even more brilliant crimson leaves of *Nyssa sylvatica*, the tupelo, or sour gum tree. The complex tonality of the woods floor increases with every shower and every gust of wind. Watching this protective potential piling up reminds me of the cover I have offered my plantings through the years, and what I have learned about the give and take of mulches.

The first mulch I ever tried was of ground corncobs, about which I had read glowing accounts. I applied it too generously and too late to help conserve the moisture from spring rains. What's more, the mulch was applied dry and unripened. I didn't realize that, unless I first put down some nitrogen-rich substance like fish meal, the stimulus for tissue breakdown would have to come from the limited nitrogen resources already in my soil. The reaction, while not particularly obvious at first in the deep-rooted perennials, was for some prime nursery-bought annuals nothing short of traumatic. No amount of watering seemed to help them establish. They grew yellower and more puny. By fall, when weeding, I came on a number of minuscule survivors, looking like the dwarfed pot plants in my old doll house. Among them were petunias, which had shrunk into miniatures, each about an inch high.

I next tried peat. But, used as a mulch, peat, as we have seen, also has drawbacks (101). With buckwheat hulls, which look charming, the situation improved—perhaps because their high cost made my application a thin one, just enough to allow a mild amount of condensation and, in all probability, to reduce the amount of nitrogen required for decomposition.

This crucial breakdown factor is most clearly seen in wood mulches. For wood bark you need just over a pound of nitrogen per hundred pounds of mulch. If the wood is in chip form you need about two pounds to satisfy the quickly released nitrogen demands of one hundred pounds of mulch.

Because wood chips are often available from utility companies for the asking when their crews are in the neighborhood shredding trimmings, their use is on the increase, not only for mulches but for path surfacing. They look well in the latter role, and are quite functional. If you have watched carefully, though, you may have observed on such paths the sudden appearance of a vast assortment of toadstools and other fungal outcrops. While it is entirely normal for all untreated wood to break down through similar activity, some authorities fear that a concentration of harmful pathogens is encouraged by excessive use of untreated wood in planted areas when the season is unusually rainy, or if drainage is poor. Where mulches mold, acids form beneath them which exclude air and inhibit the assimilation of nitrogen.

Whether you experiment with cocoa or pecan hulls, straw, bagasse, pine needles or even sweet gum balls, you may conclude, as I have, that in the long run using half-ripened compost as mulch instead is no costlier, and is far less chancy for the home gardener. Such compost definitely adds fertilization. It doesn't pack, blow, mold or form a fire hazard. It is helpfully water-retentive, and for the woods gardener it looks right—as do leaf molds, which I also use, but am careful to diversify. Not long ago warnings went out to watch oakleaf mold for toadstools, which might indicate the presence of the virulent oak root fungus. Here again a compost mulch, which has eliminated many disease factors in its "burning" process, may prove to have the added advantage of greater safety. If I have not already persuaded you to keep a compost pile going, see page 94.

Should you use mulches other than compost, the time of application is important. As with compost, it is well not to apply it when the ground is baked dry. It is best to apply mulches in the fall only after the ground freezes hard. With all organic mulches be careful not to apply them too heavily and to keep them off the crowns and away from the immediate area of bark-bearing plants, where they encourage burrowing animals and, when wet, fungi. Permanent stone and pebble mulches are increasingly suggested. They do help retain moisture but offer no fertilization and can be pesky time-absorbers when weeds or leaves need removal.

I have mentioned my delight in discovering Lob's Wood, with its far-flung daffodil tapestries. Now that fall is on the way, let me further acknowledge my debt to its owner, Carl Krippendorf, for sharing his concept of a woods garden for all seasons through the introduction of hardy exotics. Carl was an inveterate record keeper, and, fortunately, his observations and experiments are charmingly incorporated by Elizabeth Lawrence in two books based on their correspondence: *The Little Bulbs*, and the recently written *Lob's Wood*.

The fall bulb sequence, which adds so welcome a new dimension to otherwise relatively scarce native bloom, is not difficult to prepare for. The most rampant weeds can be pulled (108) or grass-whipped, so that lycoris may be enjoyed as a dominant in early August and the low-growing colchicum into October.

Colchicum's name reveals its major source of origin as eastern Mediterranean. When it's called "meadow saffron" and "autumn crocus," confusion begins, for the true spring and fall crocuses are irids and a colchicum is a liliaceous plant having its divisions in six rather than three parts as in crocuses.

There are other maddening but thrilling things about both the leaves and the flowers of colchicum: thrilling in that the flowers pop up pristinely fresh without any leaves at a time when other blooms reveal ravages of insects and summer drought; thrilling, too, in their generosity, for some corms produce from three to as many as twenty blossoms each; thrilling in their power to catch the filtered sunlight with the vibrancy of stained glass, or to deftly highlight shade;

Bulbs That Bloom Without Their Leaves

Some of our most rewarding fall florescence stems from a group of bulbs that bloom without their leaves. Masking verdure about them is so rife that the taller ones seem suspended in space. They must all be grown in areas where their foliage, copious in spring, can die back undisturbed through mid-July. Bulbs and leaves are shown here in spring condition, blooms in their fall state.

  Left to right below are Lycoris incarnata, *the fragrant lycoris, almost identical in leafage to* L. squamigera, *the early August "magic lily"—their leafage seen*

Lycoris
incarnata

Lycoris
radiata

Colchicum
speciosum

Frances
Jones
Poetker,
Arranger

Probably there is more immediately exciting beauty in a lively florist shop than in any other place of comparable size in the world. Color, all kinds of color—bold, subtle, brilliant, subdued, passionate, cool—seem to be erupting all around you. A thousand heady perfumes from all over the world fill the air. As you gaze into cooled, glass-fronted cases, roses, carnations, orchids, lilies and a hundred other blooms, each the end product of the imaginative and scientific collaboration of nature and man, strike the eye. These flowers are the result of generations of selection and crossing for color, fragrance, sturdiness and endurance. Despite their distinguished if admittedly mixed ancestry, these plants are strong, bred to be handled and arranged to beautify your home and to retain their beauty and freshness for a remarkably long period. They need no undue care. The term "hothouse," commonly used to describe someone or something as fragile or incapable of withstanding adversity, has only categorical application to these flowers. Today's highly bred plants are about as delicate as Olympic athletes.

With such magnificent yet tough flowers readily available at your neighborhood florist, why should you take the time and trouble to gather wildlings and hardy exotics to decorate your home? Many of these local plants fade quickly after cutting. They must be treated with great care. Their non-negotiable demands for proper temperature and humidity seem ridiculously pretentious; after all, many people say they are nothing but common old weeds. What aesthetic rewards do the native plants offer? Their colors rarely, if ever, match the richness of cultivated flowers. Even when imaginatively arranged, these plants born of woods and fields lack the familiar excitement generated by their relatives grown by professional growers.

For anyone who has tried one or two arrangements with native plants and found the results unrewarding, I think the key word in the previous sentence is "familiar." The flower lover who has worked only with cultivated plants from the florists' inevitably develops certain standards of beauty and performance. Somehow the native plants don't quite meet these same standards. But to appreciate the often understated beauty of native plants indoors, one develops another set of standards no less demanding than the first. In short, we learn through experience to look at wild and naturalized plants in a different way to find their special aesthetic appeal.

Working exclusively with cultivated flowers is rather like having been exposed only to academic art. The first encounter with "primitives" is likely to seem childish and uninteresting. Only after living with fine primitive art for a while and giving it due consideration do the creative sophistication of the artist and the subtle results he has achieved with exotic concepts and techniques become apparent. Arrangements with native materials require this type of understanding.

Color, for example, usually plays a diminished role. Texture, form and

A Different Kind of Beauty

189

line are the dominant interests in native plant arrangements, and therefore more than usual consideration must be given to the choice of containers and the background that will best display these traits in the finished creations. The results, I assure you, will more than repay the extra effort put into gathering the plants, catering to the exasperating care their tenderness often demands, and putting up with the frustrating difficulties of working with materials that sometimes seem as unadaptable to arrangement as cooked spaghetti. In the end you will have created something wholly your own of flora indigenous or adjusted to your immediate area, something of rare beauty that has the subtle attraction of the unfamiliar, and something that is a part of the inspiring seasonal cycle of growth. The more interesting the plants you grow the year around, the more exciting potential for rich, interesting arrangements you will possess.

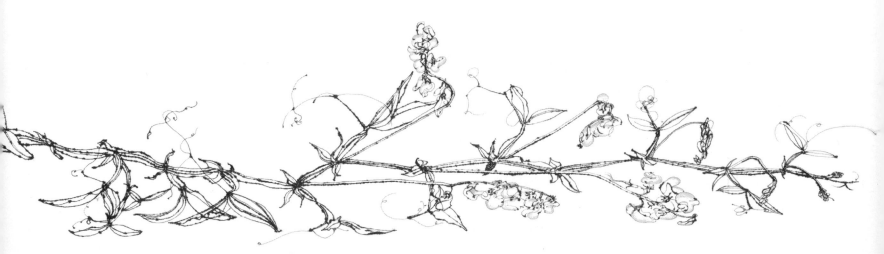

Lathyrus latifolius

The vasculum, that former symbol of botanical research, once was a great symbol; it announced to the world you were big enough to go botanizing in earnest. The tubular, tightly sealed metal case, lined with damp blotters, banged against your ribs or pulled taut as its strap caught on a twig. To the collector of native plants a vasculum used to be as necessary as a creel was to the fly fisherman, but today, an insulated ice bucket with a little water in the bottom, or even a plastic garment bag, can give one much more scope than the cramped vasculum (275).

But the principle remains the same. Almost 90% of the volume of plant structure is water, and loss of original turgidity is difficult to reestablish. So from the moment you pick, take every precaution to prevent cellular collapse. Protection from drying winds and sun and provision of a moist environment are essential.

For the short haul, in your own garden, you can use a cutting bucket (255). For the longer trip you will do well to use plastic bags. If the plastic is no heavier than the weight of a gratis dry cleaning bag, there is, even when the bag is sealed, a slight beneficial admission of fresh air which, when combined with the condensation from the moisture in the plants, keeps even the most fragile specimens in fine condition for hours.

Pre-plastic ages have faced the preservation problem in their own fashion. The Chinese, when they sent the emperor his imperial tree peonies from Lolang to Peking by horsemen that rode day and night, sealed the peony stems with wax, wrapped the blooms in cabbage leaves and protected the wrappings in bamboo cages so the blooms reached his imperial highness in prime condition.

The Medicis sent tender blooms to Marie in France. Slung on donkey back were boxes centered with hollow rods, filled with damp moss, and pierced so that stems of freshly cut flowers could be inserted. These blooms were then carried long distances.

Today in the highlands of Mexico you can imagine yourself an Aztec noble enjoying, for a mere pittance, the orchids that will travel with you for weeks when put up in a section of banana palm trunk which creates an ideal environment and yet lets you extract the flowers at your pleasure.

In the French markets it is still possible to see watercress packed by wreath-like placement in woven reed baskets—an excellent way of packing for safe, unblemished condition on arrival.

When you pack in plastic, have pipe cleaners, rubber bands, or plastic- or paper-coated wire ready for easy closures, for it is important to keep bags closed except when you add to your gatherings. It is also wise to keep the filled plastic bag out of direct sunlight. Collectors should also have with them some thoroughly dampened, porous paper—old newspapers will serve nicely. Wrapping plants in this paper before putting them in the plastic will keep them damp until you return home.

Regardless of what kind of container you use, your gear should also include

A Collector Arms For The Hunt

damp cotton, mud or sealing spray to plug the ends of plants such as wild delphinium, whose stems serve as water reservoirs, and waxed paper or foil, precut into squares, to put between blooms, like Queen Anne's lace, that would otherwise become intertangled in the carrying kit. Quite probably you'll need a book of matches or a cigarette lighter to burn the ends and halt the flow of milky sap from flowers like poppies and euphorbias, and of vital fluid from the cut stems of hellebores, bloodroot, wild lettuce and most water plants—and, from practical experience, we add maidenhair fern. Protect the upper portions of the plant from the flame and heat by the use of a dampened paper shield. For more details about packing your plastic bag or container see below.

Finally we come to the cutting tools themselves. Pruning shears or heavy scissors, a sharp knife and a foot-long handsaw with tiny teeth are basic. Without them you may fatally damage root stocks, ruin a bush or tree, or uproot entire plants when your nonlethal objective is merely to collect a blossom, a branch or some foliage. If you're going out for lofty growing plants like mistletoe or vines, you'll find a tree pruner with an extension arm is a big help.

Be sure to tuck into your basket a good field guide. Don't let your ignorance of botany intimidate you; get a book. For example, Roger Tory Peterson's and Margaret McKenny's *A Field Guide to Wildflowers* employs a visual approach, arranged by color and form with symbols for the great flower families. This book will quickly sharpen your knowledge of plant relationships and add tremendously to your acuity in sensing the individuality of plants and flowers.

And now, with the safari equipped, let's head for garden, roadside, fields and woods. If you'll be exploring on property not your own, be sure to obtain *written* collecting privileges from the owner.

Oenothera missouriensis

A collector should be an early riser, at least on days when plants are to be gathered. During the first hour or so after dawn there is usually considerable moisture on the ground and in the atmosphere, and the plant cells are at maximum distention. But if you oversleep, wait until the late afternoon for your junket. Unless conditions are right, native flowers are as temperamental as opera divas; plants gathered at midday are likely to be little more than candidates for the compost heap by the time you get them home.

When you go to the fields or woods, with your vasculum or other carrier at the ready, conservation must be the guide for everything you do. Because too many enthusiasts have collected with all the restraint shown by the Romans at Carthage, many lovely plants have been wiped out entirely and many others are in danger of extinction. If you don't know which plants are on the "protected" list in your particular region, consult your local conservation officer or write to the Wildflower Preservation Society at 3740 Oliver St. N. W., Washington, D. C. 20015. If you forget your list or are in doubt, refrain!

A final word on the subject of conservation. One segment of nature lovers, comprised largely of our younger citizens, proclaims that any picking of wild plants is ecological vandalism. This position does more credit to their concern with our environment than to their knowledge of botany. Judicious harvesting of many plants not only does no harm but in many instances stimulates growth. Wood violets and celandine poppies are just a few that fall into this category. When blooms are permitted to die and dry on the plant, production of more blooms is, on most plants other than bulbs, usually low. When flowers are picked, growth of new flowers is usually stimulated.

In taking plants that are not "protected," all you need to be a good conservationist are common sense, some slight knowledge of the physiology of flora, and a few simple skills. Obviously, you won't make all your cuttings in one small section of ground. If you take a few here and a few there, the growth will continue to be lush. Don't cut much of the foliage from bulbous plants, as the leaves are essential for survival—it's a good idea always to leave some foliage, no matter what kind of plant you cut. Naturally you don't want to pull up a plant by the roots, so don't pick or break anything by hand. A sharp knife is the best tool for most collecting, but a good pair of scissors will serve as a fairly adequate substitute. If the plants you are cutting have nodes, cut above or below them, as water intake is slower at the node itself. Plants in their very early growing stage are especially tender, and will almost never last when cut carelessly. This applies especially to spring ephemerals (65). On the other hand, material gathered past its prime, like Miss Millay's dual-lighted candle, "will not last the night."

Except for hollow-stemmed plants, all stems should be cut at an angle. We may as well deal at once with the rather special handling hollow-stemmed plants require. After you have cut them straight across, force-feed some water

In The Field

into the cut end with an eyedropper and then seal the opening with a dab of mud or with damp cotton inserted as a cork. The sealed end can be cut off when you insert the flower in your arrangement. Other plants may require their own kind of treatment in the field, but at least you don't have to wet-nurse them.

It will be helpful to remember a few other tips about cutting. If you are gathering hardy miniature gladioli, excise the top two or three buds from the tip. If possible, take appleblossoms and magnolias when they are in bud and immediately crush the stems if you're placing them in gathering cans. When you cut fairly sizable branches from trees or stalks from shrubs—anything large enough to require the use of a saw—protect the tree or bush by covering the wound with a coating of special tree paint—regular paint has adverse effects—or sealant. This precaution is usually not necessary if the branch or stalk is small enough in diameter to be taken with snips or pruning shears.

Getting cut material home in good condition should pose no difficulties if you have selected only things in bud or in a mature, prime state and have brought protective equipment with you. Flowers immediately plunged into warm or tepid water should survive nicely. But if you are using a favorite large plastic bag as your carrying case, wet newspaper wrapped around the stems will protect the plants adequately. The soggy newsprint is also excellent for preserving ferns, grape leaves and other tender foliages. Simply put them between the layers of paper and then carefully deposit them in the bag. The smaller bags, ordinarily used for sandwiches and salads, are ideal for carrying mosses, lichens, plate and other fleshy fungi. Tissue paper on the top surfaces of the latter will keep them unblemished.

In filling large containers, don't hesitate to pack materials fairly closely as long as the crowding does not cause entanglement or mechanical injury to the plants. Tangling can be a problem with lacy umbels such as dill, and therefore I advise placing plastic or lightly waxed paper between the flower heads. And now that I've made this nice, sweeping generalization about the democracy of the carrying case, let me partially nullify it by noting that certain plants, such as pansies, mignonettes, snapdragons and evergreens, are the Hatfields and McCoys of the plant world and should be packed separately; they have an unfortunate effect on other flowers. Apparently they give off vapors—to use a genteel nineteenth-century word—that cause rapid wilting. Apples are a prime example; they give off ethylene gas which hastens deterioration of other fruits or flowers near them.

But most important of all, remember the heavy moisture base of plants and do all you can to keep them turgid but not so wet that the petals will lose their bloom or the leaves decay.

When you return from a collecting trip, give first attention to yourself. Drop the carrying case in a convenient corner, grab a bar of strong soap—this is no time for the "kind-to-baby's-skin" variety—and head for the shower. During your outing you may have inadvertently handled any of a number of toxic plants or brushed them with your arms or legs. A vigorous shower, taken as soon as possible after the contact, is one way to avoid penalties. The best way, of course, is to know the enemy (121).

Unless you plan to dry the materials you have gathered—a process that will be discussed later—the job of conditioning the plants should begin as soon as you have completed your precautionary scrubbing. Most native and naturalized plants should be conditioned before you arrange them. This procedure not only prolongs their lives, but in some instances makes them easier to work with when you are arranging them.

The first order of business is to strip the plants of all foliage that would otherwise be below the waterline of the temporary containers in which they'll be placed. These containers, like the ones in which the arrangements will be made, should be of nonrusting material such as glass, ceramic, galvanized metal, wood or plastic. Use roomy receptacles for conditioning; the narrow-necked types squeeze the stems. The containers should also be absolutely clean; wash them with hot, sudsy water to which a dollop of ammonia has been added. Rinse well. Native plants suffer enough trauma being cut; don't complicate their adjustment by making them cope with a lot of unnecessary bacteria.

Stripping the lower foliage is about the only general rule that should be followed in conditioning, except that of supporting weak stems with paper cuffs until they become turgid with water. Different plants require different treatments. Among the supplies you are likely to need at one time or another are boiling and cold water, sugar, oil of peppermint, salt and a sharp knife for recutting softer plants. You may also want to crush all hard-stemmed materials with a hammer, although recent tests cast some doubt on the necessity of following this procedure. I favor crushing.

Now let's get down to specifics. For the following flora, stick the ends of the stems into boiling water for about a minute and then place in a fairly shallow container of cold water: mertensia, forget me nots, grape hyacinths, and lilies-of-the-valley. All of the narcissus or jonquils and most bulbous plants also prefer cool, shallow water, but the boiling-water treatment is not used.

With woody-stemmed plants, add a teaspoon of sugar per quart of water in the temporary container. Sugar is, incidentally, the basis of most of the commercial cut-flower preservatives.

For ilex, delphinium and asters, the water should be at room temperature. For aquilegia and daisies, add about a half-dozen drops of oil of peppermint to each quart of room-temperature water.

In principle, it is advisable to recut all stems under water to prevent air bubbles sealing the base of the stems.

Conditioning Materials

For most plants the water need be only deep enough to cover about one-half to two-thirds of the stems, but for hollyhocks and Queen Anne's lace you should immerse up to the necks of the blooms.

Get out the hammer for chrysanthemums, evergreens and lilacs and crush the stem ends before placing them in lukewarm water.

For foliage of certain trees and shrubs—and for foliage only—I recommend conditioning which actually becomes a preservative: a mixture of equal parts glycerine and water. (The usual proportions of two parts water to one part glycerine I have found unsatisfactory.) Before putting the plants into the liquid, cut out defects in the leaves and then pound the bottom 2 inches of each stem so that both the fiber and the bark are split. At least two weeks are required for the foliage to absorb all the solution necessary. During this absorption period, wipe the leaves occasionally with a cloth dampened with either water or glycerine. This will check drying before the soaking solution reaches the edges. If the humidity is low in the place where the foliage is stored, spray the plants between leaf wipings with a water-filled atomizer to further cut down the loss of moisture.

While we're on the subject of spraying, here are a few other suggestions you may find useful. Tender materials such as maidenhair fern, aquilegia and lily-of-the-valley will last longer if you spray them daily with water or once with a preservative available at your florist or garden supply shop. Such a preservative is excellent for natives like aster, monarda, rudbeckia and solidago. A floral glue may be used on seed pods or seeded heads of shrubs like sumac, and grasses like briza. This treatment helps prevent the seeds from dropping off and prolongs the decorative life of the seed head. Several drops of warm paraffin in the center perform a somewhat similar service for water-lilies. A little of the viscous fluid poured in the center of the blooms will keep them open. This is a temporary measure, for their life has a limited span (12).

A final word about additives, preservatives and such. Keep the aspirin bottle in the medicine cabinet and pennies in your purse or pocket. Aspirin will soothe at least some of the headaches that modern life induces, and pennies are useful for—well, there must be *some* use for pennies in today's world—but neither has any effect on the longevity of cut plants.

The storage area, however, does profoundly affect their life span. After you have completed conditioning, place the plants in a spot where the light is meager, the humidity is high and the temperature is low—between forty-five and fifty-five degrees is ideal. Some movement of air is also helpful, but keep the materials out of drafts to reduce drying of the plant surface. How long the plants are to remain in this conditioning limbo depends on what you have gathered. A few hours is about right for soft, fleshy plants; the sturdier variety can be kept overnight. After this period is ended, you can begin the creative job of arranging.

Many native plants can be successfully dried, but not all of them retain enough beauty to make the undertaking worthwhile. A list of those I choose for drying appears at the end of this section. The selection is, of course, subjective, so don't let these suggestions deter you from experimenting with other materials if you think they may serve your purpose.

The simplest method of drying flowers and seed pods is to hang them upside down in a darkened area with some circulation of air and low humidity, preferably not more than thirty-five percent. A clear plastic covering with some tiny holes in it to permit the entry of air will keep off most of the dust. Unless your interest in the plants is gastronomic—i.e., you plan to use them for seasoning or infusion of tea or vinegar—rather than aesthetic, I suggest the use of a retardant spray to discourage insect life.

A faster way to dry flora is with sand. But be sure the sand is clean and *dry*; either heat it in a slow oven until all moisture is gone or expose it to hot sunlight. If the sand is to be left outside overnight, cover it with plastic to protect it from dew or rain. When the sand is thoroughly dry, make a floor of it, about an inch or so thick, on the bottom of a sturdy wood or tin box. Now place the plants on the sand and carefully sift additional sand around them until they are lightly covered. If this procedure is carried out with a sufficiently considerate hand, even delicate blooms will not be damaged. The drying process will take from several days to two weeks; the fleshier the plant, the longer it must remain in the sand box.

Borax, which is somewhat faster acting than sand, can be used in the same way. Such plants as daisies and narcissus, which are light in texture, will be nicely dry in about a day and a half in borax. Others, like arums and cat-tails, will require about three to four days—even longer if they are large specimens. Incidentally, the same borax can be used over and over again. But by whatever means you dry the materials—hanging, sand or borax—be certain to spray the plants with a sealant when the drying process is over. Otherwise they will reabsorb moisture from the air like a dry sponge dropped into water. Amelia Leavitt Hill, in her book, *Arranging Flowers from the Roadside, Fields and Woods*, gives an excellent summation of particularly good material for drying, along with some of her own suggestions on effective methods of preservation.

There are certain hazards common to dried plants: large leaves tend to curl, and the petals of flowers to shatter. To prevent both phenomena, use a plastic spray or nonwater-based hair lacquer on the *backs* of petals and the *underside* of leaves before and after drying. This step will keep you from using language common in contemporary theatrical performances but inappropriate to nature lovers. In the case of bamboo the leaves may be ironed with a cool iron to keep them green and flat.

Most of my choices for drying are autumn rather than spring flowers, because they have stronger skeletons and more interestingly developed seed pods.

Drying Plants

Asters, the goldenrods, liatris, almost all grasses—foxtail, bottlebrush, oats, rye, barley, wheat—cat-tails or bulrushes (spray first with a sealer before maturity), lunaria, aquilegia, bittersweet, wisteria, oak with acorn clusters, sycamore balls, teasel, delphinium, sumac with foliage stripped from the stems, and iris and dictamnus pods are favorite materials.

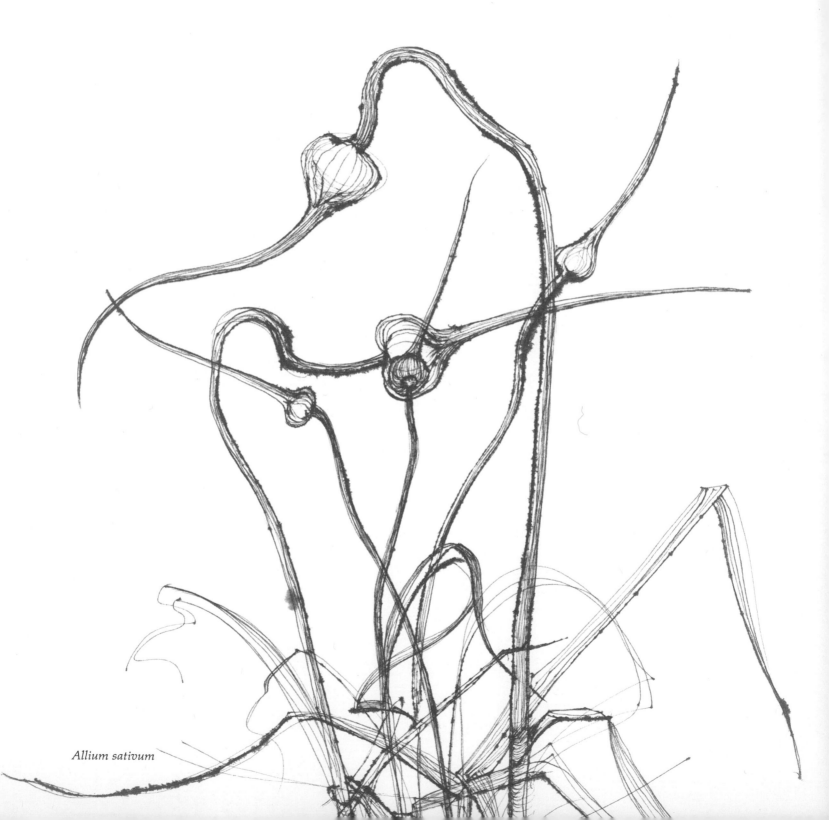

Allium sativum

When a good architect designs a building, he is concerned with sound construction, the beauty of the structure and its appropriateness to the background against which it will be seen. These are also the prime considerations of a flower arranger. Or at least they should be. The most exciting design concept in the world brings only bleak disappointment if, in realization, it begins to fall apart minutes after its completion. Similarly, a handsome, well-constructed arrangement is time wasted if it is simply plopped anywhere that's convenient with no thought given to the suitability of the background. Even the Taj Mahal would lose disastrously if surrounded by ranch-type houses.

Creating a structurally sound flower arrangement does not require a degree from M.I.T., but the designer must know how to build a foundation adequate for the demands to be made upon it, and how to provide extra support and reinforcement where needed. The latter is especially important in working with native plants, many of which lack the sturdiness of cultivated flora.

HOLDERS

As the foundation for the floral structure, the holder should be chosen with care. For heavy, large-scale and line designs (200–201), I usually find the needle-point type the best. These holders come in a variety of sizes, shapes, weights, densities and lengths of pins. When buying them, hold out for the rustproof kind if at all possible. Some are made as part of a cuplike well to serve as a container as well as the base of the arrangement; because solid weight is necessary, brass or lead is recommended. With use, the pins may become bent somewhat, but that is no reason for discarding the holder. Instead, get yourself an Oriental pin straightener, a tube that fits around the bent pin and, with a little wiggling, brings it back to an upright position.

If you have even the slightest doubt about the ability of the needle-point, or any other kind of holder, to support your arrangement, and you are as incapable as I am of figuring out the center of gravity mathematically, anchor the holder to the base of the container with modeling clay, suction cups, or stones. Or you can give added stability to the pin-type container by overlapping about half of it with a second holder of the same variety. The second holder is placed upside down so that half of its pins can mesh with half of those of the holder that will support the materials.

For lighter and smaller designs there is a wide range of commercial or homemade holders you can see. One favorite is the "birdcage" (201), which permits great flexibility of design because material can be inserted at many angles. Chicken wire, crumpled into a ball so that the holes appear at different levels, and fastened in place with tabs of adhesive tape offers the same advantage. If, however, the material you're using requires especially firm footing and additional support for the first several inches of the stems, fold the chicken wire into layers. For certain kinds of flowers, like reeds, rushes and clusters of grasses, I'm fond

Holders,
Containers
And
Settings

Shown on the left are holders that resolve one of the greatest problems in flower-arranging stability. With heavy shrub branches use two large needle pinholders, called kenzans (f). Use one so the branch can be impaled on the projecting pins. Use the other, with its heavy metal base uppermost, to counterbalance the weight. There are similar models with plastic bases, but these usually prove to be too light and fragile. If plastic or any other light holders are used, and they tend to tip, anchor the holder with very sticky florist's or modeling clay rolled into a ribbon before adding water to the container.

A more sophisticated kenzan of brass (b) with an adjustable bar adds control at a higher level. The lead strip, shown here (a) in glass to clarify the explanation, is a highly versatile support. If necessary, more than one strip can be used; they can be clipped anywhere along the rim of the container and wrapped around the stem.

The geometric Oriental models in (c), (g) and (h), decorative in themselves, are good for small arrangements in shallow bowls. They sometimes need a supplementary piece of stem within the interstices to brace individual flowers. In contrast, (d), while not so attractive, is more practical because of its less rigid wire holders and rubber-suctioned base. Foliage can be used to hide the holder.

Well-types (e) and (i) are useful on flat trays or wood and stone slabs. If tall material is used, it can be further braced with a spiral wire inserted in the pin or support area as seen in (i).

Birdcage holders (j), most practical in rustproof heavy metal, come in round, oval or rectangular shapes. Stems may be inserted at an angle. Additional control can be given by using crumpled chicken wire (k), available in hardware stores. Chicken wire is most suitable when the arrangement is light in weight. Use 1½- to 2-inch wire mesh, preferably in galvanized, nonrusting material. One- to 1½-inch narrow lead strips (l), slit for stem insertion, permit you to improvise holders for irregularly shaped or free-form containers.

For arrangements of lilies and similar plants whose long stems you resist cutting because the bulb really needs them to mature for the next season's growth, (m) solves a problem. Again shown in glass only to make the mechanics clear is a suction-based pinholder whose height is adjustable to compensate for the lack of stem.

(a)

(b)

(c)

(d)

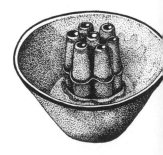

(e)

(f)

(g)

(h)

of the hole-type holders, glass or pottery, some of which come in the forms of fishes, frogs and other water animals, and all of which have holes in the body for the placement of stems. These are classic Japanese forms. Such a holder made of glass is especially effective when the container is clear crystal; the holder tends to disappear (202).

If you are using a container with a moderate-sized opening and you want the holder to be all but invisible, with the plant material rising from the center, try a small Y-shaped branch, the sort which, if permitted to grow, might become good slingshot material. Let the overall length of the Y be slightly greater than the diameter of the mouth of the vase. Then bend the branch, insert it an inch or two in the neck of the container and release. The resilience of the wood will hold the branch firmly in place. Insert the stems in the crotch of the Y (204). If you don't have an incipient slingshot handy, narrow strips of lead or transparent tape across the mouth of the vase will serve almost as well. The lead strips may be stretched across or looped at the edge of the container to hold stems in place. Water-holding synthetics, or foam, can be made into quite satisfactory temporary holders by punching flowers right into the material. If the stem ends are still not stiff enough, make the holes with a nail or icepick. Incidentally, this material usually crumbles after several usings. Cut the foam into small pieces for strangely shaped containers which defy the insertion of conventional holders.

I sometimes like to improvise holders. A potato or grapefruit, for example, cut in half, works well when nothing else is handy. The flat side, of course, goes on the bottom of the container, and holes punched in the upper surface serve as slots for the stems. Coral and sponges, which obviously need no additional openings, also work well if your material is light in weight or if you bind the sponge to a flat stone to give ballast. If the stems of the plants you are using are sufficiently strong, you can simply employ a pile of stones, marbles, pebbles or sand as your holder. These also make an attractive finish around less sightly holders.

Because of the flexibility of their stems, a number of wildflowers can't be arranged without some sort of stiffening device. Thin strips of lead or wire, wound about the stem in corkscrew fashion and anchored at the base, are one

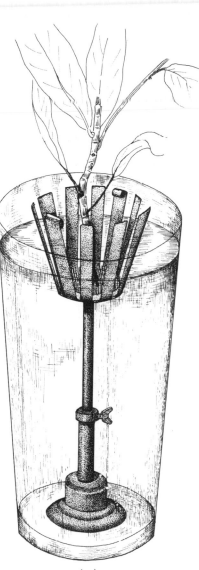

(m)

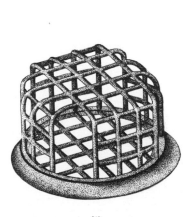

(i)

(j)

(k)

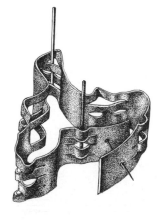

(l)

If no holder is available, one can be improvised by stretching florist's or adhesive tape over the rim of a vase or bowl as in (n). Well-type ivy rings in sections, half-rounds or double circles of glass, plastic and pottery, with holes made in the top to secure stems, as in (o), are extremely useful when one wants to minimize the effect of a container, leaving the accent on the foliage or flowers themselves.

Ceramic, metal and glass holders as in (p), (q) and (r) come in a variety of shapes. These are the generic "frogs" of the arrangers' lexicon. Holes of a variety of sizes and angles dictate the type of material they are to hold. Here again, to increase stability, any of these holders may be affixed to a dry container with strips of sticky tape for the glass ones and clay for the others.

A bulb spray (s) for misting and floral preservatives—which usually come in their own containers—and for coating and cutting down water loss adds to the longevity of most arrangements.

Shown next is a series of practical aids: a spool of florist's thread (t) for binding tender stems; paddle wire (u), 22 gauge, for small, slender stems; coiled wire (v), 18 or 20 gauge, for heavier branches; stick wire (ee), 18 to 30 gauge, for reinforcing individual stems; tin snips (y) for cutting wire; and pruning shears (w) for cutting branches. Now a piece of florist's clay (ff) from which a portion has been removed and coiled as in (z). This is the type of coil one places under a holder to make it stick to the vase.

Following is a knife (gg), invaluable for cutting and slitting stems. For an extraordinarily firm bond between, say, a holder and a container, there is an adhesive clay (aa) that comes on a roll. One kind of florist's tape (bb), available in a variety of colors, is used to wrap stems. Another type (cc) is a much stronger material and is usually used to bind a holder to a container. The bond is not so permanent as that created with adhesive clay. Waterholding foam (dd) is saturated and wedged into vases or natural containers such as bamboo or gourds and is easy and practical to use. The nonmoisture-holding expanding plastic (x) works well in dry arrangements. It may be used repeatedly. Stuck in this block of foam is a pointed translucent tube called a florist's pick, which holds water in a combination wet-and-dry floral arrangement. Other florist's picks in various lengths, some with wire attached, are used for extending short-stemmed plants. Rubber bands or plastic-coated wires are additional helps in supporting, extending, binding and strengthening flowers and branches.

(n)

(p)

(o)   (q)   (r)   (s)

means of providing support. Use twenty-two-, twenty-four-, or twenty-six-gauge wire on weak or slender stems and eighteen- or twenty-gauge wire on heavier or very firm stems. Another is the "in-unity-there-is-strength" method: just tape or wire a number of stems together. The fabled father who taught his sons not to try to break bundled sticks was well aware of this principle. If, however, you are working with hollow-stemmed plants and you don't want to bind them together, you can give them extra rigidity by inserting wire, broom straws, toothpicks or sharpened twigs into the stems.

It is possibly more important to have a practical and extensive collection of man-made flower holders and stem-controlling devices than it is to have an abundance of vases or bowls. Sketches of most of the holders described and a few additional ones, with further identification, appear on pages 200–204.

CONTAINERS

Containers are obviously as much a part of an arrangement as accessories are of a woman's costume. Yet too many floral designers, including, I blush to say, some professionals, seem to be satisfied with almost any receptacle that's handy, so long as it doesn't leak. The role of the container is subtly to complement the arrangement, not dominate it. In working with native plants or naturalizers, the choice of receptacle is especially important. Line, form and texture are usually the primary considerations; color's function, if any, is secondary. Therefore any overly ornate, eye-catching container will often overshadow the flora.

Because they do not detract from the plants, and suggest the natural environs, earth-toned containers are among my favorites. When the stem is particularly attractive, however, I turn to transparent or translucent glass so as not to hide any of the beauty of the material. For arrangement or plantings of mosses, liverworts, lichens and small vernal flora, traditional Oriental containers of iron or

(x)

(t)

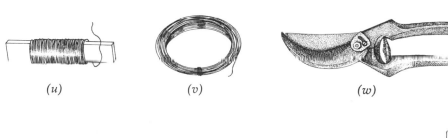

(u)

(v)

(w)

(y)

(z)

(aa)

(bb)

(cc)

(dd)

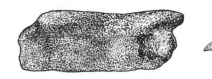

(ee)

(ff)

(gg)

Holders made from natural materials are often highly utilitarian. Shown left in (hh) and right in (ll) are twigs braced against the sides of containers. Heavy florist's string or spool wire wrapped around the base of the cut may be used to control the length of the slit in both instances. In the glass jar (hh), the split stem of a branch to be arranged is hooked into the similarly slit branch holder. In the top of a classic metal usubata (ll), a forked stick, called a kubari in Japanese, is placed under tension horizontally by fitting it to the width of the vase. Willow branches make good springy cross braces. An upright branch wedged into the crotch as shown will receive the necessary support to stay in position.

A spongy holder can be made of fern or huckleberry fronds as in (jj). The fronds are bundled up to the general size of the container and then bound with thread. This is the temporary equivalent of a birdcage holder. Stems may be inserted from all directions if one keeps the weight of the arrangement balanced. Pebbles or sand may be sifted around the fronds for added weight.

Vertically packed snippings of twigs or evergreens as in (kk) serve much the same purpose as folded wire netting but decompose in time.

A curved burl as in (ii) or a stump of wood into which moss may be forced will hold short flower stems. Not shown are cork circles which may be used to support floating flower effects. Pebbles, stones, and sand of different shadings may be kept ready for use in glass jars or boxes to add weight to or hide unsightly holders.

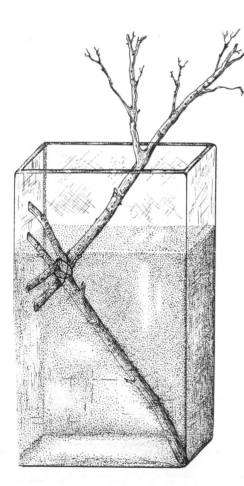

(hh)

(ii)

(jj)

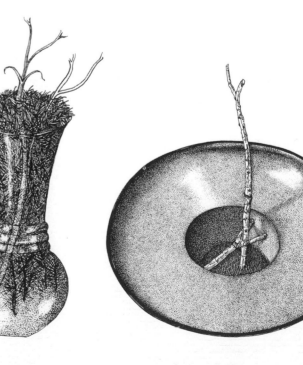

(kk)

(ll)

bronze or eighteenth- and nineteenth-century glass dome effects are excellent. I am also enthusiastic about pewter and copper for hellebores, and pressed or cut glass for capturing the delicate charm of such old-fashioned flowers as blue-eyed Mary and wood violets. A more modern note can be struck with some of the handmade containers which incorporate well-type holders. Among my favorites are those made from oddly shaped stones (251) and wooden slabs (289).

Because native flora is usually at its best when displayed casually, it is often rewarding to ignore conventional containers and look around the house for un-orthodox receptacles. Old bottles, carafes, pitchers and eighteenth- and nineteenth-century teapots, cooking vessels and stoneware jars, for example, will sometimes lend exactly the right touch (272). Or put a water-holding container inside a woven basket that has been weighted with bricks or stones (243). Some of the more sensitive native materials survive best in covered or enclosed receptacles that retain moisture. For such plants, try a fishbowl or battery jar (269) covered with a glass plate and placed on a mirror or tray. In the book, *Wildflowers in Your House*, by Josephine Von Miklos, many excellent suggestions for containers for every room are made and illustrated.

For small arrangements, designers have successfully used such unlikely ob-jects as wooden cups, medicine bottles, and eggshells supported on a tripod of toothpicks—the toothpicks are held together with thread or string—and boxes of ceramic, metal and glass. A miniature chest with the drawers pulled out staircase fashion can be a fascinating receptacle for tiny flowers or vines. To hold the water inside the drawers, I use refrigerator dishes, plastic pill bottles or water-retaining foam wrapped in aluminum foil. If the material has extremely fine stems, you may want to try the tops of salt and pepper shakers, old-fashioned hatpin holders, liqueur glasses singly or in groups, or miniature jugs. These few suggestions will at least give you an idea of the kinds of things to look for when you begin ransacking the attic, basement and cupboards. Beware of receptacles that have charm in themselves but are not sufficiently functional and tend to tip, especially when a tall or curving element is included in the plant material.

SETTINGS

We won't waste any time with a floral argument that's akin to the poultry ques-tion about the relative priority of the chicken and the egg. It really makes no dif-ference whether you choose a background and then design an arrangement appro-priate for that setting, or first complete your design and then select a proper placement. What *is* vitally important is that the background and the arrangement be harmonious. Cultivated flowers, especially if brilliantly colored and arranged boldly, can often compete with a less than ideal setting. But native plants, whose visual appeal is more subtle, are usually lost against a poorly chosen background. A strongly patterned wallpaper, a vividly colored painting nearby, a grouping of ceramic ornaments, for example, would provide far too much distraction for such an arrangement.

Because I normally select the setting before making the arrangement, we'll

Because I normally select the setting before making the arrangement, we'll deal with settings first. I repeat, however, that this is purely a personal quirk, no more meaningful than putting on the left shoe before the right. A plain wall is a good place to consider first, particularly if natural or artificial light is available to cast fascinating shadows of leaf patterns on the undecorated surface. Imaginative lighting, I should add, can contribute enormously to the effectiveness of wild-flower arrangements (301). The small high-intensity lamps—the kind recommended for bedroom reading—can be especially useful because they are unobtrusive and function somewhat like a spotlight. Experiment. Try lighting from above, from the sides, from below. A dramatic effect with shadows can often be achieved with even the simplest design. Lights, however, are hot—if brought too close they will wilt tender material.

If you find the plain wall too severe or its color not right for the arrangement you have in mind, hang a piece of linen or burlap to serve as the background. Both fabrics have a pleasant, natural look that enhances native plants. Wooden, stone and brick surfaces also have good rapport with wildflowers, as do clear- and ground-glass panels. The rough textures of stone, brick and some woods provide a particularly good contrast to the glossy sheen of magnolia, holly and mahonia leaves. Glass, either clear or ground, is an excellent background for shrubs and the gaunt lines of bare winter branches.

The table or pedestal on which the arrangement will rest is, of course, a part of the setting. Wood, marble, metal or woven materials all serve well as bases, so long as they look informal. In a formal setting, wildflowers can seem as out of place as hiking boots with a cocktail dress, whereas the elegant, exotic accent plants, such as crown imperial, are completely at home.

Accessories around the arrangement can contribute to the natural appearance you seek. Mineral or rock specimens such as geodes, crystals and corals, in either crude or polished form, are excellent. I also occasionally use ceramic, metal or wood figurines of birds, insects and roots for this kind of stage dressing. Other interesting and appropriate accessories are birds' nests, butterflies or moths, dried cicada or dragonflies, snail shells, fossil or ferrous stones, even an abandoned hornets' nest, shed snake skin or broken birds' eggs. Bark peeled from dead trees may be used as an accessory for your natural arrangements or when coiled as a wrapping. The bark can convert an ordinary container into the perfect vessel for wildflowers. As with containers, try out unlikely things as part of the setting to see if they work. Not every experiment will be a success, of course, but even a big league ballplayer is usually happy if he gets three hits for every ten times at bat.

Forgive me if I begin this section while standing on a soapbox. When designers say that native plants look lovely when arranged in a way that approximates the natural setting of the flora, I am the soul of agreement. But I become a strong dissenter when anyone insists that *only* such an arrangement is appropriate for wildflowers. To my mind, this is akin to holding that only realistic painting is valid and that abstractionism and other forms of nonliteral art are without equal worth. In working with native plants, as with any other materials, there is no one "right" way to make arrangements. This point of view has been developed and discussed in *The Art of Flower Arrangement* by Beverley Nichols.

Traditionalism has many virtues, but it should never serve as a tether around the neck of creativity. If you want to experiment with geometric patterns or abstract forms with the plants you have gathered, by all means do so. You can always remind an unfriendly critic of the wide variety of styles employed by Picasso over the years. In the following pages you will find arrangements of all kinds. The orthodox designer should, therefore, be prepared to avert his or her eyes from time to time.

Any floral design, whether conventional or abstract, falls into one of two basic categories—line or mass—although some arrangements do have elements of both. A line composition is sparse, bold, disciplined. The amount of material used is minimal. In fact, the success of such an arrangement depends as much on what is left out as on what is used. The emphasis is on the forms of individual branches, leaves, seed pods or buds. The lines are sweeping, but a visual balance is provided by the compact weight where the branches come together. Space is, of course, a vital component of the design. The open areas, which should be irregular in size, must be given as much consideration as the selection of materials. In other words, don't disregard the voids. *Flower Show Ribbon-Winning Arrangements* by Mrs. Raymond Russ Stoltz illustrates some of the standards of excellence adhered to in successful flower arrangement competition.

Any discussion of line design automatically brings to mind the Japanese, for they are among the world's masters of this art form. Certainly their influence is evident in many of the arrangements that follow. But because Japanese designing is based largely on a formalistic symbolism that has little meaning for most Westerners, any lengthy analysis of the basic concepts would serve no useful purpose here. It is enough to study the principles of Japanese design for the beauty of form and balance achieved with a minimum of materials and imaginative use of space.

If line designs, including those created by the Japanese, can be compared to chamber music, then mass design is a symphony, an all-out affair. Abundant material is needed to create the mass. The effect is striking, often dramatic. The individual components can, of course be examined at leisure, but the first impression is of the composition as a whole. Colors are normally massed, not spotted throughout the arrangement—a string section, not soloists. If small

Sculpting With Flowers

flowers are used, they are bunched to serve as a counterbalance to large blooms. The heavy materials are at the center, and the weight becomes progressively less toward the outer edges of the design.

Whether the arrangement is line or mass, almost all good design starts with a concept. A happy accident can occur if you start out devoid of an idea, yet filled with hope that something worthwhile will evolve as you work with the materials. But the likelihood of success with this method is minimal. Assuming, then, that you are not the sort of person who bases his retirement plans on the expectation of winning the Irish Sweepstakes, I suggest you begin by becoming familiar with as many design forms as possible. Develop a retentive eye as you read magazines and books on arrangements. Make mental notes of the designs you admire in the homes of friends. Become a private eye when you visit your florist shop and carry away all the good ideas you observe. I am not proposing, of course, that you become a mere copyist. Your observations are only to provide a framework for your own creativity.

I often find that a sketch pad is the best place to begin a design. With the available materials and the planned location of the arrangement well in mind, I start by trying out a number of basic, overall forms. Perhaps circular or fan shaped would be best. Or how about doing something triangular and, if so, should it be an isosceles or a right angle? Now let's see how these plants would look in a vertical design. Not too good? Maybe horizontal would be better. The things I gathered are fairly long and flexible; maybe an S-shaped structure would be ideal. Ah, here's a thought. Why not make up a number of small units and put them together to create one massive triangular picture? Or, if that won't work, arrange a number of small units in identical design and place them in juxtaposition to produce a horizontal effect; in that way, the arrangements can be considered individually or collectively.

All such decision-reaching can be done with a minimum of effort on your sketch pad and thus save the plants from the unnecessary handling that takes place when you change your mind in the middle of an arrangement. Your drawing paper can also be useful when you are in the field. In preparation for a natural-setting design, make sketches of the actual grouping of plants as they grow in the wild. Thus you can combine flora that exist side by side in nature.

In developing your concept, whether on paper or in your mind's eye, you should be aware of certain elements common to all good designs. Visual balance is, perhaps, number one on the list. There is, of course, frequently a difference between visual and physical balance; a slight woman wearing an enormous hat may *look* topheavy but she's really not likely to fall on her face. Visual imbalance, however, does make the viewer feel uneasy. If, for example, the base seems too light for a tall, rather heavy-looking design, or there is too much weight on one side of a broader creation, we get the impression that the arrangement may topple, even though it may be perfectly sound structurally. And remember that dark colors, as well as the length and thickness of the materials, contribute to this feeling we have about weight.

This does not mean, however, that the base of every vertical design must be massive, or that all sides of a design must have the same color balance and extend the same distance from the central axis. Dark colors or a striking bloom near the base will usually provide the necessary visual balance for a tall arrangement. A broad, asymmetrical design, which may seem slightly lopsided on its own, is often brought into balance by the placement of a bird's nest, some pine cones, an appropriate figurine or a bloom in a separate container near the "light" side of the arrangement.

The problem of visual balance is made less troublesome in many contemporary arrangements because large flowers are usually given the low position and spiky blooms the high. This automatically gives weight to the fulcrum, and therefore a sense of stability. This is a perfectly sound concept, but it should not become an absolute. Sometimes it's well to remember that flower arranging *rules* are made to be broken. History also has something to teach us. In sixteenth- and seventeenth-century drawings and paintings of arrangements, large and rare blooms, like the fritillaria, are often shown at full stem length, with the less dramatic flower near the base. In most instances, a dark, rather heavy-looking container provides the balance. This approach of our forefathers has considerable relevance to working with wildflowers when, to emulate nature, tall, spiky plants must frequently be used at full length.

Proportion is, of course, closely related to visual balance. There are certain general principles worth knowing, but they should be ignored without a second thought if circumstances warrant. For a vertical arrangement, the rule of thumb is that the highest bloom should not be more than one and one-half to two times the height of the container. For a horizontal design, the tradition is that the height should not be greater than the width plus the breadth of the shallow container. But, I repeat, these are only guidelines, not eternal truths.

After visual balance and good proportion, "rhythm"—the feeling of life and movement in an arrangement—is the next most important element in design. (I have a literal-minded friend who objects to this practice of ascribing mobility to an immobile object, but I convinced, or at least silenced, him with a picture of a Thoroughbred racehorse standing alert but absolutely still in a pasture, the powerful muscles beneath the animal's gleaming coat clearly poised for action. Even my prosaic friend could not deny that rhythm and a sense of motion were conveyed in a still photograph.) Rhythm can be made part of a flower arrangement through various means. Repetition of more or less parallel lines or a series of graded curves are among the ways of imparting this quality to a design. A number of grasses bent in the same direction can give the feeling of wind sweeping across a meadow. Using the same type of flower in various

Hosta
ventricosa
seed pods

stages of development—from bud to full bloom—is still another technique for incorporating rhythm into an arrangement.

Depth in a design will also contribute to the rhythm, and will add variety and character as well. Depth is created by variations in length and shape of materials, and by the use of unusual, almost bizarre examples of branches, seed pods and flowers. The delicate tips of shrub branches, the threadlike ends of grasses and curving sections of vines are among the easily found materials that can be made to project or retreat from the design's center of interest and thus add to the three-dimensional appearance.

Color, too, can play an important role in the creation of depth. Colors tend to advance or recede, depending upon the amount of light each reflects. Because white, pink, yellow, orange, some reds and bright magenta bounce back much of the light striking them, they seem to advance, to be nearer to the eye, than violet, dark blue and green, and purple. These latter shades give a feeling of shadowed distance to the arrangement. Incidentally, in choosing colors, give some thought to the light that will be falling on them at the time you want the design to be seen at its best. Normally, light colors should be dominant for an arrangement to be seen under artificial light; give the dark ones stage center when they'll be bathed in bright daylight. Some flowers, like the purple aster with a yellow "eye," have both advancing and receding qualities, and therefore are effective in either natural or artificial light.

"But you often tout arrangements with monochromatic colors," comes a voice from the balcony. "How do you get depth in one of those?"

Borrowing a phrase hallowed in political circles, I reply, "I'm glad you asked that question." It's true, I am enthusiastic about monochromatic designs in greens, reds, brown, grey-browns and other shades. And it's also true that such designs present some minor problems in achieving depth. But the problems *are* minor. The previously noted variations in length and shape of materials—combining round and pyramidal blooms, for example—will help enormously. Depth is also achieved by placing the flowers at various angles, ranging from full-faced to profile. The greatest boon to this kind of placement, however, is that it avoids monotony. Flowers are never at their best when they're lined up like Rockettes, all facing the audience. Now that I think of it, even Rockettes are monotonous in this formation, but this is probably not the time to attack cherished American institutions.

If you are planning to combine several plants in your arrangement, take the time to look at your materials with no preconceptions of what goes with what. Sometimes an alliance of unlikely components produces a striking design of rare beauty. Also, an imaginative addition to a rather uninteresting plant can bring about a Cinderella-like transformation. A plate fungus combined with beautiful grasses, for example, has all the freshness of the natural scene. Thorns in an arrangement with silken petals, like those of the colchicum, take on a wholly new excitement (291).

Fascinating contrast can also be achieved by combining material like sweet William—as stiff in style and character as a maitre d'hotel in a posh restaurant—with something soft and flexible like clematis or honeysuckle. Similarly, variety in line can lead to an interesting arrangement. Don't, for example, scorn plants with crooked stems. Instead, use them with straight members to effect unusual patterns. Long stems are, of course, to be cherished; many otherwise excellent designs are marred because there aren't enough lengthy pieces to provide good proportion and balance. This variation in stem length is important with all materials, but it is especially so with blossoming plants since the objective is to have each flower show up to advantage. And because every bloom should star individually, don't place one directly above the other; group them so that they are spaced at irregular intervals.

All too often foliage is used almost as an afterthought instead of being incorporated into the basic structure. This is rather like staging a theatrical production in which the set and costume designers are not on speaking terms. When you sketch your design, either actually or mentally, know exactly where the foliage is going and how it fits into the general scheme. Various kinds of foliage can be effectively mixed as long as there is a relationship in texture and/or color. Almost any foliage will add distinction to an arrangement, but among my favorites in natural plant designs are coppery begonia leaves, sheaves of grey-green iris and yucca leaves, interesting succulents and glossy beech, velvety mullein, ivy, rhododendron and magnolia leaves, hosta and ginger.

I usually find that branches, shrubs and spirelike flowers are the best materials to delineate the basic lines of the arrangement. But in planning your composition, keep in mind the distance from which it will normally be seen. If, for example, the arrangement is most likely to be viewed from another room, a bold, uncomplicated design is usually advisable. Save your intricate patterns for works that will be looked at from close range.

Among the rewarding aspects of working with native plants is that one can constantly reflect the current season in arrangement. In spring, for instance, I like to emphasize the vigorous growth and surging strength of the various leaves and blooms thrusting upward from bulbs. The lateral growth of summer plants, spreading like a carpet over the earth, makes me want to fill all available containers with foliage so placed that the design takes on an almost mosaic character. In autumn, there is an almost infinite variety of color and form in leaf stems, seed pods and blooms, thanks to the different maturation periods of the various plants. And for winter there are the dried arrangements, plus some handsome groundcovers and a few volunteers, like the spice bush, to brighten the short days and long nights. The author Nelson Coon, in his field manual, *Using Wayside Plants*, suggests using natural accessories such as the lichen-covered stone.

Before we deal with the specific arrangements that are illustrated and described on the following pages, I'd like to make a few general comments about this nebulous art of sculpting with flowers. As with all arts, there are certain basic techniques to be mastered—the proper cutting of plants, caring for them, drying them if desired, and the pure mechanics of arranging them. The rest of the learning process in becoming a good designer is almost wholly subjective and, I should add, endless. However, a proper approach to the subject will make the job far easier. Creativity is nourished by observing and analyzing the interesting work of others, by a willingness to experiment and to accept the inevitable percentage of failures. And, in the case of native plants, there must exist an ability to put aside, at least in part, familiar standards of beauty and appreciate new and unfamiliar forms and combinations. But from the very beginning, make every design your own, a reflection of your personality, taste and convictions. In flower shows, judges place major emphasis on originality, distinction and style. These qualities can be present in an arrangement only when a designer expresses himself in a way that is uniquely his own—whether he tends to asymmetry or to a beautiful balance as shown in the seeded dandelion.

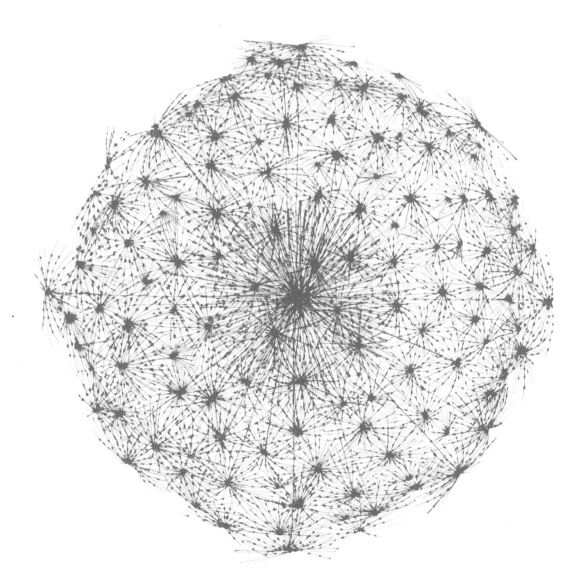

Arrangements For All Seasons

We present flower arrangements here as an art that brings flowers to the eye of the viewer in a pleasing, unusual or thought-provoking manner. In the pages that follow you will see specific examples that rely almost entirely on the rich variety of materials gathered from exquisitely planned groupings by Marion Becker at her living laboratory at "Cockaigne" in the Cincinnati, Ohio, area. Tree blooms, ferns, wildflowers, grasses, fruits, pods and branches comprise a large percentage of the most effective native materials combined with many of the distinctive introduced plants which have adapted themselves to local mesophytic conditions. Because Marion Becker's interest is particularly strong in the field of bulbs, you will find that we have been able to combine those plants which are integral to the climax plant community with beautiful hardy exotic specimens. This is a satisfactory, practical and innovative situation, one we hope you will care to explore for yourself. Let's begin with winter and work our way through the seasons.

Glass Shelter for Arrangements

Container: Rounded, narrow-necked glass jar, apothecary jar
Holder: Small needle holder in water receptacle (201)
Plants: Five to seven Lenten roses, 3 to 6 inches in length
Water: Only a little, as jar reduces evaporation
Other Materials: Small leaf or tuft of moss to hide receptacle; raffia, or rust-
    proof wire

In late November, Christmas roses, *Helleborus niger* (58), and by February the Lenten roses, *H. orientalis* hybrids (59), appear amid the snow patches. Steal a march on spring and bring in a few of these blossoms. Arrange them in a glass-covered container, which cuts the moisture loss. Placed close to a cool window, preferably east or northeast, where the sun is not too hot, the flowers will last for an amazing length of time. A small needle holder in its own or in a separate small receptacle is easily inserted in the container and covered by a leaf or few tufts of moss. Should you use a rounded jar with a narrow opening, similar to the containers for cotton puffs or guest soap, cluster the stems, then bind them lightly with coated rustproof wire, or tie with raffia and impale the bunch as a single flower onto the holder. If the opening is too small to permit entrance for your hand, position the blooms with ice cube tongs or tweezers.

Try yellow winter aconite, *Eranthis hyemalis*, in one container, snowflakes, *Leucojum vernum* in another, and the greenish-brown, white, purplish-rose of hellebores in a third. Stack them like a miniature apartment building—with the coarser blooms on the lower floors. The tallness of the container makes up for the shortness of stem characteristic of many winter-blooming flowers.

Later in the season the seed pods of these plants (59) are equally effective for use in free-air arrangements. When harder in texture they will be much more tolerant of the dry air of our houses. For a more enduring arrangement, one that may last for several years, plant tiny ferns and mosses from your wildflower garden in the glass bell jar on a shallow bed of soil to make a terrarium. As moisture from the soil and plants condenses, the terrarium finds its atmospheric balance and needs only an occasional misting. Should you over-water and find condensed moisture excessive, wipe off the lid and inner sides of the jar.

Wild Flowers to Know and Grow, by Jean Hersey, develops the pleasures of creating a terrarium which the author calls a small world under glass.

Winter Scene

Container: Glass building block cut in half
Holder: Grey-green plastic water-holding foam
Plants: Buds, magnolia leaves, moss, teasel
Water: Moistened foam
Other Materials: Milkweed, 3½-inch-long magnolia pods, pheasants' breast feathers, cockscomb, acorns, beech leaves, Queen Anne's lace, prairie blazing star

From the edge of the roadside, blown by the winter winds, one can gather fascinating plant forms in warm and subtle tones of beige, brown and quiet greens. In the foreground of this arrangement are American beech leaves, *Fagus grandifolia*. Behind them are a rosette of magnolia leaves, *Magnolia grandiflora*, with a handsome red-seeded magnolia pod, bits of teasel, *Dipsacus sylvestris*, long-lasting and prickly-proud, and a milkweed pod, *Asclepias syriaca*, half filled with down. The base is comprised of pheasants' breast feathers inserted in patches of moss, and a few lichen-covered stones. The sturdiness of acorns and the laciness of the dried Queen Anne's lace blooms, *Daucus carota*, which curl into a bird's-nest shape, bring familiar forms into this winter mosaic. I couldn't resist tucking into the water-holding foam a segment of rosy-red cockscomb, *Celosia cristata*, and terminal tips of the prairie blazing star, *Liatris pycnostachya*.

Late winter is also the time to enjoy the subtle shapes and colors found in seed pods, fallen leaves and the evergreen rosettes of the forest floor. Collect some of these just as you might pretty pebbles and bring them home to arrange in one of the sections of your collector's table. As illustrated opposite, a substitute for a collector's table can be readily fabricated by lining the top of an ordinary bench with halves of glass building bricks—these are usually available at a building supply company or your local florist. And in among the dried leaves you will find a few evergreen materials and some dried flowers and fruits which retain a surprising amount of color. Your next arrangement could be the instant spring landscape created by combining some of the more or less permanent items discussed above with a few of the very early flowering bulbs of spring.

Raye Miller Underwood makes excellent suggestions on what materials to collect in the helpful volume, *The Complete Book of Dried Arrangements*.

Forecast of Spring

Container: ½ glass block

Holder: Oriental lead holder with small sectional divisions. Segments of twigs

Plants: Eight or nine snowdrops, 2½ to 3 inches; three miniature daffodils, 1½ to 2 inches; seven winter aconite, 2 to 2½ inches; two large-leaved waterleaf leaves, 2 to 2½ inches, and moss

Water: Shallow

A mere handful of bulb blooms, those first precious specimens that can re-create in the mind's eye an entire spring landscape, are shown in a setting scaled to their size. Snowdrops, *Galanthus nivalis*, miniature daffodils, *Narcissus asturiensis*, two or three *Hydrophyllum macrophyllum* or large-leaved waterleaf leaves, winter aconite, *Eranthis hyemalis* (55), and fragments of moss are enough to give the vernal illusion. The stems are inserted in an Oriental lead holder with small sectional divisions (200) and held gently but firmly in place by wedging them at the base with segments of twigs. Moss is filled around the stems and over the holders. Deep water is not desirable for flowers from bulbous plants, and in most cases a preservative is not helpful. It can even be injurious in some instances. Keep your plants in air as cool and moist as possible without losing your family to lobar pneumonia.

The Watery Image

Container: Porcelain-lined saucer-shaped pewter bowl
Holder: Pinpoint on needle-type lead base
Plants: Five netted iris, 3½ to 5 inches; three large-leaved waterleaf leaves, 3 inches
Water: Shallow
Other Materials: Florist's clay, pebbles

In nature, pools of melted snow reflect the cool beauty of early iris. In this arrangement a similar silvery look is captured by using a shallow pewter-faced porcelain bowl filled to the brim with water. The four *Iris reticulata* (64) stems are grouped, then lightly bound together with a piece of water-resistant tape, thus presenting a broader base to be impaled on the needle holder. Smoothly worn pebbles are used around the holder base to disguise the prongs. These pebbles may be smooth, shiny ones imported from Japan, or river-polished stones collected on your own travels. A vertical slit through the base of the iris stem, past the first constricting nob, permits the water to enter the plant, a treatment helpful in prolonging the life of the iris. A beautifully mottled, pointed leaf of large-leaved waterleaf, *Hydrophyllum macrophyllum,* projecting over the outer edge of the container gives visual emphasis and balance. In this arrangement I follow the orthodox rule that flowers be one and one-half to two times higher or broader than the greatest vertical or horizontal dimension of the container. In many current arrangements a more exaggerated height is used. The reedlike foliage of these bulbous irises is extremely important in giving a graceful natural look to the composition.

Budded Branches

Container: American Indian clay jug
Plants: Two red maple and two spice bush branches, 2 to 3 feet
Water: Deep
Other Material: Lichened branch, 2 feet

Seen against the sky, the swelling buds of red maple, *Acer rubrum,* bring great excitement to the pattern of their lead-colored branches. This same vernal magic will take place in your own home when you cut these branches and bring them indoors. There is a beautiful and characteristic pattern of movement to the terminals of the budded branches as they arch and reach up. In your own design, try to recapture this typical movement of harmoniously repeated curves. In the arrangement illustrated, the branches are shown in a patterned red and dull-blue earthenware jug of American Indian origin, an ideal foil for this arrangement. But red maple is also magnificent when used alone in an un-adorned container, or when the branches frame a single choice blossom of early spring, such as a tulip—pink or red if the vase is a dark value, white if the vase is light. To increase the color area of the single bloom, spread the petals by rolling them back gently before tucking the flower into the arrangement. Note the similar use of a single flower branch on page 229. The color of the branches becomes more pronounced as the buds swell and mature. Recently some authorities have advocated skipping the presoaking of the branches, but I find covering the entire branch for several hours in lukewarm water hastens the bud-bursting process.

Ohio buckeye, *Aesculus glabra* (97), forces well under kitchen windowsill conditions. A few branches will develop into a leaf pattern of primitive force.

Acorn Cup Container

Container: Two acorn caps of bur oak
Holder: One inverted maple sugar mold
Plants: Three pepper-and-salt stems, 1½ to 2 inches, and one Angel's tears daffodil, 1½ inches
Water: Small piece of water-holding foam
Other Materials: Florist's clay and moss to cover clay

One of the fascinating challenges of flower arrangement is finding a way in which to make a limited amount of material interesting, even memorable. This 2-inch wonder does just that. Two acorn cups of *Quercus macrocarpa*, one inverted on top of the other, create a pedestal or formed hourglass container. The two cups are held firmly together with a dab of florist's clay. The joint is concealed by smearing the clay with powdered leaf mold and tucking in a few strands of moss. A thimbleful of wet florist's foam holds firm the pepper-and-salts, *Erigenia bulbosa* (66), and *Narcissus triandrus* var. *albus* (70). The acorns are based on an inverted maple sugar mold and are secured to the container with florist's clay. A wide-mouthed, overscale glass or bowl may be inverted over this tiny arrangement to preserve it. The pepper-and-salt, which in many places is one of the earliest of spring flowers, has another common name, harbinger-of-spring. The leaves, which come up from a corm, not a bulb, develop fully after umbels of small flowers appear. The bewitching appearance of the plant justifies your late winter and early spring search for it.

An Early Autumn Version

Container: Acorn cup or cups
Plants: Three cyclamen stems with seed pods, 3 to 4 inches, and moss
Water: Small piece of water-holding foam
Other Materials: Florist's clay

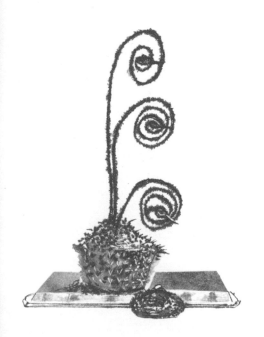

A contrast to the preceding spring grouping is this arrangement for fall. Again I utilized a bur oak acorn cap mounted on a man-made rectangular base and cemented to it with florist's clay. I filled the acorn with a water-holding foam and inserted the spiral immature coiled seeds of cyclamen species in a repetitive manner so that attention would be focused on the fascinating snaillike structure of the stem and seed pod. The grouping will last for three, four and even five weeks if the basal material is kept moist. This type of arrangement provides a close-to-nature experience for those who have difficulty in making field trips.

Small Arrangement for Single Species

Container: Small, pale-blue glazed vase
Plants: Five stems blue-eyed Mary, 5 to 8 inches
Water: Deep

Small arrangements have a very special charm, but their success depends largely on having a proper scale between the container and the plant material. A collection of small vases, bowls, cruets and jugs can be extremely helpful if you are willing to use some of your cherished containers as flower receptacles. If you are a collector of American glass, you will find this particular flower with its delicate stems especially effective in a piece from your collection. History is on your side: for centuries, some of the handsomest art works have been designed to hold flowers.

This arrangement features the delicate beauty of blue-eyed Mary, *Collinsia verna*, in a small handsome ceramic vase with a soft blue glaze. By not mixing this flower with other materials, I focus attention on a single species, and invite detailed inspection. One advantage of this arrangement is its easy portability. Often I carry a small vase of flowers with me from one part of the house to another—from a wilting desk in the study to a spot near the piano, to a card table, tea cart or end table. It is a constant pleasure to see the varying effects that changing lights have on blue and lavender flowers. But I prefer their bright, clear appearance in intense natural light, because they tend to recede, fade away, or vanish in dim or artificial light. A bit of foliage used near the rim of the container serves to bind flower and vase together. Blue-eyed Mary lasts in prime blooming condition in the garden for an amazingly long period of time and may be enjoyed from early October, when its tender dicots form a fresh green groundcover, until late April, when its whorled seed pods take on considerable stature (130). Even in a vase it keeps on growing.

Miniature Reflecting Pool

Container: Ceramic cigarette box with inverted lid
Holder: Birdcage type
Plants: Two small branches of spice bush, 9 to 12 inches; one small branch of viburnum, 5 to 6 inches; two white trout lily blooms and leaves, 3 to 4 inches; three bloodroot blooms with leaf, 2½ to 3½ inches; one blossom double snowdrop, 1 inch
Water: Shallow
Other Materials: Florist's clay

A cluster of spring flowers discovered in a natural setting brings a start of delight and amazement to the viewer. Try to capture that same unexpected quality in arrangements made of these materials. The spring bulb flowers need less water than those of any other season, and therefore permit the use of a shallow container. Fasten your holder to the bottom of the dry cigarette box with a ribbon of florist's clay pressed down firmly enough to bind container and holder together. Then add the budding branch of spice bush, *Lindera benzoin* (221), at a height and angle which have verve. The delicacy of the branch design and the spice scent of the yellow blossoms make this plant doubly enjoyable. Early American settlers used the bark, leaves, twigs and berries to brew a strong tea. It was referred to by French botanist André Michaux in 1796 in his American wilderness diary. Of the spice bush tea he said, "This beverage restores strength, and it had that effect, for I was very tired when I arrived." It is closely related to sassafras tea, still adored by many but recently banned by the U.S. Department of Agriculture as carcinogenic. The brown-green mottled leaves of the *Erythronium albidum* (66) illustrate the reason for the common name of the trout lily or dog's-tooth-violet. The bell-like blooms seem to ring as they sway on slender stems.

Take care that the sap from a broken root or leaf of bloodroot, *Sanguinaria canadensis,* a rusty red used by the Indians as a dye, doesn't stain you.

In the inverted water-filled lid of the container lies a single blossom of the double snowdrop, *Galanthus nivalis* 'Flore Pleno,' floating like a miniature water-lily. A branch of sweet-smelling *Viburnum farreri,* an easily grown vase-shaped shrub which blooms intermittently from December through March, is placed so that it reflects itself in the box lid, now transformed into a small vernal pool. One, two, or three tulip tree blooms (93) make a lovely substitute for the bloodroot in this arrangement.

Backdrop Setting

Container: Arched, shell-shaped white ceramic with shallow rim in front
Holder: Fitted block of water-holding florist's plastic foam
Plants: One branch of juniper, 12 to 15 inches; two branches of juniper, 9 inches; two dozen daffodils of contrasting form and color; six to twelve daffodil leaves which may be of common varieties other than those of the flowers
Water: Shallow
Other Materials: Piece of moss 6 inches wide by 9 inches long, or equivalent

I find it pleasing to arrange daffodils in twos and threes, simulating their natural habit of growth, or I use two or three different varieties placed in adjacent positions for contrast in silhouette, color and design. Four smaller blossoms will often balance one very large or two medium-sized flowers. Differences in cup or trumpet will give the desirable variation in depth. A group of stems with a bud or two may be used for balance or variety of form. The juniper, or red cedar, *Juniperus virginiana* (133), our only local native evergreen tree, is naturally kept higher in position than the level of the bulbs. A heavy pin or lead holder underneath the foam may be necessary to give support to those tree branches, especially if they are quite extended and heavy. In this arrangement, the curved daffodil leaf repeats the shell-like curve of the far side of the container. A daffodil leaf may be induced to curl or curve by drawing it over the blade of a dull knife. If the leaf is somewhat limp, you may want to hold a sharp knife against it as you sink it into the foam to supply necessary rigidity for this insertion. It is usually wise to press the slimy substance out of the bottom 2 or 3 inches of daffodil stems before placing them in an arrangement. The water will then rise easily in the bulb stems.

Presoak the foam before fitting it into your container. Most foams absorb water quickly, so this soaking need not be long. Never put cut flower stems into dry foam, or decay and rotting will occur at the surface. Never change the position of the plant stem in foam by pulling 'it out a short distance. This creates an air block through which no water can be absorbed. If a change is necessary, pull the stem out completely and reinsert in a new, firm area. Foams serve ideally when the container is too shallow to hold an adequate water supply. With the limited moisture available it may be necessary to prune excess foliage to cut down on water intake; you may discover in so doing that you have created a more interesting line. Moss and small pebbles can give a natural finish to the surface of the foam into which the flower and branch stems are inserted. Should arrangements be seen from more than one point of view or from all sides, almost twice as much material is needed to give a feeling of depth to the composition.

Weighted Container for Spreading Branches

Container: One antique iron mortar
Holder: One large lead-based pinpoint
Plants: Three branches redbud, 3 feet long
Water: To brim of container
Other Materials: Two narrow strips of sheet lead cut into 8-inch lengths; one slab of lichen-encrusted hackberry bark, 2½ to 3 feet long

The blooming of the redbud, *Cercis canadensis*, establishes spring's reality for many of us. These branches are easily arranged, for the contrast of magenta-pink, almost red blooms, clustered along the ebony-black stems, produces an intermittent combination of line and color. There is an angularity about these native branches and twigs that gives a particularly Oriental character to the redbud branch pattern.

To create this design, choose branches that will extend three, four or even five times the height of the mortar. The lateral extension can be of the same proportion. Make several cuts up into the ends of the stems. This division makes it possible to insert the stem on and between the pins of your large long-pronged pinpoint holder. If the branch does not seem secure, wire or bind another very short branch to it at the base to give a broader area of support. In choosing branches for arrangement, strive for interesting patterns, curves or angles. This is not always easy to achieve, but with a little careful pruning and the elimination of unwanted lines, the pattern will emerge. Group the branches so that they seem to be issuing forth as a single large stem. Some modern Oriental designers use a heavy staple gun to bind stems together. The same effect can be achieved with strips of sheet lead wrapped below the rim of the container. I have placed a segment of bark at the base of the arrangement for additional texture, balance and a feeling of the out-of-doors. If you don't have an iron mortar, and the container you are using is not heavy enough to counterbalance the branches, add small stones as needed.

Contrasts of Form and Color

Container: Antique brass

Holder: Birdcage

Plants: One trillium, 3½ inches; three stems squirrel corn, 6½ inches; three clusters delphinium leaves, 5 inches; three grape hyacinths, 4 inches

Water: Shallow

Arrangements of early spring flowers bring to your home the subtle shapes, sharp fragrances and clear, light colors of the new growth. A small bowl containing a few vernal flowers makes it possible to focus on the structure and beauty of the individual blossoms, stems, and leaves. The dull red, clear white, and soft blue color scheme is unusually pleasant. The clustered bells of *Muscari paradoxum*, or grape hyacinth, combine well with *Trillium sessile*, the maroon sessile trillium, or toadshade, as it is often called. Common names are apt, colorful and descriptive, but they sometimes fail to convey relationships as well as scientific names. The squirrel corn, *Dicentra canadensis*, for example, gets its common name from its golden-kerneled root. But as its Latin name indicates, it is related to the Dutchman's breeches, *Dicentra cucullaria*. One can tell the difference, however, by the basal spurs of the flowers. The squirrel corn blossom is like the shape of a bleeding heart, while the Dutchman's breeches do look like pantaloons or "cucullaria."

The first choice for plant names, ever since Linnaeus made his famous classification, is dependent on the time of initial publication (124). Since researchers and taxonomists are constantly going through ancient documents, they inevitably discover names older than the ones that are familiar. Thus names change, much to the confusion of the layman.

Double Theme

Container: Two crystal vases with elliptical opening

Plants: Eight stems of violets with foliage, 2½ to 8 inches; one fritillary, 4 to 8 inches

Water: Shallow

Other Materials: One knitting needle or crochet hook

Arrangements of flowers that grow in moist woodlands may be made and enjoyed for days in your own house if you create the conditions in which the plants thrive. Here is one easy way. Gently position the flowers and foliage in a transparent container. Place them out of strong sunlight. Different colored violets, in this case *V. canadensis*, *V. papilionacea*, the common blue, and the greyed Confederate, *V. priceana*, are easily and quickly placed if you guide the stems into the cavity of a vase with a knitting needle or crochet hook. These tools extend the use of your fingers in areas too small for the hand to operate. In this very narrow oval opening I permitted the stems, blossoms and leaves to be supported by the sides of the vase. The reticulated blossom of the *Fritillaria meleagris*, the guinea-hen flower or checkered lily, with its brownish-purple coloring, is a splendid contrast to the simpler coloration of the violas. The interlacing pattern of curved lines can be varied without limit. Try this type of design to make maximum use of a very limited amount of material. The vases are particularly effective when used as a pair in front of a mirrored area. By this device, all sides of the plant may be seen and enjoyed simultaneously. Very little water is required in the base of the container, just enough to touch the stem ends and to keep the air within the vases very moist.

Enveloping Leaves Frame Small Blossoms

Container: Free-form ceramic bowl
Holder: Birdcage
Plants: Three Japanese butter-bur leaves, 10 to 15 inches; three stems shooting
  star, 9 to 11 inches
Water: To rim of container
Other Materials: Twigs or matchsticks for wedging

The arrow-shaped shooting star, *Dodecatheon meadia*, which is also called
Indian chief or American cowslip, provides a striking contrast to the wavy, almost circular mature leaves of the Japanese butter-bur, *Petasites japonicus* (151)
—a boldness of design remote from the usual concept of arrangements made with
so-called wildflowers. Note the almost metallic grey unfolding leaves which support the base of the shooting stars. The extreme differences of form and volume
bring out the individuality of the various materials. The trick is to find a neutral
and harmonious container that not only supports but gives emphasis to the
design by reinforcing the major motif in the plant material. Here the larger, con-
spicuously veined leaves seem to frame the emerging rocketlike blooms of the
shooting star. The large fleshy stems are wedged firmly with little sticks in the
squares of the birdcage holder (201). A misty spray of water squeezed over the
plants keeps the lovely foliage from shrinking.

The butter-bur bloom, not shown here, has a fascinating prehistoric look
that would make it an intriguing choice to use with lumps of coal or with the
shelf fungus often found on old locust trees. Such arrangements lend themselves
to contemporary settings.

Reflected and Doubled Effects

Container: Green-tinted glass cylinder with leaded base, 6 inches
Holder: Pinpoint
Plants: Four stems large-flowered trillium, 6 to 10 inches
Water: Shallow
Other Materials: Mineral fragments, clay, one large mirror with 10-inch base

Trillium grandiflorum is one of spring's loveliest blossoms. It lasts well, unless the flowers have been pollinated. Senator George D. Aiken mentioned in his newest edition of *Pioneering with Wildflowers* that snow trillium turns pale pink and then deeper pink as it ages, giving unexpected variety of color. The trillium also has decorative pinkish pods which can be seen in late summer. Frequently the true beauty of the bloom is missed because all parts of the bloom are not observed simultaneously. To make one's view more complete we have used mirrors in a rather abstract design to demonstrate a technique of arrangement that seems to have particular visual appeal. The four blossoms of varied heights are pushed onto a pinpoint holder painted green, which is inserted into the base of a clear green-tinted glass cylinder. The prongs are disguised with segments of mineral fragments used between them and the glass. Two of the stems barely reach the top of the container and the white blooms seem to float above the water level. The third bloom stretches up in a vertical line. The fourth blossom bends over the rim of the container in an arc so that it is reflected in the elliptical mirror plateau on which the container rests. Thus, two views of the same flowers are readily available. Other smaller, variously shaped mirrors placed at random will reflect other views from still different positions. Overhead light, candlelight, and highlights from the ░░░░░░░░ the visual aspects of this arrangement. Ethereal in effect, it has an *art*░░░░░░░ ░░articularly lovely for dinner table settings. Colchicum, lycoris, da░░░░░░ ░emones and poppies are all perfect materials for mirror-reflected de░░

The native and rare exotic materials used which you have ░░░ ░urself or which have been given to you by a generous grower may ne░░ ░imum amplification. Certainly, one wishes to present them as the jewels they ░░ Enjoyment of their beauty will encourage others to care for, plant and develop such native plant groupings. Obviously, if the trillium is on the "protected" list in your area, don't use it at all.

Arrangement for Terrace or Courtyard

Container: Shallow, shell-like thick pottery bowl
Holder: Leaded birdcage type
Plants: Three stems Japanese fritillary, 15 to 24 inches; Lady's-mantle leaves, 3
    to 4 inches; ten Greek anemone stems, 4 to 6 inches
Water: Two to three inches
Other Materials: A stone stele (slab)

This arrangement is best seen and enjoyed out-of-doors, especially on a small terrace, the patio of a vacation house, on a loggia or in a small area garden currently without blooming flowers. For the ladderlike structure of the *Fritillaria verticillata* (see endpapers), I use here a handsome 40-inch stele-shaped stone both as a background and as protection against the prevailing wind. This protection is especially important for an out-of-doors arrangement. If you don't happen to have such a stone as shown here, devise a windbreak of bamboo, shutters, screening or a section of log, but be certain your choice of accessory fits in well with the overall design. The container for this arrangement is a flat, seashell-like, mustard-brown pottery bowl. A well-shaped round container of lightweight Mexican tufa could serve equally well. Anemones, *Anemone blanda*, provide spotlights of captured light at the base of the fritillary. The scalloped, shell-shaped leaves of Lady's-mantle, *Alchemilla mollis*, blend into the shape of the bowl and also catch the dew in a most entrancing manner.

While we're on the subject of outdoor arrangements, a couple of other ideas you may want to consider. Place a smaller glass tic cylinder inside a larger one and put interesting leaves between the two parent surfaces. This gives wind protection. Also, that discarded iron pot in the basement still has its uses. Fill the pot with a melange of flowers, plants and mosses to form a miniature garden. Or plant a strawberry jar with hardy succulents and creeping thymes. These evergreen plants will withstand winter weather and so will fiberglass containers and certain other pots provided they have a drainage hole.

The Cantilevered Curve

Container: Japanese bough vase
Plants: One spray pruned red pine, 17 inches; one tree peony bloom, 4½ inches
Water: Deep

The red pine branches, *Pinus resinosa*, form a foil for the silken petals of a single tree peony blossom, *Paeonia suffruticosa*. As indicated in the drawing, there is an aesthetic, if not always a physical, bonus to this arrangement: the dropping pollen forms a kind of golden shadow under the circular blooms. Although this pollen is beautiful, its charm will be lost on anyone who is allergic to it. With proper lighting, this arrangement will provide fascinating shadow patterns, so do a little experimenting. Incidentally, the peony will last longer if the end of the stem is flamed or held momentarily in boiling water before positioning it in the design. In either case protect the blossom from heat or steam during the searing process.

Unnecessary pine needles were relentlessly pruned to give a lighter, more graceful and balanced look to the design, very much as the gardeners in the old temple gardens of Kyoto, Japan, thin the branch pattern of pines seen against the sky. Peonies combined with pine have the symbolic meaning of eternal youth in Japan.

Before I hear complaints about including red pine in this book, I'd better state that I'm aware that this pine is not a native of our part of the country. But it can be grown without difficulty—even without acidifying our limestone soil.

A Garden Spot in a Basket

Container: One two-level basket 30 inches high with carrying handle
Holder: Crumpled chicken wire, two pieces covered wire or green pipe cleaners
Plants: Seven lilac stems, 6 to 18 inches long; five dwarf larkspur stems, 6 to 9 inches, and foliage; nine lily-of-the-valley stems, 5 to 7 inches; four hosta leaves, 6 to 8 inches; five lily-of-the-valley leaves
Water: Very shallow
Other Materials: Dish liners to fit basket

An effective floor decoration that simulates a garden spot is achieved by use of a two-level basket. This arrangement has the added advantage of being readily portable; it can be moved from room to room and will be equally lovely in the foyer, living room or patio. By using low-growing plants such as lily-of-the-valley, *Convallaria majalis,* and the wild dwarf larkspur, *Delphinium tricorne,* at the lower level of the basket and by placing French hybrid blooms of the common lilac, *Syringa vulgaris,* in the upper section, I suggest the varying heights at which these flowers grow. Use whatever liner you have that will fit the two sections of the basket. Crumple chicken wire to give several layers of support. Lilies-of-the-valley, which are at their best when clustered, require very shallow water. Use the variegated *Hosta undulata* leaves and lily-of-the-valley foliage to create a background for the delicate bell-like flowers and the somewhat taller purplish-blue wild delphinium. At the upper level, two kinds of lilacs are massed with blooms concentrated in the center and foreground. The heavy panicle of a double lilac bloom hangs gracefully over the edge of the container, well above the short-stemmed flowers, a juxtaposition one sees in a real garden setting. The basal foliage of the lilacs is eliminated to provide more water for the full bloom clusters. The stems are bound to the handle of the basket with florist's green pipe cleaners to provide a permanent curving line of leaves and flowers.

Modified Mass Arrangement

Container: Dull-gold, melon-shaped vase

Plants: Three wild hyacinths, 9 to 13 inches; two buds and leaves Japanese roof iris, 11 to 14 inches; four spires synandra, 10 to 14 inches; two lycoris leaves, 12 to 15 inches

Water: To the top of the vase

Somewhat surprisingly, the elegance of a formal, semi-mass arrangement can be achieved with simple native flowers and foliages and a few pet exotics. In a dull-gold, exaggerated melon-shaped container, the interplay of foliage and bloom stalk, large flower and small, makes this arrangement diverting. In general, as a matter of design, I try for a somewhat varied silhouette with deep indentations. The interesting variety of outline and volume shown in the illustrations in Germain Bazin's *A Gallery of Flowers,* taken from flower paintings of the Louvre, shows us the continuity of appreciation of a style of arrangement that has existed through art history. At this time of year, a few leaves of lycoris are amazingly useful; they give height and strength, and the cutting of two or three, not all from the same clump, will not materially diminish the amount of growth next fall. *Iris tectorum* blooms of distinctive character are used high, in the style of the Flemish painters. Wild hyacinth, *Camassia scilloides,* stalks provide strong silhouettes as well as beauty in the individual blossoms. The delicate green of the *Synandra hispidula* leaf, and the variation in texture which it affords, serve both as a pleasant type of filler and as a substitute for a round or radial form. The square-stemmed stalks of synandra are featured in low positions, where the intricacy of their veining shows to maximum advantage. Crumpled chicken wire used as a holder keeps the materials well spaced within the container.

Wreath Form in Flowers and Leaves

Container: Smoky black-brown oval ceramic bowl
Holder: Water-holding foam
Plants: Nine May apple blooms, 2 to 2¼ inches; about fifty ivy leaves,
    2 to 3 inches
Water: To brim

The contrast of the true, clear white of the May apple, *Podophyllum peltatum*, against the shiny dark ivy foliage is emphasized by placing the plants in a
smoky blackish-brown oval ceramic bowl. The ivy leaves are inserted first to
cover the foam and can be sculptured with considerable variation of height. The
blooms of the May apple are then interspersed among the leaves. This arrangement is particularly suited for use as a table decoration for public functions such
as a church dinner or a museum tea, as well as for your own enjoyment. The
foliage and blooms arranged in a simulated wreath shape are equally decorative
on a round, oval or rectangular table. The use of water-holding foam in the container makes for easy carrying if the arrangement is to be transported any distance.
Water should be added daily. Keep these blooms out of extremes of temperature,
strong sunlight and drying wind.

Ivy-covered foam islands shaped like those of the Japanese Inland Sea can be
placed in a larger traylike container so that their shapes complement one another.
Or variations of this arrangement can be equally effective in round, rectangular
or even segmented containers. With the latter, a geometric or serpentine pattern
can be used, with figurines interpolated between the parts. But be sure to choose
accessories that are not overwhelmed by the bold scale of the flowers. The large
number of separate leaves required makes this a time-consuming design to
arrange.

The Whimsical Container

Container: Small white glazed mustard jar or child's teapot
Plants: Five stems false-rue anemone, 5 to 7 inches
Water: To rim
Other Materials: 26-gauge wire, toothpick

For the last-minute arrangement, a small container with a definite personality is as gratifying and reliable as one of the sound, time-tested recipes for a quick cake or casserole. This tiny mustard jar with a mouse attached is one of my favorite receptacles for hasty flower designs. Almost any small blooms look attractive in it, and in this instance I have used dainty white blooming false-rue anemone, *Isopyrum biternatum*. Isopyrum arranges more gracefully than the similar blossoms of rue anemone, *Anemonella thalictroides*, because its flowers are distributed widely over its matted foliage rather than rising in a dense cluster from a single stalk. In either case wire is needed to bend the stems, but to avoid cutting them, toothpicks are used at the base as reinforcers. The 26-gauge wire is bent into the shape of a hairpin. One side is placed alongside the stem and toothpick, thus giving still greater strength, and the other side of the wire is wrapped corkscrew fashion around all three.

Almost every household has a number of small containers suitable for such arrangements. Teapots from a child's set, for example, or liqueur glasses are excellent, doubling as miniature vases when filled with minute blooms that reflect their scale. Such receptacles are the perfect answer for arrangements to go on breakfast and luncheon trays for convalescents or, in the Continental style, at individual places at the table.

Flower Texture Contrast with Stone

Container: A stone with a well-like depression
Holder: Pinpoint cup holder
Plants: Clematis spray, 10 inches, and giant sedum, 7 inches
Water: To rim of cup

One of the more astonishing phenomena to be seen during a woodland walk is a rock split by seemingly delicate growing plants. Here we have duplicated this impressive action of nature by anchoring a *Clematis henryi* vine to a pinpoint cup holder set in the cavity of a stone. Stones with such circular depressions are often found in creek beds, or you can get man-made facsimiles in florist or hobby shops. The stone base is especially effective with plants that are notable for the beauty of their stems, leaves, flowers or seeds. In this instance the visual and physical hardness of the stone serves to point up the sinuous curves of the clematis and the succulent thickness of the giant sedum, *S. maximum* 'Atropurpureum,' which is combined with it.

Invisible Support

Container: One overscaled champagne glass, 1 or 1½ feet high
Holder: One glass block flower holder
Plants: Three stems clematis, 4 to 8 inches long; six to eight stems cypress
spurge, 5 to 10 inches long
Water: To rim

Ethereal flowers are particularly beautiful in glass or crystal containers, but the beauty is sometimes marred by the obvious methods used to keep the flowers in place. One simple and almost invisible method is illustrated here. An old-fashioned glass block flower holder is placed at the bottom of the container. Flowers are then simply inserted in the apertures, avoiding, if at all possible, the crisscrossing of stems under water. If the holes of the glass flower holder are too large, woody green stem ends are wedged into the openings until the flower is kept in the desired position. Because the holder is not fastened to the bottom of the glass, place the flowers in such a way that an actual physical balance is maintained. Do this by adding a few plants at a time, first to one side and then the other, rather than by following the usual technique of completing one side and then revolving the container and arranging the other. If a glass flower holder is not available, the balance may be built up by making a grid of transparent plastic tape over the top of the bowl. This is slightly more difficult than using a glass holder, but becomes easier when one learns to balance two or four elements against each other in the center. Occasionally a temporary union of two stems can be made with gummed tape or wire.

The *Euphorbia cyparissias* or cypress spurge is one of the milky-sapped flowers that bleed when cut. Therefore, seal the stem by burning or dipping in boiling water (195) before placing it in the arrangement. Otherwise the water will become milky and discolored, spoiling the lovely clarity of effect. The tendrils of the *Clematis X* 'Ramona' vine curl gracefully over the rim of the bowl and provide an attractive contrast to the spurge. The baroque curves of the stem and leaf of the clematis also lead the eye back into the arrangement.

Arrange as You Pick

Container: Gardener's picking can
Plants: Three stems Jacob's-rod, 20 to 27 inches; one giant sedum, 6½ inches; two honesty stems, 20 to 30 inches; one broad-leaved glaucous spurge, 10 inches
Water: To top of container

Borrow an idea from the practical British gardeners and flower arrangers: when in your own cutting garden pick and then immediately arrange your materials. In other words, cut to the desired lengths and place the plants in the water-filled cutting cans at once. As you place the material in the cans, superfluous basal foliage may be shucked off with a quick movement of the hands, stripping the plant of leaves below water level. An attractive grouping, uncontrived in appearance, will reward your efforts. The plants shown here are all very long-lasting, and they undergo interesting developmental changes with the passage of time. The color contrasts are attractive, an important consideration when selecting your material for this type of design. The *Lunaria annua* stems may be cut when the moon-shaped discs are a soft, pale green—when the seeds are semiformed—instead of waiting for them to ripen. All the plants will dry in this condition and retain their engaging forms for many months. The Jacob's-rod, *Asphodeline lutea,* which is a glaucous green with intermittently opening giant starlike pale-yellow blooms, curves at the unopened tip of the bloom head in a form reminiscent of a peacock feather. The giant sedum, *S. maximum* 'Atropurpureum,' grey-green to rosy purple-pink, gives substance, weight and focus to the base of the arrangement, and the *Euphorbia myrsinites* picks up the grey green of the asphodeline leaves.

This apparently casual design, reinforced by the slender, straplike carrying handle on the cutting can, makes a design that is suitable for many informal areas, for a terrace or enclosed court, as well as for a raised stone or brick fireplace, or for a low shelf. Best of all, the arrangement is completed on the spot and material is handled only once with this procedure. Do keep in a cool dark spot for several hours to "harden off" before putting it on display.

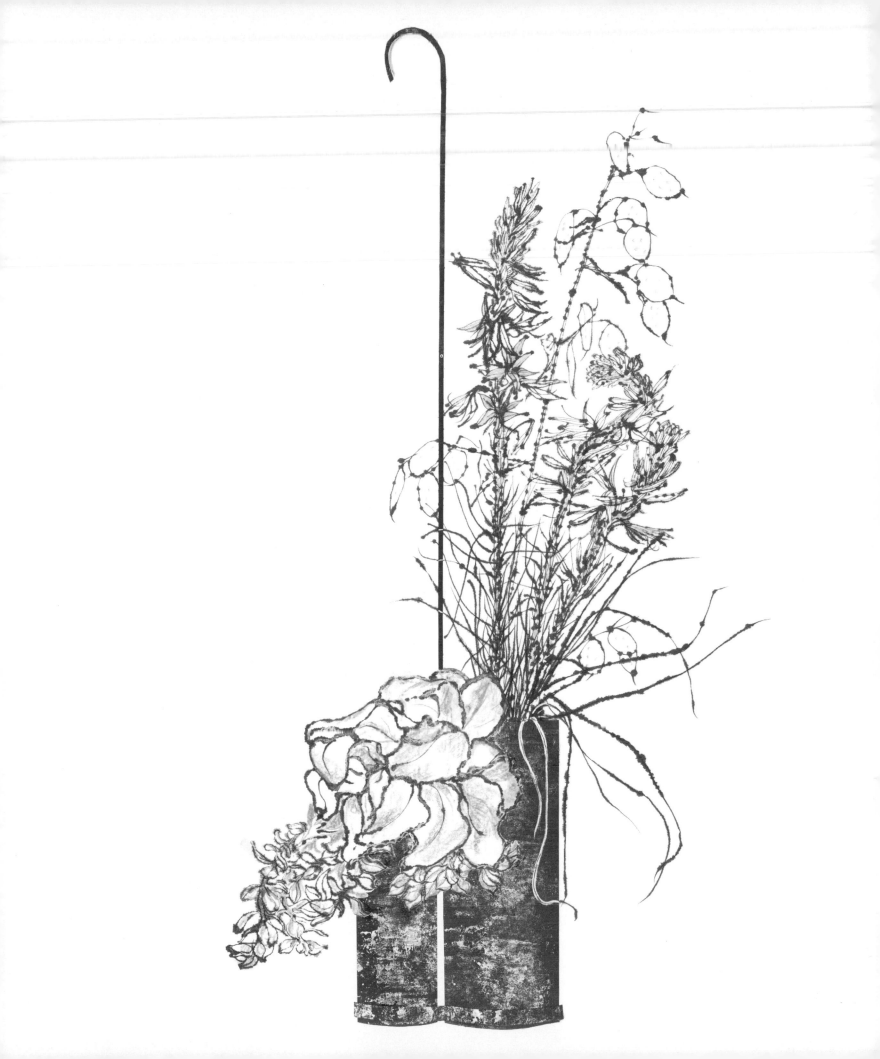

Glass Protection for Fragile Flowers

Container: Glass apothecary jar, old medicine jar or fishbowl
Holder: Small needle holder with suction ring attachment
Plants: Columbine, 17 inches; two spotted Italian arum leaves, 5 to 7½ inches, and bloom
Water: Shallow cup holder in jar

Winter gardens, courtyards, driveway plantings are all made interesting by the triangular white-netted, glossy leaf of *Arum italicum* 'Marmoratum,' which remains beautiful throughout our southern Ohio winters. In late spring, with the appearance of the 8- to 10-inch pale green spathe and ivory spadix looking like a beautiful jade calla lily, the plant reaches its apogee and thereafter withers and disappears until the following autumn, when the dark green arrowhead-shaped leaves make their appearance again. Meanwhile the spadix has ripened its airy but tight-packed blooms into layers of red seeds almost indistinguishable from jack-in-the-pulpit clusters. A gardener may choose this last stage of beauty to cut one or two leaves for an arrangement, although it is a six-month-long temptation. Simultaneous with this bloom appears the equally dramatic but lighter and airier columbine growing at a higher level. This *Aquilegia* 'Hensol Harebell,' a strong blue with sturdy spurs, is a great naturalizer, as is *A. vulgaris* var. *nivea* 'Grandiflora,' whose long white spurs would recall the marbled white veining of the arum leaf. These prima donnas can be arranged together to create a glorious floral *pas de deux*.

See them here in an old medical jar which has measured markings. But a cylinder of glass, a large wine balloon or overscaled brandy snifter, or even a rounded fishbowl also affords the moist air that keeps these materials fresh for a maximum period of time. The plant material may be arranged by bracing it against the sides of the container so that no obvious method of support shows.

I use a small needle-type holder imbedded in a plastic base and anchored to the bottom of the container with a suction ring attachment. Columbine leaves camouflage the holder.

Grasses, Sedges and Reeds

Container: Incense pot with grilled lid
Holder: Pin-type
Plants: Two dozen stems of Kentucky blue or other grasses, sedges or reeds,
   11 to 21 inches
Water: Container one-third filled, then water is permitted to evaporate

The poetry of grasses, sedges and reeds is apparent to most nature lovers. Even those who appreciate the undulating movement and currents of the wind's passage through a prairie grassland or mountain meadow are amazed to observe the forceful beauty of a mere handful of grasses arranged simply in a handsome container. About the bluegrass, *Poa pratensis*, shown here, whose luxuriant character has given its name to a whole region, no one knows if it is a native or an alien to the Kentucky cane areas (39). A bona fide native, the big blue stem (14), placed in an umbrella stand or large pickling jar can bring you a feeling of prairie spaces.

Here the ascending pyramidal line of the bluegrass is contained as in a frame by the widespread handles of the Oriental container. The squat, rather heavy proportions of this metal bowl provide balance for the exaggerated slender height of the delicate grass stems.

The grasses may be bunched in the hand and tied at the base with a string, or held with an elastic band. Then the whole group is impaled on a pin holder. An alternate method is to place the grasses one at a time in a metal, glass or pottery flower holder with more widely spaced apertures into which the grass stems might be inserted. If the openings are too large, wedge auxiliary twigs or rolls of paper at the base of the stems to add bulk.

This type of arrangement will last for long periods of time. It is wise to place it in water originally so that the stems do not become limp and collapse. Then let the water evaporate and the plants dry in place. For long-term preservation, many arrangers spray the dried grasses with a clear sealer or plastic spray. This also helps retain form and rigidity. It is possible to use various grasses as a "filler" between other flowers or leaves, but I find them most beautiful alone.

Straight Lines Meet Circles

Container: Round earthenware container
Holder: Well-type pinpoint holder
Plants: Eight stems field horsetail, 12 to 17 inches; four stems yellow Missouri
   primrose, 6 to 7½ inches
Water: In well-type holder only
Other Materials: Florist's clay

There are some plants that communicate a sense of history. *Equisetum arvense*, field horsetail or scouring rush, with its beautiful cylindrical, jointed stems, is one of these. This plant was in existence in the millennia when the coal measures were laid down, and somehow it has survived to the present day, in the very select company of a few club mosses, ferns and the gingko tree.

To provide contrast to the linear pattern of the equisetum stems, I use blossoms of the soft yellow Missouri primrose, *Oenothera missouriensis*, as a focusing device. Most experienced flower arrangers utilize this idea without consciously thinking about it. It is almost a rule of thumb to contrast round or radial forms with vertical ones, since one will complement the beauty of the other.

The actual pattern of nature may be simulated by bending or utilizing a wind-bent equisetum stem. A round earthenware container is chosen to repeat the circular form of the primrose blossoms, and a radiating pattern of yellow ochre on the base of the container reaffirms the beautiful coloring of the blooms. The rough, greyish-brown texture of the exterior recalls the ribbing of the equisetum. A well-type pinpoint holder, fastened off-center inside the bowl, makes it possible for the interior coloring and design of the waterless container itself to be seen. This technique can be employed whenever the lining of the container is important in color and design. In this case, the equisetum may be permitted to dry in place and will remain strikingly beautiful in pattern long after the primroses have faded.

Roses-of-Sharon, handsomely marked mallow flowers, tuberous-rooted begonia blooms or hollyhock blossoms are all quite acceptable substitutes for the less frequently seen primrose.

Plants Chosen for Rhythmic Rapport

Container: Rectangular brown Oriental terra cotta container
Holder: Pinpoint holder
Plants: Three giant garlic, 12 to 20 inches, and six dried wisteria tendrils, 15 to 18 inches
Water: To top of pebbles

The flower arranger usually looks for material that has an interesting curve or dramatic and appealing line. Because giant garlic, *Allium sativum*, has both, it is one of the great favorites. These glaucous pale-green allium stems, which have been impaled on a pinpoint holder and held in place by trickling pure white stones around the stems, are balanced at the right by the penmanshiplike circles of dried *Wisteria sinensis* tendrils. These stems may be saved and reused many times. The trick in making an arrangement like this is to control and eliminate. Having selected the right stem and the proper container, reduce the stem length without hesitation when a shorter piece will benefit the line and proportions. Unnecessary and distracting side branches or leaves should always be removed. This type of arrangement is best placed in front of a plain wall surface and lit as dramatically as possible to provide interesting shadows.

Container as Design Reinforcer

Container: Columnar vase with hooded rim
Holders: Well-type needle-point flower holder and loosely crushed chicken wire ball
Plants: Two pinellia, 13 to 14 inches; green dragon leaf, 9 inches; two sedge seed-heads, 9 to 10 inches
Water: To top of container
Other Materials: Square-topped Japanese flower stand

The two-hooded *Pinellia ternata* blooms rise dramatically from the mouth of the ceramic columnar container with a sheathed lip which repeats the semicovered motif of the spathe. A strong, cantilevered green dragon leaf, *Arisaema dracontium*, curves around the base of the vase. A matching green well-type needle-point flower holder, shaped in an arc, affords both moisture and support for the broadly stretched leaf. The simple pedestal of classic form provides a base that serves to unify the two elements into a single arrangement. The round, spiked seed-heads of *Carex grayii*, one of the sedges, has a diagonally compelling Dali-esque thrust that delights me. Some of the sedge's slender foliage has been clipped to emphasize and clarify the design. Mist with an atomizer to keep the foliage fresh and crisp looking.

Floor Vases for Impressive Arrangements

Container: Pottery floor vase, umbrella stand or metal cylinder
Holder: Heavy stones, half bricks and chicken wire
Plants: Five stalks yucca, 24 to 40 inches
Water: One-half the depth of container

The stately, commanding blooms of *Yucca filamentosa*, Spanish bayonet or Adam's needle, as it is sometimes called, give dramatic accent to our steep and sun-washed hillsides in late June. They give the same look of grandeur in a 20-inch terra cotta floor vase, with the 3- to 4-foot bloom stalks simply arranged in a manner that recalls their natural growth. Coils of rolled-up chicken wire, mashed inside the container, keep the bloom stalks in place. Because of the weight of these bloom stalks, a very heavy container is required to prevent the arrangement from tipping over. When it is impossible to obtain a sufficiently heavy receptacle, I weight the vase or bowl with bricks or stones to provide ballast. Precaution for providing ample weight is especially important since the container should be only half filled with water. The fleshy stems will rot if deeply immersed. The heavy leaves are placed around the bloom stalks, recalling their growth at the base of the stem. The seed pods of this yucca are particularly good in dried arrangements. They will last for several years and may be used again and again.

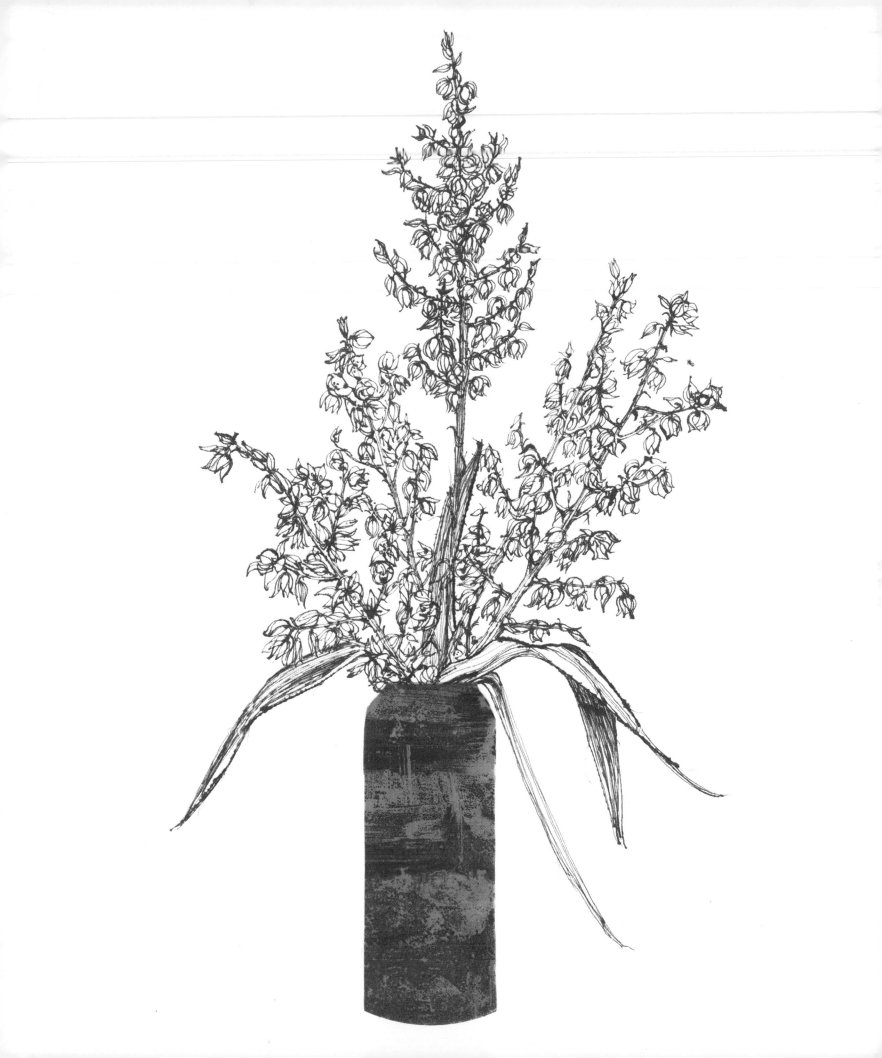

Strength with Simple Materials

Container: Aquarium
Holder: Pinpoint
Plants: Seven fresh garden onions, 12 to 20 inches; four dried onion blooms, 3 inches
Water: Only in well-type pinpoint holder
Other Materials: Stone

Whether the plants are native, exotic or cultivated, the feeling of movement and rhythmic repetition of form is one of the important considerations in any serious designing. Certain flowers, usually those of bold, dramatic outline, have such force that auxiliary foliage is not necessary or even advisable. The common onion, *Allium cepa*, with its strange and beautiful curves, is such a plant. The curves are part of the arrangement, and are as effective as the bloom. This design requires a glass container of definite outline; in this case I have used a heavy rectangular fishbowl. The arrangement is achieved by attaching a well-type lead holder with pinpoint base to the glass aquarium with a small amount of florist's clay. The tallest stem, which defines the maximum height, is added first. Then the more extended lateral stems at left and right are placed. The stems are kept closely grouped at the base and as parallel as possible to keep a look of strength and simplicity. Although the height and width are great in relation to the size of the container, the forms are so airy that this proportion is visually acceptable. An attractive heavy stone is placed at the base, partially in front of the holder, which is further disguised by the massing of extra bloom heads at this level.

This rectangular fishbowl can also be used for the growing of moisture-loving plants, as well as for arrangements of dried and fresh material which extend well above the rim. For small growing plants, such as woodland groundcover, a sheet of glass should be placed over the top of the container to minimize water loss. Let the terrarium touch the glass at a north window with good light. The glass will absorb coolness from out of doors. Also give the plants a sprinkling every week or so if they seem dry, and lift the lid every few days for a minute or two to let in air.

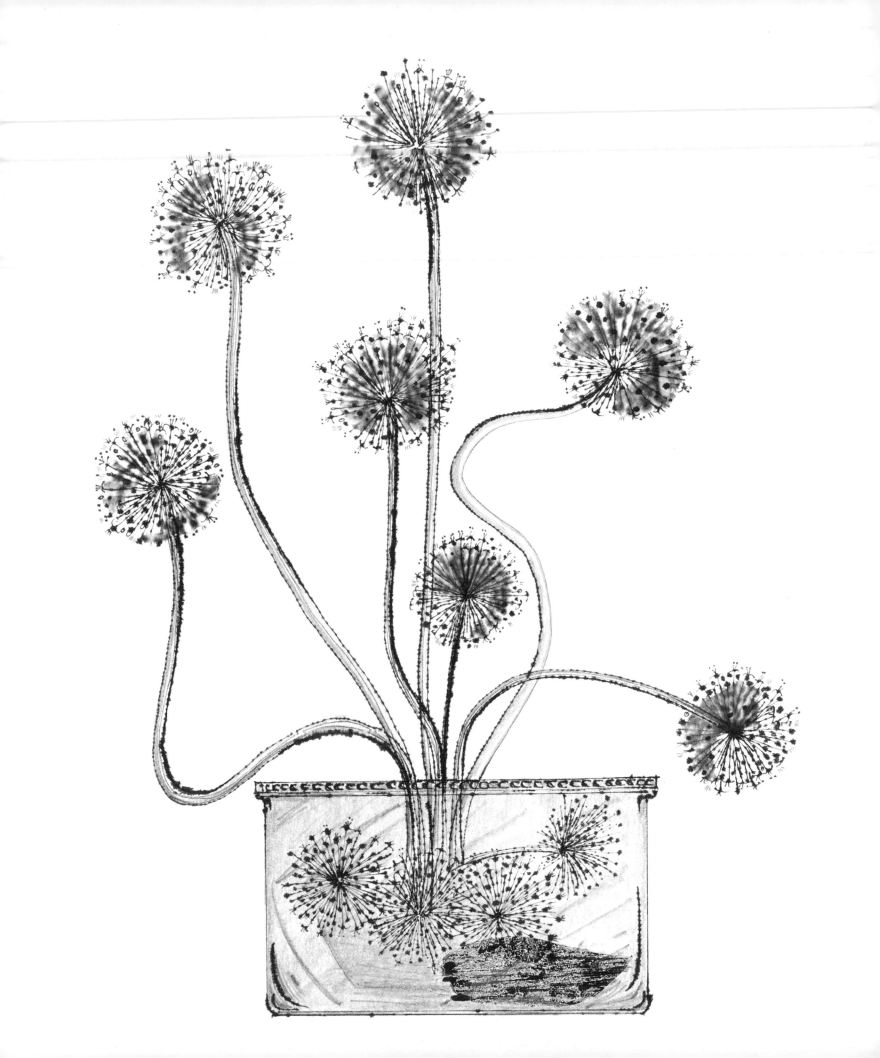

Growth Form Dictates Design

Container: Narrow-necked container
Plants: Three berried Solomon's-seal sprays, 15 to 28 inches
Water: Full, for ballast

Great Solomon's-seal leaves, *Polygonatum canaliculatum,* with their parallel venation, beautifully arched with pendant berries and blooms and patterned precision at the leaf nodes, almost place themselves. It is interesting to use plants of this type at almost their full length to create the illusion of a growing specimen. A narrow-necked container was chosen to hold the stems in position.

The foliage of the false Solomon's-seal, *Smilacina racemosa* (119), looks much like the authentic version and lends itself to a similar type of placement. In large arrangements, these two foliages are frequently utilized to establish a fan-shaped or vertical background for other plants.

Wine Jug Arrangement

Container: Wooden wine jug or bottle, copper bound, 12 to 15 inches
Plants: Three stems everlasting or perennial peas, 18 to 20 inches; two stems gas plant, about 18 to 30 inches
Water: Filled to top

The vinelike tips of *Lathyrus latifolius,* the perennial or everlasting pea, twine and fall in a fashion difficult to control. One solution to the arranging of these wiry legumes is to use them in a narrow-necked pitcher such as this French wooden wine jug. The plants are given a certain degree of support and the articulated stems fall in their own natural lines. The stems of the rigid, vertical *Dictamnus albus,* or gas plant, provide contrast by establishing a strong upright pattern which is crossed by the curved one. The aromatic dictamnus pods dry in an interesting way and repeat the natural wood tones of the jug, which must be kept filled with water at all times to prevent the wood from shrinking.

Double Duty for a Vasculum

Container: Metal vasculum

Holder: Foam blocks in refrigerator containers

Plants: Two stems pink single roses, 6 to 8 inches; butterfly weed, 8 inches; three stems yellow single roses, 5 to 8 inches; three stems field daisies; red clover, 6 inches; honeysuckle, 8 to 10 inches; black-eyed Susan, barren strawberries, thistles, daisy fleabane, St. John's-wort, golden rain tree blooms; two stems bouncing-Bet, 8 to 10 inches

A vasculum filled with a water-holding foam and moist moss provides the background for a collection of the riches available on the first of July. Incidentally, these materials have, for me, all the color and explosive beauty of a great fireworks display.

The arrangement of this great variety can be difficult; here are a few suggestions which may be of assistance. Group materials rather than divide them in a helter-skelter fashion. Pink and yellow single roses are kept to the right side, along with red clover, *Trifolium pratense,* and graceful tips of the prolific honeysuckle, *Lonicera japonica.* Butterfly weed, *Asclepias tuberosa,* field daisies, *Chrysanthemum leucanthemum,* and black-eyed Susan, *Rudbeckia hirta,* give startling color to the other end of the box. Daisy fleabane, *Ergeron annuus,* and *Hypericum patulum* 'Hidcote' sparkle in the center of the upper layer. The beautiful leaves and blossoms of *Koelreuteria paniculata,* the golden rain tree, lend distinguished grace to this tapestrylike combination. Skyrockets of prickly thistle blooms, *Cirsium arvense,* reach upward, while stems of tiny strawberries, *Duchesnea indica,* with their characteristic leaves, cling to the rim of the container and fall forward. Bouncing-Bet, *Saponaria officinalis,* soon to end its blooming cycle, registers in a final burst of sprightly bloom. Some water-filled glass tubes, elevated on twigs or wooden sticks, may be used to supplement the stems when greater length is needed. The gardener's picnic table would sparkle with such a comprehensive decoration.

Showcase Container

Container: Multiple-necked ceramic container
Plants: Four 'Gloriosa Daisies,' 7 to 12 inches; two dried stems gas plant, 18 to 20
    inches
Water: To brim

The arrangement of *Rudbeckia hirta,* 'Gloriosa Daisies,' and *Dictamnus albus* in this multiple-necked container—a type that is almost self-arranging—proves that the short stems may be an advantage rather than a disadvantage if the result prompts the viewer to look down on the handsome flower forms and examine them more carefully. The daisies, with their brilliant color, rest directly on the container. The daringly simple use of the flowers carries out the vertical axis of the container with two oppositional lines of last year's gas plant seed pods for contrast. Unusual starkness of effect is achieved by the complete elimination of any softening auxiliary foliage. Again, do disregard the old saw about using the largest flowers only at low points. They can be used high just as well when needed for balance or emphasis.

Blossoms against Mats

Background: Translucent discs, circular-cut boards or tray
Holder: Two water picks or tubes
Plants: Flower heads from two stems dill, 3- to 6-inch diameter
Water: Tube or pick filled
Other Materials: Adhesive, transparent, plastic or florist's tape, wire or glue to fasten tubes to background, eyedropper to refill tubes

Fresh flowers and seed pods may be used as living botany prints. The beautiful circular design of the dill, *Anethum graveolens,* an introduced annual from Asia which has become naturalized and grows along roadsides and waste places as well as in cultivation, lends itself to a circular plaque-like wall treatment. The compound umbels of yellow flowers and the finely dissected fennel-like leaves combine to give a delightfully lacy look. In the accompanying drawing, you will see one method of designing the plaque-like arrangement. Affix a water-holding tube to the translucent discs, tray, or circular-cut board with florist's or masking tape, wire or glue, depending on the permanence of the arrangement and the surface of the background. These tubes of plastic or glass may be obtained from any florist or saved from drug supplies. The florist's tubes come equipped with a rubber cap with a hole through which the plant stem can be inserted. The tube may be painted to match the stem color or background color if you feel it is too conspicuous. An eyedropper will be needed to refill the tube, as it holds relatively little water. Spraying the flowers with a sealing preservative, which cuts down on water loss, will also enhance the keeping qualities. Dried materials such as allium, hydrangea, yarrow or the perennial fennel may be used similarly, but then the tube is unnecessary. Only transparent tape is needed to fasten the dry stems to the background.

Showy Specimen Arrangement

Container: Shallow silver-lined copper bowl
Holder: Lead loop strips covered with sand
Plants: Two stems lilies, 12 to 20 inches; 'Gloriosa Daisy' stems, 7 to 10 inches
Water: Shallow

The attractive Golden Clarion hybrid trumpet lilies prove eye-compelling material for flower arrangements. The regal height and balance of the stems suggest that this natural dignity be maintained. Often I find that the design is improved if some of the buds and blooms are removed and used at the base of the arrangement, as shown here, or reserved for another grouping. The lily foliage is crisp and beautiful and usually needs no additional greenery. *Rudbeckia hirta,* 'Gloriosa Daisies,' used at the base of the arrangement are strong enough in design, form and color to balance the vigor of the lilies. These flowers were beloved by many artists: Minoan potters used them as decoration on vases; Byzantines incorporated them into exquisite palace mosaics; great Italian painters of the Renaissance portrayed them on canvas; designers of *art nouveau* recreated them in metal and jewelry.

In the arrangement shown, the flowers are held in place in a shallow silver-lined copper bowl with a holder made of looped strips of lead hooked over the upper edge of one side of the container (200). This method is firm and inconspicuous and can be made almost invisible by covering the lead strips with sand.

If you are the victim of lily pollen smears on your clothing, lift the clinging powdery substance from the stained garment with a fluffy dab of cotton. Trying to rub or brush the pollen away can be disastrous.

Vine Curtain

Container: Scooped-out bamboo stalks, 36 inches
Holder: Foil-covered foam wedged into bamboo sections
Plants: Five blooming or seeded ivy strands, 8 to 24 inches; two wild or escaped
    cultivated grape strands, 12 inches; two akebia vines, 28 inches; one white
    wild potato-vine, 12 inches; one dried wisteria stem, 10 inches; one bristly
    greenbrier, 12 inches
Water: Enough to soak foam
Other Materials: Cord around ends of bamboo for hanging

The grace of vines can be utilized in a pendant arrangement which focuses attention on the beauty of the individual leaves and the varied, rhythmic motions of the strands. To create this curtain of hanging vines, I use a split, scooped-out bamboo stalk filled with a saturated water-holding foam. The foam is bound in place with adhesive tape sprayed or crayoned to match the bamboo, thus rendering the binding almost invisible. Grapevines, both the native fox grape, *Vitis labrusca*, and the escaped cultivated grape, add familiar charm. I usually keep the vines between layers of dampened newspaper until they are ready to be used; they do not last well when exposed to the drying air of the average household. Once the vines are in place, misting them with a florist's bulb spray helps to maintain the necessary high humidity level. The residue will give a visual effect of dew.

Bristly greenbrier, *Smilax hispida*, upper left, and smilax species with their distinctive clinging tendrils, wreathe the trees and shrubs of the second-growth community in a cobweblike curtain. It is important, therefore, to include them in any vine arrangement that is typical of the area. Another evergreen vine that is ubiquitous in its escaped and naturalized form is the English ivy, *Hedera helix* (113). In blooming condition, the ivy is highly attractive, but it must be remembered that the pollen is poisonous if ingested. Seen above the bamboo holder are the seeded blossoms and mature ovate leaves of arborescent ivies. The braided habit of the *Akebia quinata* is a pleasant contrast to the ivy and smilax, and the coiled curves of the old wisteria stem, *W. sinensis*, are a true decorator's delight. Morning glories, like the giant wild potato-vine, *Ipomoea pandurata*, cut in bud in the evening, will open for the next morning. They are a beautiful addition to any vine arrangement.

The same considerations of design apply in making arrangements of hanging vines as in making those in which the stems are self-supporting. Avoid isolated elements; lead the eye in an easy transition from one vine to another, and try for interestingly varied leaf and bud forms.

The Built-In Holder

Container: Ceramic container with multiple bottle-necked openings
Plants: Six 'Gloriosa Daisies,' 13 to 24 inches; two purple coneflowers, 28 inches;
two dried poppy pods, 26 inches
Water: To brim

Strength meets strength in a striking flower arrangement designed for a boldly patterned container. The geometric pattern of this thin, rectangular block, pierced at the top to provide a built-in flower holder, is relieved by a texturally raised circle of glazed clay. The surface and form of the container dictate the choice of flowers and seed pods used in it. The coneflowers, *Echinacea purpurea*, *Rudbeckia hirta*, 'Gloriosa Daisies,' and the immature poppy pods, *Papaver orientale*, are all distinguished by their textured centers. Incidentally, the poppy pods, similar to pepper shakers in function, may be saved and used repeatedly in varied designs. The stems of these plants are carefully arranged at a diagonal slant that repeats the designs on the container. This pleasing division of space brings the eye to the point at which the stems meet and emerge from the container. Here I have placed one particularly choice sunflower-like bloom. The rhythmic quality of the design gives it a studied feeling, quite different from casual designs. Foliage which would confuse or complicate the strong stem pattern is deliberately removed, a permissible act when a designer is working to achieve a severe line effect. A few containers of this type are an addition to any collection, for they allow the use of a minimal amount of material so grouped that the flowers, and especially grass forms, can be individually relished. Because of their small necks, holders or braces are seldom necessary. As demonstrated, not every neck need be filled. When they are, guard against too much diagonal crossing of stem lines.

Live Flowers That Turn into a Dried Arrangement

Container: Antique copper flat-sided coffeepot

Holder: Chicken wire, crumpled

Plants: Nine stems goldenrod, 12 to 22 inches; five stems wild aster, 15 to 21 inches; three stems Queen Anne's lace, 12 to 16 inches; five blooms Jerusalem artichokes, 8 to 10 inches; and stems of burdock burs, 12 to 16 inches

Water: To brim of container

Massed arrangements seem to reflect the luxuriant beauty of late summer and fall flora. Asters, *A. ericoides* and *A. azureus,* and goldenrod, *Solidago ulmifolia,* found in many species at the edge of the woodlands, in open fields and along the roadsides, serve to establish the maximum height and spread of this arrangement. The asters and burdock burs of *Arctium minus* are used as starry "filler flowers." Focus and a strong basic pattern are given by the brilliant blooms of Jerusalem artichoke, *Helianthus tuberosus,* and Queen Anne's lace, *Daucus carota.* Excess foliage has all been pruned away. All varieties lend themselves to drying in borax or hot sand (197); they will keep their color as well as their form exceptionally well for a long time.

A Bow to the Orient

Container: Traditional black iron usubata in two pieces
Holder: Pinpoint metal holder with Japanese name of kenzan, and forked flower
holder called a kupari
Plants: Three stems plume poppy, 20 to 48 inches, and two stems blackberry-
lily, 24 to 28 inches
Water: To brim of container
Other Materials: Usuban-kwaban, a black teakwood square base used under
container

The fragile beauty of the plume poppy, *Macleaya cordata*, with its soaring arched stem and beige seed tassel, provides a delicate yet effective contrast to the mature late-summer pattern of the fanned-out, irislike foliage and the shining black seed pod of *Belamcanda chinensis*, so like a blackberry that it gives the plant the name of blackberry-lily. These two diverse forms dramatically illustrate the power of exaggerated linear elongation in floral design. In this case the rather extreme height of the plant materials indicates the end of a lush growing period. The technical aspects of this design are simple. The irislike leaves of the blackberry-lily are regrouped to simulate the natural habit of growth and are then impaled on a sharp-needled pinpoint flower holder. At the base of the well in the top of the usubata a forked Y-shaped kupari could have been used alone or with the kenzan. The plume poppies are placed at an angle on the holder to achieve lateral emphasis as well as dramatic height. The black teakwood base, an usubankwaban, is used to give visual balance to the composition in the traditional Japanese manner. The usubata consists of two main parts, the vase proper and a flat, panlike top in which water is filled to the edge. Either part may be used alone. It is generally made of iron or bronze and is often identified with nineteenth-century classic Japanese arrangements.

Thorns as Holders for Blooms Needing Almost No Moisture

Container: Aluminum and stainless steel serving platter
Holder: Pinpoint holder
Plants: Three locust thorn branches, 20 to 24 inches; colchicum blooms in variety, 3- to 4-inch diameter
Water: To top of well-cup in pinpoint holder
Other Materials: Moist cotton, twig-colored florist's tape, sand-polished driftwood

The varying pattern of the colchicums (174) is one of the magic beauties of autumn and it is pure excitement to maintain that mood of wonder in an arrangement.

Here is one way to do it. Impale all but six blooms on the needle-sharp thorns of the honey locust, *Gleditsia triacanthos,* that rests on the base of wave- and sand-polished river driftwood, a setting that provides an interesting contrast to the slightly iridescent texture of the blossoms. Small blossoms are best balanced on the terminal thorns. A clusterlike bouquet of the six larger flowers, in both rare white and lilac-mauve, issue from a well-like opening in the driftwood base. The methods are simple. Use well-type needle holders, partially tucked under the driftwood, for maximum ease of placement. The holders are disguised with pebbles or bits of moss. An oval serving platter of dull antique or tarnished finish is a perfect foil for the stellar beauty of the colchicum. These are among the few flowers that will keep almost as well out of water as in it. But for added security, especially if the flowers are known to be several days old, you might add a bit of wet cotton to the base of the petiole. The blooms will usually last two or three days without the damp cotton, if they are not placed in strong sunlight, heat or a drying draft. Twig-colored florist's tape may then be wrapped around the bloom end to fasten it to the thorn. Other blossoms that may be similarly used are mallow, hibiscus, morning glory and daylily (for short-term effects), and many of the small chrysanthemums and native thistles, which will last one to two weeks. For a really long-lasting effect, impale dried allium pods on the thorns, choosing the allium species best in scale with the size of your thorn grouping.

Garlands

Container: Pair of two-tiered tole containers with foot, one central tole container
with lion's head decoration

Holder: Water-holding foam

Plants: Sedum in variety, 5½ to 12½ inches; leadwort, 6 to 8 inches; ebony
spleenwort, 5 to 7 inches; common houseleek, 3 inches; gill-over-the-ground,
4 inches; baby cyclamen stems, 4 to 6 inches; thyme, 6 to 8 inches, and ivy
leaves, 2½ to 3½ inches

Water: Enough to saturate foam

Other Materials: Fine wire

The "graceful garland" has dressed table, wall, and pillar for centuries.
Sedum sieboldii, which grows in a continuous, evenly patterned manner, may be
picked and recombined into a half-circle to create a garland. Bind together a

number of sprays with spool wire looped around the stems to form a curved foliage connection from one container to another. Strands of *Thymus serpyllum* wired together make two graceful arcs looped from the central container. The fronds of ebony spleenwort, *Asplenium platyneuron*, the thyme and *Cyclamen neapolitanum* 'Album' afford rich, handsomely patterned forms. A pair of tiered containers of tole are combined in this design with a central matching single-level container. The lion's head with ring decoration repeats the formal circle pattern of the rosetted *Sempervivum tectorum*, or common houseleek, below and circlets of *Glechoma hederacea*, gill-over-the-ground, in the top layer. Leadwort, *Ceratostigma plumbaginoides*, echoes the drooping lines of the *Sedum sieboldii* above. Moisture-holding foam packed into the containers furnishes a medium in which the succulent plants will last for weeks, and even continue to grow. These arrangements are splendid for formal tables, mantel shelf, or credenza treatments. Virgin's bower, *Clematis virginiana*, with its graceful strands and pleasant fragrance, also lends itself to this type of arrangement.

Hanging Arrangement

Container: Japanese reed basket with liner
Holder: Water-holding foam or crumpled chicken wire
Plants: Four stems dogwood, 10 to 16 inches long in leaf and seed
Water: To rim of liner
Other Material: Rope or wire to suspend basket

Red drupes of the beloved flowering dogwood, *Cornus florida*, and the brilliant pinkish-flame to burgundy-red leaves which range from ovate to acuminate, make the flowering dogwood as beautiful in late September and early October as it is when the creamy white bracts drift across the spring landscape. This shrub-tree is easily identified by the horizontal, or layered, growth of the branches, blooms and fruits. Thus it is an interesting and challenging problem to arrange it in such a way that these branches have a natural appearance. A horizontal hanging basket or a basket placed on a high shelf is an ideal container. When a burst of autumn color is needed for an indoors effect, choose this time for necessary pruning of your own dogwood tree. Unless the indoor humidity is high, the leaves will curl in a relatively short period. It would be advisable to make this

arrangement as close as possible to the time when you wish it to be viewed. If you choose branches from which the leaves have dropped but which still retain their colorful seeds, you will have a good contrast with the spring bud and branch form. This kind of viewing, very close to eye level, gives one a new assessment of the beauty of this cornus.

Hamamelis virginiana, the witch-hazel, which blooms in late autumn (50), is another shrub that we would suggest cutting and enjoying in a similar way. Hollies too are too rarely used in containers that permit us to enjoy their branching habit. The trumpet creeper, *Campsis radicans*, is an ideal midsummer material for the hanging arrangement. It is gracefully at home in this setting. A light syringing with a spray atomizer, placement out of hot sunlight—and certainly not over a radiator—and protection with a cellophane sheet when not being viewed will keep these treasures looking handsome for several days.

Wind-Shaped Arrangement

Container: French tin-lined copper mold
Holder: Chicken wire crumpled to fit container
Plants: Eight stems of teasel, 6 to 20 inches; five stems of aster, 10 to 20 inches, and yarrow, 6 to 8 inches long
Water: To brim of container, allowed to evaporate when materials have dried
Other Materials: Florist's tape to hold wire in place, pebbles to weight arrangement

Many native materials and their naturalized companions dry in graceful curves and in subtle blonde to beige and brown colorings which are reminiscent of the autumn and winter woods. It is wise to choose materials that have already taken on a directional curve like the *Aster ericoides,* shown here, or to collect a sufficient amount of material to permit a choice. By stressing a specific line, one creates an impression of wind-bent branches. Thus, projection of a right-angled triangle, made with *Dipsacus sylvestris,* or teasel, and reinforced by yarrow, *Achillea millefolium,* may be used to fit a certain end of the mantel shelf, buffet or hutch to take on a casual look and avoid a too rigid feeling.

A chicken wire base filling the cavity of the mold affords maximum angle of insertion of the flowers and pods used. It is important to keep the wire slightly below the rim of the container. It is easy to fasten the loosely crumpled wire in place by taping it to the side with florist's or masking tape in a color that is close to holder or flowers. A tiny bit of sticky clay on the outside of the tape, where it meets and projects into the holder, will keep a camouflaging leaf or seed pod in place and help to disguise the methods used. Gravel or sand weighting the container will provide necessary ballast.

Golden rain tree pods, sumac seed heads, iris seed pods, fern fruiting bodies and cat-tails all lend themselves to arrangements of this kind. This is an excellent way of using and displaying some of your favorite antique pieces, for interest in the container is often greater with dried materials.

The Two-Linked Container

Container: Shallow two-level ceramic container
Plants: One star-of-Persia seed head, 10 inches; two Schubert onion blooms, 10 inches; and common houseleek, 4 inches in diameter
Other Materials: Brownish-olive florist's tape, florist's stick wire

The lasting blooms and seed heads of *Allium christophii*, also known as *A. albopilosum*, or star-of-Persia, recommend themselves to us throughout the year. The purplish-grey metallic blooms are beautiful at first flowering. Later the plant produces some starlike seed pods that resemble a bursting sky rocket. *A. schubertii* is pinkish while fresh. Either of these alliums, fresh, or dried as shown here, are cut at a length that fits in with the overall size you wish for your own setting. Insert a piece of florist's stick wire in the stem to make it possible to bend the stems slightly and to give them mechanical support. Push the wire all the way up to the seed head. There is a point near the dried bloom at which the stem will shrivel or break. It is here that the wire stem becomes most important. I cover the wire with a brownish-olive florist's tape that is twiglike in color. A two-level compartmented ceramic container like the one shown has many advantages. A dry arrangement may be used in one section and a planted one in the other. Very short-stemmed dried materials may be massed in one side or, as shown here, reinforced with the common houseleek, *Sempervivum tectorum,* and taller materials used with greater support and water depth in the second side. Tiny trailing vines or succulents may be draped down from the taller side. One fresh *Lycoris incarnata* (170), similar in silhouette but different in color, would be easy to use as an alternate in the flower design shown here.

Shadow Pictures

Container: Rectangular pewter container, 9 inches
Holder: Pinpoint holder
Plants: Queen Anne's lace, 7 to 10 inches; American bittersweet, 5 to 12 inches
Other Materials: Florist's clay; brown, white or black sand

The fascinating curves and angles of dried plant stems can be dramatically heightened by placing a light in such a position that the shadows emphasize and exaggerate the forms of the stems. There is an element of movement in this flower shadow play that is the result of the original choice of plant stems. Small terminal tips of dried Queen Anne's lace, *Daucus carota*, turn as figures in tableaux of a wildly choreographed ballet. Stems of bittersweet, *Celastrus scandens*, true to their vinelike nature, have hardened into loops and angles that permit them to seem to advance and retreat in this half-humorous, half-grotesque dance. A pinpoint holder is anchored with clay to the base of the rectangular pewter container which forms the stage for this dance macabre of orange bittersweet and grey-brown autumn-dried flowers. Brown, white, or black sand, funneled unevenly into the container to cover the holders, adds interesting basal texture and color.

Composition in a Shadow Box

Container: Shadow box or frame around shallow flat or drawer

Plants: Collection of dried commonplace growths such as lady's-thumb, bottle-brush grass, peppergrass seed pods, dandelion, tragopogon, clematis, black-eyed Susans, mullein pods, sugar maple and hawthorn leaves, pussy willow, cat-tails, cedar gall, nightshade, velvet-leaf, pokeberries, white boneset, honey locust and a plate fungus

Other Materials: Paint, wallpaper, gift wrapping paper or felt, silica gel, borax, sand, florist's aerosol spray or nonwater-based hair lacquer, florist's clay, glue and stapler

For some people, the commonplace plants found along a roadside, open field or hedgerow are just weeds. For an observing, creative designer, they can be the components of a rewarding composition of great aesthetic appeal. The container can be a purchased shadow box, or you can make your own by placing a frame around a shallow drawer or seedling flat. The interior of the box can be painted a neutral or brilliant color, or you can glue or staple wallpaper, gift wrap paper, velvet, felt or other fabrics to the inside of the box to provide an interesting setting for your display.

In this arrangement, I have used velvet-leaf, *Abutilon theophrasti;* bottle-brush grass, *Hystrix patula;* peppergrass seed pods, *Lepidium virginicum;* lady's-thumb, *Polygonum persicaria;* dandelion, *Taraxacum officinale;* cedar gall (133); and *Tragopogon major,* all of them dried. The tragopogon will dry most satisfactorily if picked before the pods open, when they are just showing white. When drying these plants, place them in a carton with the heads supported and they will dry in such a way that they can be used without the need for wire to support the stems. Fix the pods by misting with florist's aerosol glue or a plastic-based hair lacquer. *Clematis tangutica,* black-eyed Susans, *Rudbeckia hirta,* and mullein pods, *Verbascum thapsus,* are dried in silica gel or borax (197). Sugar maple leaves, *Acer saccharum,* and hawthorn leaves of a native *Crataegus* species have been used to add lustrous color. These were pressed in the old way, between the pages of a thick dictionary or family Bible. The newly peeled pussy willow, *Salix discolor,* and small cat-tails, *Typha angustifolia,* kept dry, establish firm central lines in this permanent arrangement.

I have also added a cluster of the bright berries of the nightshade, *Solanum dulcamara,* and the inky blue-black pokeberries, *Phytolacca americana,* which have been dried in sand or silica gel. Dried, fluffy white boneset, *Eupatorium perfoliatum,* which lingers until late fall, gives contrast and looks as though it were rimed with frost. To cover the stems and to simulate a bowl or sconce, I have used a bracket or plate fungus. The entire composition is kept in place by spraying the back of each item with florist's aerosol glue before pressing that item in place. The heavy honey locust bean, *Gleditsia triacanthos,* will require considerable glue. A tack or pin inserted under the fungus will provide additional support for this larger item.

Dried Arrangement on a Tray

Container: Pewter tray

Holder: Dry plastic foam and pinpoint holder

Plants: Ten stems goldenrod, 16 inches; five stems bittersweet, 5 to 11 inches; nine stems Roman wormwood, 13 to 15 inches; two rosettes mullein, 9 to 12 inches

Other Materials: Florist's clay

Color and form combine to make this dried and lasting arrangement express the mood of tongues of flame and puffs of smoke. Bloom ends of goldenrod, *Solidago caesia*, and wormwood, *Artemisia pontica*, permitted to dry in the arrangement, take on a silver-beige coloring and a billowy contour. This radiating design, streaked with the vivid orange and red berries of the American bittersweet, *Celastrus scandens*, issues from a clump of the dried biennial rosettes of common mullein, *Verbascum thapsus*. These materials were pushed into a plastic foam which had in turn been impaled on a pinpoint holder fastened to a dry pewter plate with sticky florist's clay. If hair lacquer is sprayed on an arrangement of this type, it may be retained for a considerable period of time—a year or two is not unusual. If storage space is available, I suggest that the arrangement be stored and reintroduced from time to time, possibly with the addition of some fresh materials to prevent its becoming too familiar from constant viewing.

Wreaths

Holder: Heavy-gauge copper florist's ring, 12-inch diameter
Plants: Pine cones, locust seed pods, acorn clusters, buckeyes, sycamore balls,
   beech nuts, golden rain tree, tulip and jimsonweed pods, Kentucky coffee tree
   pods, sweet gum burs, sumac clusters, leopard's claw
Other Materials: 22- or 24-gauge florist's stick wire and florist's tape

Wreath making is a time-consuming job, but it is a rewarding one when you use the beautiful and long-lasting seed pods of our native and introduced trees, shrubs and herbaceous plants. Red, instead of the usual green, is dominant in this wreath which is comprised primarily of velvety red sumac seed clusters, *Rhus typhina*, with just a bit of American holly, *Ilex opaca*. The technique is quite simple. A heavy-gauge wire copper ring is used as the base. This can be purchased from a florist shop or you can make your own by using a coat hanger, or by clustering long slender willow, birch or hornbeam twigs together and binding them with wire. With 22- or 24-gauge stick wire—to be found at the florist's, hobby shops or hardware stores—make a hairpin shape. Place one end of the wire straight and parallel with the stem of the individual pieces to be used, and bind the other end around the stem end of the pod, using the straight wire as a brace. If the pod has little or no stem, provide one by piercing the pod with a hairpin-shaped wire and twisting it into a stem. Florist's tape in a neutral twig color, spiraled around the wired stems, gives a smooth, natural-looking finish. These stems are then twisted around the ring base in such a way that the individual beauty of each pod and piece of greenery is exploited. At the top of the wreath, two plumelike seed pods of sumac are featured. These seed clusters tend to drop unless fixed in place by spraying with floral glue.

Leaf clusters of American holly have been wound into the wreath to impart a Christmaslike mood and to bring out the form of the other elements. Tufts of the blue-berried juniper, *Juniperus virginiana* (36), can be substituted or added for a fuller, more evergreen look. Ohio buckeyes, *Aesculus glabra*, make glossy additions to the wreath; drill through them off center and insert a wire and bend back to make a stem. Jimsonweed burs, *Datura stramonium*, capped acorn clusters, painted sweet gum burs, *Liquidambar styraciflua*, locust pods, *Robinia pseudo-acacia*, tulip tree blossom pods, *Liriodendron tulipifera*, and channeled, four-angled pods of the golden rain tree, *Koelreuteria paniculata*, also add a variety of forms. *Martynia annua* or leopard's claws, with curved hooked talons, simulate ribbon loops, and pierced wisteria pods, *W. sinensis*, strung on wire or thread, become "ribbon ends." Greyish-brown Kentucky coffee tree pods, *Gymnocladus dioica*, whose slight bloom gives them a somewhat dusty look, are added for strength of outline.

Both lycopodium and mistletoe could be blended into this wreath if you

desire a fuller effect and a greater contrast of color, form, and texture.

For contrast against dark walls, try spraying the wreath lightly with white spray paint or an antiquing compound.

And thus the year comes full circle with a composition of winter materials. But the appearance of such plants as aconite, snowdrop, trout lily and hellebore is only weeks away; a wholly new process of growth is about to begin. With care, love and skill, this seasonal cycle of beauty can continue to enrich our lives indefinitely.

Bibliography

Abelson, Philip. "The Inexorable Exponential." *Science,* October 11, 1968.

Aiken, George D. *Pioneering with Wildflowers.* Englewood Cliffs, New Jersey: Prentice-Hall, 1968.

American Chemical Society. *Cleaning Our Environment, The Chemical Base for Action.* Washington, D.C., 1969.

American Horticultural Society, Inc. "Daylily Handbook." *The American Horticultural Magazine,* Vol. 47, No. 2, Spring 1968.

Anderson, Edgar. *Plants, Man and Life.* Boston: Little, Brown & Co., 1952.

Bacon, Francis. *Essays.* New York: E. P. Dutton & Co., Inc., 1947.

Bailey, L. H. *The Standard Cyclopedia of Horticulture.* New York: Macmillan Co., 1935.

Bazin, Germain. *A Gallery of Flowers.* Hudson, New York: Appleton-Century, 1960.

Blossfeldt, Karl. *Urformen der Kunst.* Berlin: Ernst Wasmuth, 1936.

Blunt, Wilfrid. *The Art of Botanical Illustration.* New York: Charles Scribner's Sons, 1951.

Bowles, E. A. *A Handbook of Crocus and Colchicum for Gardeners.* New York: D. Van Nostrand Co., 1952.

Bowles, E. A. *My Garden in Spring.* London: T. C. & E. C. Jack, 1914.

Braun, E. Lucy. *Deciduous Forests of Eastern North America.* Philadelphia: The Blakiston Company, 1950.

Braun, E. Lucy. *The Monocotyledoneae.* Columbus: Ohio State University Press, 1967.

Braun, E. Lucy. *The Woody Plants of Ohio.* Columbus: Ohio State University Press, 1961.

Brown, Harrison; Bonner, James; and Weir, John. *The Next Hundred Years.* New York: Viking Press, 1957.

Čapek, Karel. *The Gardener's Year.* London: George Allen & Unwin, 1931.

Carson, Rachel. *Silent Spring.* Boston: Houghton Mifflin Co., 1962.

Cato, Marcus Porcius. *On Agriculture.* Harvard University Press, 1934.

Clifford, Derek. *History of Garden Design.* New York: Praeger, 1966.

Conway, J. Gregory. *Conway's Encyclopedia of Flower Arrangement.* New York: Alfred A. Knopf, 1957.

Coon, Nelson. *Using Wayside Plants.* New York: Hearthside Press, 1960.

Deam, Charles. *Flora of Indiana.* Department of Conservation, Division of Forestry for the State of Indiana. Indianapolis, 1940.

Dowden, Anne Ophelia T. *Look at a Flower.* New York: Thomas Y. Crowell Co., 1963.

Ellacombe, Rev. Henry N. *In My Vicarage Garden and Elsewhere.* London: John Lane: The Bodley Head, 1901.

Elliott, Clarence. *Rock Garden Plants*. New York: Longmans, 1935.

Farrer, Reginald. *On the Eaves of the World*. London: Edward Arnold, 1917.

Fernald, Merritt Lyndon. *Gray's Manual of Botany*. 8th Edition. New York: American Book Company, 1950.

Fischer, Helen Field, and Harshbarger, Gretchen Fischer. *The Flower Family Album*. Minneapolis: University of Minnesota Press, 1941.

Gleason, Henry A. *The New Britton & Brown Illustrated Flora*. The New York Botanical Garden. New York: Hafner Publishing Co., 1963.

Gordon, Robert. "Map of Original Vegetation of Ohio." Columbus: Institute of Natural Resources, Ohio State University.

Graf, Alfred Byrd. *Exotica*. Rutherford, New Jersey: Roehrs Company, 1957.

Guilcher, Jean Michel. *The Hidden Life of Flowers*. New York: New York Philosophical Library, 1954.

Hall, A. Daniel. *The Genus Tulipa*. London: The Royal Horticultural Society, 1940.

Hay, Roy, and Synge, Patrick M. *The Color Dictionary of Flowers and Plants for Home and Garden*. New York: Crown Publishers, 1969.

Hersey, Jean. *Wild Flowers to Know and Grow*. New York: D. Van Nostrand Co., 1964.

Hill, Amelia Leavitt. *Arranging Flowers from the Roadside, Fields and Woods*. New York: The Studio Publications, 1958.

House, Homer D. *Wild Flowers*. New York: Macmillan Co., 1935.

Hunter, Beatrice Trum. *Gardening Without Poisons*. Boston: Houghton Mifflin Co., 1964.

Jacobson, J. S., and Hill, A. Clyde. *Recognition of Air Pollution Injury to Vegetation*. Pittsburgh, Pa.: Air Pollution Control Association, 1970.

Jekyll, Gertrude. *Wood & Garden*. London: Longmans, Green & Co., 1904.

Jones, Frances. Unpublished Master of Arts thesis: "Vegetation and Habitat Contrasts of a North and South Slope in Southwestern Ohio." Cincinnati: University of Cincinnati, 1934.

Kern, G. M. *Practical Landscape Gardening*. Cincinnati, Ohio: Moore, Wilstach, Keys & Co., 1855.

Klein, Isabelle H. *Wild Flowers of Ohio and Adjacent States*. Cleveland, Ohio: Cleveland Museum of Natural History and Case-Western Reserve University, 1970.

Koerner, Gustav. *Memoirs of Gustave Koerner, 1809–1896*. Edited by Thomas J. McCormak. 2 vols. Cedar Rapids, Iowa: Torch Press, 1909.

Lawrence, Elizabeth. *The Little Bulbs*. New York: Criterion Books, 1957.

Lawrence, Elizabeth. *Lob's Wood*. Cincinnati, Ohio: Cincinnati Nature Center, 1971.

McCaull, Julian. "Mix with Care." *Environment*, Vol. 13, No. 1. St. Louis, January/February 1971.

March-Penny, John. *Japanese Flower Arrangement Ikebana*. England: Hanlyn Publishing Group, 1969.

Marsh, George Perkins. *Man and Nature*. New York: C. Scribner & Sons, 1864.

Mattoon, H. Gleason. *Plant Buyer's Guide, 6th Edition*. Boston: The Massachusetts Horticultural Society, 1958.

Maw, George. *A Monograph of the Genus* Crocus. London: Dulau & Co. 1886.

Michaux, André. "American Wilderness Diary." From the *Journal of André Michaux, 1793–1796*. Edited by Reuben G. Thwaites. Cleveland, 1904.

Ministry of Agriculture, Fisheries & Food. "Narcissus Variety Trials. Ist Report 1955–63." Great Britain.

Nichols, Beverley. *The Art of Flower Arrangement*. New York: Viking Press, 1967.

Nicolson, Philippa. *V. Sackville-West's Garden Book*. London: Michael Joseph, 1968.

Ohwi, Jisaburo. *Flora of Japan*. Washington, D. C.: The Smithsonian Institution, 1965.

Perry, Frances. *Water Gardening*. New York: Charles Scribner's Sons, 1938.

Peterson, Roger Tory, and McKenny, Margaret. *A Field Guide to Wildflowers*. Boston: Houghton Mifflin Co., 1968.

Pfeiffer, Ehrenfried. *Bio-Dynamic Farming and Gardening*. New York: Anthroposophic Press, 1938.

Pückler-Muskau, Baron. *The Regency Visitor*. Edited by E. M. Butler. New York: Dutton, 1958.

Repton, Humphrey. *Sketches and Hints on Landscape Gardening*. London, 1795.

Richter, Conrad. *The Trees*. New York: Alfred A. Knopf, 1940.

Rickett, Harold William. *Wild Flowers of the United States, The Northeastern States*. Vol. I. The New York Botanical Garden. New York: McGraw-Hill Book Company, 1966.

Robinson, W. *The Wild Garden*. London: John Murray, 1870.

Rohde, Eleanour Sinclair. *The Story of the Garden*. Boston: Hale, Cushman & Flint, 1933.

Royal Horticultural Society. *Classified List and International Register of Daffodil Names*. London, March 1969.

Royal Horticultural Society. *Dictionary of Gardening*. Oxford: Clarendon Press, 1956.

Sackville-West, Victoria. *How Does Your Garden Grow*. New York: Doubleday, Doran, 1935.

Sears, Paul B. *Deserts on the March*. Norman, Oklahoma: University of Oklahoma Press, 1935.

Sears, Paul B. "Natural Vegetation of Ohio." *Ohio Journal of Science*, Vol. 26, No. 4, 1926.

Sedgwick, Mabel Cabot. *The Garden Month by Month*. New York: Frederick A. Stokes Company, 1907.

Sitwell, Sacheverell; Blunt, Wilfrid, and Synge, Patrick M. *Great Flower Books 1700–1900*. London: Collins, 1956.

Stern, Sir Frederick C. *A Chalk Garden*. London: Thomas Nelson & Sons, 1960.

Stern, Sir Frederick C. *Snowdrops and Snowflakes*. London: Royal Horticultural Society, 1956.

Steyermark, Julian A. *Flora of Missouri*. Ames, Iowa: Iowa State University Press.

Stoltz, Mrs. Raymond Russ. *Flower Show Ribbon-Winning Arrangements*. New York: Scribner's Sons, 1958.

Synge, Patrick M. *Collin's Guide to Bulbs*. London: Collins, 1961.

Thomas, Graham Stuart. *Plants for Ground-cover*. London: J. M. Dent & Sons, 1970.

Thompson, D'Arcy. *Growth and Form*. New York: Macmillan Co., 1942.

Trollope, Frances. *Domestic Manners of the Americans*. New York: Dodd, 1927.

Underwood, Raye Miller. *The Complete Book of Dried Arrangements*. New York: M. Barrows, 1952.

United States Department of Agriculture. *Climate and Man*. Yearbook of Agriculture, 1941.

Von Miklos, Josephine. *Wildflowers in Your House*. New York: Doubleday & Co., 1968.

Wyman, Donald. *Ground Cover Plants*. New York. Macmillan Co., 1956.

Wyman, Donald. *Hedges, Screens and Windbreaks*. New York: Whittlesay House, 1938.

Wyman, Donald. *Shrubs and Vines for American Gardens*. New York: Macmillan Co., 1958.

Index

Bluebell: English, 70
   Spanish, 70, **73**
   Virginia, **84, 85,** 195
Blue-eyed grass, 148
Blue-eyed Mary, 52, 93, **130, 131, 223**
Bluegrass, Kentucky, 19, 258, **259**
Bluets, 134
Blunt, Wilfred, 127
Bone meal, 100
Boneset, 108, 302, **303**
Borax for drying, 197
Border planting, field, 157
Botrychium dissectum, 51
   multifidum, **42,** 107
   virginianum, 107
Bottlebrush grass, 302, **303**
Bouncing-Bet, 274, **275**
Bowles, E. A., 49, 56
Box-elder, **121**
Bracken, 107, 109
Branches, to arrange, 228
Braun, E. Lucy, 24, 124, 127
Bromus purgans, 154, **155**
Broom-sedge, 111
Brown, Harrison, 4
Bryant, William Cullen, 43
Buckeye: bottlebrush, 96, 157
   Ohio, 96, **97,** 157, 220, 306, **307**
   red, 96, 134, 157
Bulbocodium vernum, **62, 64, 70, 71**
Bulbs: bloom without leaves, **170, 171**
   exotic introductions, 49
   fall, 169
   in pots, 74
   spring, 68, **70-73**
Burbank, Luther, 30
Burdock burs, 286, **287**
Butler, E. M., 91
Butomus umbellatus, 154
Butter-bur, Japanese, 68, **69, 151,** 154, 234, **235**
Buttercup, creeping, 51, 152, **153,** 154
Butterfly weed, 157, 274, **275**

C

Cactus, 24, 30, **31,** 33, 58, 62
Calla palustris, 122, 154
Caltha palustris, 154
Camassia scilloides, 50, 67, 73, 244, **245**
Campanula americana, **166,** 167
Campion, 51
Campsis radicans, 113, 134, **135,** 137, 157, 295
Camptosorus rhizophyllus, **116,** 117
Cane: giant, **39,** 137
   Kentucky, 258

Čapek, Karel, 184
Cardiocrinum giganteum, 138, 161
Carex grayii, 264, **265**
Carpinus betulus, 134
Carson, Rachel, 11, 144
Cassia marilandica, 157
Catalpa speciosa, **112,** 113, 157
Catalpa tree, northern, **112,** 113, 157
Cato, Marcus, 183
Cat-tails, 154, 296, 302, **303**
Caulophyllum thalictroides, **172,** 173
Cedar, red, 24, 51, 133, 182, **227,** 306
Cedar gall: dried, 302, **303**
   and apple trees, 133
Celandine: lesser, 68, **69**
   poppy, 93, 104, **105,** 193
Celastrus scandens, 113, **301, 305**
Celosia cristata, **217**
Ceratostigma plumbaginoides, 116, **292, 293**
Cercis canadensis, 228, **229**
Chamaemelum nobile, 118
Chamomile, 117
Chemicals, 22, 137
Cherry, Cornelian, 68
Cherry tree, fall color, 182
Chestnut, 24
Chickweed, sylvan, 52, 131
Chicory, **23,** 157
Chionanthus virginicus, 90, **91,** 157
Chionodoxa luciliae, **72**
Chives, Chinese or garlic, 139
Chrysanthemum, 51, 196, 290
Chrysanthemum leucanthemum, 274, **275**
Cichorium intybus, **23,** 157
Cicuta bulbifera, 110
   maculata, 110
Cigar tree, **112,** 113
Cincinnati, Ohio, 47
Cincinnati Nature Center, 115
Cirsium arvense, 274, **275**
Claytonia virginica, **42,** 65
Clematis, 51, 113, 136
Clematis henryi, 250, **251**
   heracleifolia var. *davidiana*, 136
   X *jackmanii*, 144, **145,** 157
   'Ramona,' 252, **253**
   recta, 136
   tangutica, dried, 302, **303**
   virginiana, 292
Clifford, Derek, 184
Climate, map, **20**
   succession, 38
   variations, 22
Clover: Korean and white, 117
   pink, 157
   red, 274, **275**
Club moss, creeping, **26**

Cockaigne, 43, 47
Cockscomb, **217**
Coffee tree, Kentucky, 306, **307**
Cohosh, blue, **172,** 173
Colchicine, 82, 178
Colchicum, 62, 139, 140, 169, 173, 290, **291**
Colchicum agrippinum, 173, **174**
   autumnale, 173, **174, 177**
   byzantinum, 173, **174**
   'The Giant,' 173, **175, 177**
   'Lilac Wonder,' 173, **174**
   sibthorpii, 173, **175**
   speciosum, **170, 171,** 173, **175, 177**
   'Water Lily,' **175,** 176
Collecting wildflowers, 191-194
Collector's bench or table, 216, **217**
Collinsia verna, 52, 93, **130, 131, 223**
Color: for design, 209, 210
   garden, 68, 87, 136, 183
   monochromatic, 210
   seasonal: fall, 182; summer, 157, 158
Columbine, 51, 147, 256, **257**
Communities, plant and animal, 28
Compost: about, 94-101
   for hardiness, 61
   for mulching, 169
   periodic enrichment, 61, 62
Conditioning flowers, 195-196
Coneflower, purple, **166,** 167, **285**
Conioselinum chinense, 28
Conium maculatum, 28, 110
Conservation of wildflowers, 193
Containers: about, 203-205. *Also see*
   individual arrangements, 214-306
   miniature, 248
   usubata, 288, **289**
Convallaria majalis, 242, **243**
Convolvulus arvensis, 158
Coon, Nelson, 211
Cornus florida, **88,** 89, 294, **295**
   mas, 68
Coronilla varia, 157
Corydalis, 67
Cottonwood, 30
Cowbane, spotted, 110
Cranesbill, seed pod, **100**
Crataegus, 135, 302, **303**
Crinum X *powellii* 'Album,' 140
Crocus: autumn, 51, 169
   fall-blooming, 62
   pests, 56
   spring, **62,** 63, **63**
Crocus kotschyanus, 62
   sativus, 56
   tournefortii, 57
   zonatus, 62

Flowers: arranging, 206-212
   conditioning, 195
   field, 157
   holders for, 199, **200-204**
   "hothouse," 189
   picking, 193
Foam: plastic, in arrangements, 226
   ivy-covered, 246, **247**
Foamflower, 51, 102, **103**
Forbs: and chemicals, 137
   prairie, 17
Forcing bloom, 220
Forest: beech-maple, 41
   climax, 41
   Eastern complex, 24, 30, 31
   floor, **8, 9**
   "second growth," 40
   succession, 33, **36, 37**
   types of, 24
Forget-me-not, 154, 195
Forsythia primulina, 136
   suspensa, 136
Franklinia tree, **156,** 157
Fringe tree, 90, **91,** 157
Fritillaria imperialis, **132,** 133, 138, 139, **140**
   meleagris, 139, 232, **233**
   verticillata, 139, 238, **239, Endpapers**
Fritillary, Japanese, 238, **239, Endpapers**
Fuki, 68, **69**
Fungicides, 141
Fungus, plate or shelf, **42,** 302, **303**

G

Galanthus. Also see Snowdrop
   elwesii, 52
   nivalis, 52, **55, 70, 217, 225, 308, Endpapers**
   plicatus, 52
Galium aparine, **42,** 108
   odoratum, 116
Garden: catalogs, 68
   green, 87
   levels, variety in, 89
   maintenance of, 90, 108
   paths, 90
   planning, 89, 128
   reference books, 127
   water or streamside, 152
Garlic: field, to remove, 108
   giant or serpent, 139, **198, 263**
Gas plant, 272, **273,** 276, **277**
Geology, lessons from, 27
Geranium: strawberry, **142,** 143
   wild, 50, 98, **99**

Geranium 'Johnson's Blue,' 98
   maculatum, 50, 98, **99, 100**
   platypetalum, 98
   pratense, 98
   sanguineum, 98
Gigantism, 178
Gill-over-the-ground, 67, 176, **292, 293**
Ginger, wild, 65, 68, **84, 85**
Ginkgo, fall color, 182
Glacial effects, 18, 24, 38
Gleason, Henry A., 127
Glechoma hederacea, 67, 292, **293**
Gleditsia triacanthos, **291, 303**
'Gloriosa Daisy,' **277, 281, 285**
"Glory of the Snow," **72**
Glycerine and water preservative, 196
Golden rain tree, 100, 157, 274, **275,** 296, 306, **307**
Goldenrod, 158, 286, **287, 305**
   blue-stem, 176
Goodhue, Bertram, 38
Gordon, Robert, 24
Goutweed, 108
   variegated, 116
Graf, Alfred B., 114
Grapevines: arranged, 282, **283**
   as barrier, 136
   as groundcover, 136
Grass: brome, 154, **155**
   foxtail, yellow, **23**
   and grasslands, **14, 15,** 16, 18, 30, 62, 67, 117, 258
   to preserve, 196, 258
   triple-awned, 100
   western, 31
Gray, Asa, 127
Green belts, 11
Green dragon, 123, 264, **265**
Greenbrier, bristly, 282, **283**
Grey-leaved plants, 116
Groundcovers, 51
   about, 111-118
Growing seasons, 19, 22
Growth, continuous, dangers of, 6
Guilcher, Jean Michel, 162
Guinea-hen flower, 139, 232, **233**
Gymnocladus dioica, 306, **307**

H

Hackberry, 67
Halesia carolina, 157
Hall, A. D., 70
Hamamelis mollis, 50
   vernalis, 50
   virginiana, **50,** 295
Hanging arrangement, 294, **295**

Harbingers-of-spring, 48, **66, 222**
Hardiness: about, 57-63
   siting for, 59
   zones, 20
Hardwoods, Ohio, 16
Harmony, man and nature, 6
Harshbarger, Gretchen, 162
Hawthorn, 302, **303**
   as hedging, 135
Hay, Roy, 127
Hedera helix, 113, **247,** 282, **283**
Hedges, about, 128-136
Helianthus tuberosus, 133, 158, **287**
Hellebore, 67, 98, 192
   bear's foot, 56, **60**
   culture of, 54
   seed pods, arranging, 214
Helleborus corsicus, 60
   foetidus, 56, **60**
   macranthus, 58
   niger, 52, **53,** 54, 56, **58,** 59, 214
   orientalis, 54, 56, **59,** 214, **215, Endpapers**
Hemerocallis, 144, **145,** 157
Hemlock: tree, 33
   hedges, 133
   poison, 28, 110
   water, 110
Hemlock-parsley, 28
Hepatica acutiloba, 51, 56, **57,** 65
Herbicides, 137
Herbs, 116
Hersey, Jean, 214
Hesperis matronalis, 81
Hibiscus: arranging, 290
   palustris, 157
   syriacus, 134, 136
Hickory, 19, 31, **35, 182**
Hill, A. Clyde, 143
Hill, Amelia Leavitt, 197
Holders, flower, about, 199-204, **200-204**
Holly, 295, 306, **307**
Hollyhocks, 157, 196, 260
Honesty, to dry, 254, **255**
Honeysuckle, 112, 133, 274, **275**
   winter, as hedging, 133
Horizontal design rule, 209
Hornbeam, European, 134
Horsetail, field, 97, 260, **261**
Hosta, 67
   culture of, 163-167
   "August lily," **163**
Hosta lancifolia, **165,** 167
   plantaginea 'Grandiflora,' 163
   sieboldiana, 164, **165**
   undulata, 128, **129,** 167, 242, **243**
   ventricosa, 157, **165,** 166, **209**
"Hothouse" flowers, 189

The Authors and Illustrator

MARION ROMBAUER BECKER, a Vassar graduate best known as co-author with her mother of JOY OF COOKING, is equally respected in the world of gardening. Presently a director and a member of the Rare Plant Committee of the Garden Club of America, she won from that organization in 1961 the Amy Montague Medal for Civic Achievement. For four years she edited the Cincinnati Garden Center *Bulletin*, and she now serves at the Cincinnati Nature Center as horticultural chairman.

Formerly Director of Art at the John Burroughs School in St. Louis and later at Hillsdale, Mrs. Becker was for ten years Director of the Cincinnati Modern Art Society. At Cockaigne she and her architect husband have created a woodland garden of great beauty.

FRANCES JONES POETKER, botanist and ecologist, is also a graduate of Vassar, with a master's degree in plant ecology from the University of Cincinnati. She is currently a board member of both the Society of American Florists and the American Academy of Florists and the only living woman member of the Floricultural Hall of Fame.

Mrs. Poetker, a frequent lecturer on TV and radio, is a winner in flower shows here and abroad and has been honored by the United States Department of Agriculture for fostering foreign understanding. She is remembered by many as the author of the nationally syndicated column FUN WITH FLOWERS. She and her husband own a florist shop in Cincinnati which specializes in rare exotics.

PAUL BIGELOW SEARS, recipient of many doctorates, is a prominent pioneer in plant ecology. Author of several books, including the well-known DESERTS ON THE MARCH and THE LIVING LANDSCAPE, Dr. Sears is honorary president and past chairman of the board of the National Audubon Society and past president of both the Ecological Society of America and the American Association for the Advancement of Science. He received the Eminent Ecologist Award of the Ecological Society of America from that body and the Richard Prentice Award for writing in the field of popular science.

Director of the Yale Conservation Program from 1950 to 1960, he now makes Taos, New Mexico, home base for his writings and his nationwide lectures and consultancies.

JANICE REBERT FORBERG, a native Ohioan, comes from a family with artistic traditions. At the Art Academy of Cincinnati, where she studied more than three years, she was impressed by the residual trend toward the teachings of Nikolaides, which a number of the faculty who had advocated his methods had left ingrained there, and engrossed herself in his book *A Natural Way to Draw*. Later there was a brief but vital encounter with Sohaku Ogata, who visited Cincinnati from the Zen Study Center in Kyoto.

Mrs. Forberg has exhibited many times in the Cincinnati Vicinity Show, and her work has appeared in nationally distributed magazines. She has mingled her art interests with civic activities such as past presidencies of the Woman's City Club and Seven Hills Neighborhood House. She is currently a member of the Cincinnati Community Chest Board of Trustees and the Playhouse in the Park.

SB439
S43
Wild wealth

1243
Sears, Paul Bigelow